INTIMATE
AUDREY

Also by Sean Hepburn Ferrer

Audrey Hepburn, An Elegant Spirit
Little Audrey's Daydream
Mauricio of Uruguay

Also by Wendy Holden

The Teacher of Auschwitz
I Give You My Heart
The Cruelty of Beauty
Born Survivors
The Sense of Paper

INTIMATE AUDREY

AN AUTHORIZED BIOGRAPHY

SEAN HEPBURN FERRER
and WENDY HOLDEN

GRAND CENTRAL

New York   Boston

Copyright © 2026 Wendy Holden and SHF Entertainment, Inc.

Cover design by Amanda Kain
Cover photo © Philippe Halsman / Magnum Photos
Cover copyright © 2026 by Hachette Book Group, Inc.

Hachette Book Group supports the right to free expression and the value of copyright. The purpose of copyright is to encourage writers and artists to produce the creative works that enrich our culture.

The scanning, uploading, and distribution of this book without permission is a theft of the authors' intellectual property. If you would like permission to use material from the book (other than for review purposes), please contact permissions@hbgusa.com. Thank you for your support of the authors' rights.

Grand Central Publishing
Hachette Book Group
1290 Avenue of the Americas, New York, NY 10104
grandcentralpublishing.com
@grandcentralpub

First Edition: April 2026

Grand Central Publishing is a division of Hachette Book Group, Inc. The Grand Central Publishing name and logo is a registered trademark of Hachette Book Group, Inc.

The publisher is not responsible for websites (or their content) that are not owned by the publisher.

Grand Central Publishing books may be purchased in bulk for business, educational, or promotional use. For information, please contact your local bookseller or the Hachette Book Group Special Markets Department at special.markets@hbgusa.com.

Library of Congress Cataloging-in-Publication Data

Names: Ferrer, Sean Hepburn author | Holden, Wendy author
Title: Intimate Audrey : an authorized biography / Sean Hepburn Ferrer and Wendy Holden.
Description: First edition. | New York : GCP, 2026. | Includes bibliographical references.
Identifiers: LCCN 2025049619 | ISBN 9781538775073 hardcover | ISBN 9780306837814 ebook
Subjects: LCSH: Hepburn, Audrey, 1929–1993 | Motion picture actors and actresses—United States—Biography | LCGFT: Biographies
Classification: LCC PN2287.H43 F474 2026 | DDC 791.4302/8092 [B]—dc23/eng/20251222
LC record available at https://lccn.loc.gov/2025049619

ISBN: 9781538775073 (hardcover), 9780306837814 (ebook)

Printed in Canada

MRQ-T

10 9 8 7 6 5 4 3 2 1

To the children of the world—our future

Every child is proof that God has not lost hope in man.

—Audrey Hepburn, inspired by Rabindranath Tagore

CONTENTS

Foreword xi
Authors' Note xv

Chapter 1 1
Chapter 2 19
Chapter 3 39
Chapter 4 65
Chapter 5 81
Chapter 6 101
Chapter 7 125
Chapter 8 143
Chapter 9 167
Chapter 10 185
Chapter 11 211
Chapter 12 229
Chapter 13 249
Epilogue 273

Acknowledgments 283
Bibliography 285

FOREWORD

by Sean Hepburn Ferrer

BEFORE AGREEING TO WORK ON the definitive examination of someone who is often referred to as 'the woman behind the sunglasses,' I reminded myself that there are already more than a thousand books about my mother, Audrey Hepburn. Few women apart from the queen of England were as photographed in their lifetimes as she was, and it turns out that few celebrities have ever been so written about either.

Aside from the biographies, comics, cookbooks, fictional representations, and illustrated lifestyle guides, there are fashion books featuring the numerous magazine covers she graced and the hats she wore. Many of these publications have been translated into multiple languages. There's even one about her neck, would you believe?

My first book, *An Elegant Spirit*, arose out of a thirty-page memoir I wrote shortly after she passed away more than three decades ago. At the time, I penned it for the children I hoped I'd have one day. I imagined them looking up at a giant screen in a square in Tokyo or New York, a billboard in a Milan railway station, or a poster in a hair salon anywhere, seeing her smiling down at them, and wondering, *What was Audrey truly like?*

Never could she—or I—have imagined how ubiquitous her image would become on everything from T-shirts to artwork, coffee mugs to style features in magazines. It got to the point where, I am almost embarrassed to admit, while I was traveling with my children, we used to play a game titled "three minutes to find Granny." It was a game few ever lost, and one I still play occasionally while out and about on my lonesome, delightedly sending my wife, Karin, a photo of each new discovery.

Despite the fact that my mother is everywhere and always watching over us, the best books about her are mostly no longer in print. Even though she would have considered any biography of her preposterous and said—with a grimace—that the world needed it "like a hole in the head!" she could never have envisaged the insatiable appetite for her around the globe. "I wanted to work, and I behaved nicely," she said, summing up her life. "I was polite and normal. I think that communicated a certain something to people. That's all."

As the guardian of her image, name, and likeness in the years since her death, however, I have witnessed something truly remarkable—the crystallization of her myth as an icon and a legend, not just internationally but also from the previous generation, through mine, and on to tweens and teens. Having "Audrey Hepburn" on Google Alerts bloats my inbox daily with hundreds of notifications in English alone, so I can only imagine how many others there are.

Hundreds of photographs of her in films like *Breakfast at Tiffany's*, *My Fair Lady*, and *Roman Holiday* portray her as a pretty lady with a pretty smile wearing pretty clothes. Journalists frequently speculate that someone like singer Ariana Grande or actress Lily Collins must have been cast as Audrey in the latest rumored biopic simply because they wore vintage Givenchy.

How did such enduring fame happen? What brilliant marketing made it so? I wish I could claim credit for having cleverly plotted all this, but the truth is that I had little to do with it. My mother is being carried aloft into each new generation by millions of children and young adults, a fitting tribute to the Pied Piper she became as a legendary ambassador for UNICEF.

And how much more impressed they might be if they knew that the real Audrey—the one who overcame enormous hardship to grow into a woman far deeper than the image they are drip-fed—was a true champion of starving children.

As her eldest son and best friend, I felt that the organic shift in the Audrey dynamic had placed newfound responsibility at my feet. Did something more need to be said about the woman who'd defied all trends and crossed decades unknowingly long after her death? Was it time to take a different approach, a fresh look at her life and the intimate experiences that shaped this ethereal creature, seemingly made from air, yet so completely human and vulnerable?

Ultimately, it was my friend and literary agent Alan Nevins who offered a solution. "There is yet to be *the* authorized biography," he reminded me.

The final word? I pondered. And could it be in some way truly *final?* I am in my sixties and will soon no longer have a taste for trying to maintain an accurate course for the oftentimes derailed narrative about my mother. I refer to stories that she had an eating disorder, was Katharine Hepburn's sister, was Marilyn Monroe's best friend, or got married three times.

I liked the idea that this manuscript above all could be the one that sits on the top of the pile, like a history book, to ensure that there will always be an accurate account, some of it in her own words from never-before-seen letters. And what better time to reinspire the world with her than now, as we seem to be spinning back into the kind of events that sparked the fires that helped forge this extraordinary woman?

Like a good doctor who knows he should never treat a member of his own family, I asked Alan who might be the perfect filter—an objective narrator and guide. Without hesitation, he suggested the British author Wendy Holden, his client and friend. Since my mother's life had essentially started and ended with war, I was immediately drawn to Wendy, who'd been a war correspondent before shifting to become a writer of more than forty books, many of them bestsellers about those who'd survived the Second World War.

As my mother often referred to her years as a UNICEF ambassador as her second and most important career, it made perfect sense to have someone by my side who didn't have to guess what the fear, hunger, and stench of death are like. This book is as much Wendy's as it is mine, if not more so.

You might think that these things—fear, hunger, death—don't sound very "Audrey Hepburn." But it is precisely because of her dark experiences that the sublime was created. Like Anne Frank, someone she identified strongly with and who became the Malala of her generation, my mother strove to make the world a better place. The tragedy is that every day, in every generation, as wars continue around the world and children continue to suffer, there is still an urgent need for the light of these remarkable individuals to shine in the darkness.

My mother's legacy now sits atop a tripod pedestal that elevated her from a childhood under Nazi occupation to a career as an actor bathed in grace. Her elegance and beauty as a timeless beacon of style helped maintain the universal esteem in which she is held, and she was gilded further by her glorious humanitarian last chapter. Without any one of these elements, she would have lost her steadfast poise—and her longevity.

It is precisely the combination of these things that allows us all, no matter how old or from which continent, to feel the same way—that this shy survivor who began her teens as a typical girl from across the landing courageously stepped out into the world but always remained one of us. Here you will learn how and why.

◆

AUTHORS' NOTE

The chapter openings are written in screenplay style to bring to life events that proved pivotal to Audrey's development, character, and choices. In places, dialogue based on memories, testimonies, letters, and interviews has been created for narrative purposes. As far as we are able, we have re-created these moments accurately.

1.

Being without food, fearful for one's life, the bombings—all made me appreciative of safety, of liberty. In that sense, the bad experiences have become a positive in my life.—AH

EXT. BAIDOA, SOMALIA, September 1992

Under a relentless sun, wide-eyed women and children huddle in the shade of an acacia tree, languidly batting away flies as they wait for their next meal. Slumped onto cracked earth the color of terra-cotta, they look like ghostly figures from a biblical tableau.

A tall, slender woman in her sixties wearing a polo shirt and slacks climbs from a dented four-wheel-drive vehicle policed by armed Somali bodyguards. They are carrying AK-47s and chewing green khat leaves that brown their teeth.

After giving her unlikely protectors a nod of thanks, **AUDREY HEPBURN** is led into the eerily still clearing by UNICEF field officers who shepherd her toward the crowd.

She is accompanied by her companion, **ROB WOLDERS**, and a handful of media representatives who emerge stiff-limbed from similar vehicles.

Jaw clenched, **AUDREY** is wide-eyed at the scenes all around her as the smell of unwashed bodies, excrement, and sickness pervades the stifling, dusty air, catching in the back of her throat.

Treading a careful path through those too frail to seek protection from the midday sun, she sees skeletal toddlers held limply in their exhausted mothers' arms. There are very few babies.

AUDREY
(giving the mothers a small smile)
How far have these people come to get here?

FIELD OFFICER
(brushing flies away from his face)
Many days with little food or water. Maybe weeks. Most are close to death by the time they arrive.

AUDREY
They seem to have waited until the very last moment to ask for help! Why?

INTIMATE AUDREY

                FIELD OFFICER
      Out of shame...for not being able
          to look after themselves.

AUDREY gasps as he leads her forward.

                FIELD OFFICER
     Let me show you the feeding station.

Spotting a careworn **NURSE** trying to encourage a naked boy to open his lips for what looks like porridge as his mother watches, **AUDREY** steps forward and holds out her hands.

                    AUDREY
                      May I?

The **NURSE** looks up, and her face registers immediate recognition.

                    NURSE
         Miss Hepburn!...Of course...

AUDREY cradles the child in her arms and tenderly brushes away the flies clustered around his mouth as she attempts to slip the spoon between unresponsive lips.

                    AUDREY
     Oh my...he weighs nothing! He's so
                    fragile.

>   (sniffs at the spoon)
>   UNIMIX?

>   **NURSE**
> Yes, and it tastes better than it smells.
> The older kids get protein biscuits, and
>   the adults can have rice and beans.

Staring into the child's unseeing eyes as his head lolls to one side, **AUDREY** begins to gently swing the boy to and fro, humming something faintly.

>   **AUDREY**
>   Will he make it?

The **NURSE** gives a small shake of her head. **AUDREY** looks up with tears in her eyes.

>   **AUDREY**
> How do I tell his mother that I'm deeply sorry?

>   **NURSE**
>   (to the mother, who remains expressionless)
>   Waan ka xumahay.

AUDREY looks despairingly at similarly malnourished children lying in the dust with sunken eyes.

>   **AUDREY**
>   What about the others?

INTIMATE AUDREY

                    NURSE
It depends how quickly we can get them rehydrated. Many are beyond food. Eating even the smallest amount can have fatal consequences. We've lost at least ten of the youngest overnight.

AUDREY turns away, her eyes closed.

                  FIELD OFFICER
There are almost 250,000 people here now, all made worse by a plague of locusts and the civil war. In Somalia, a child can be killed for a bowl of rice.

Their conversation is interrupted by the sputtering arrival of a battered truck, its exhaust pipe spouting acrid fumes.
AUDREY watches men get out and start loading bodies. Shrouded in old UNIMIX sacks and stacked like logs behind a camel-thorn fence, the corpses exude a pungent stench as people cover their mouths.

Staring at the bundles, many of them tiny and weightless, **AUDREY** swallows against a constriction in her throat.

                  AUDREY
How can we allow this?!

FIELD OFFICER
There's no easy answer. We can only
carry on alleviating the suffering,
one human being at a time.

Followed by the **FIELD OFFICER**, the **NURSE**, and
ROB, **AUDREY** slowly picks her way around the camp.

AUDREY
I didn't expect this deafening silence.
That is something I'll never forget.

FIELD OFFICER
They're too weak and too traumatized
to speak, especially the children.

AUDREY watches as volunteers measure the arms
of children to try to identify the most severely
malnourished.

FLASHBACK:
INT. CANDLELIT BASEMENT, ARNHEM, HOLLAND, 1944

Teenage **AUDREY** encircles her emaciated arms with
her fingers as she lies on her mattress on the
floor, weak from hunger. The sound of bombshells
reverberates all around.

Her aunt, **MIESJE**, shuffles over to where **AUDREY**
lies, carrying a teacup filled with water, and
encourages her to drink.

INTIMATE AUDREY

> **MIESJE**
> *Fill yourself up with this, my dear.*
> *We have run out of food. All we can*
> *do now is drink and sleep.*

EXT. RETURN TO THE FEEDING STATION:

AUDREY comes upon the curled-up shape of a boy lying on a grubby square of sacking. His rib and hip bones show through his skin, and he is fighting to breathe. Squatting beside him, she tenderly strokes his cheek with the back of her finger before resting her hand on his.

> **AUDREY**
> (shaking her head)
> I had asthma as a child. I know how
> frightening it is being unable to breathe.
> I only wish I could help him.

As she watches, the little boy rolls away from her, gives a little shudder, and gasps his final breath.

> **AUDREY**
> (rising slowly, visibly overcome)
> This is unbearable.

> **FIELD OFFICER**
> (stepping forward)
> Yes, but we deal with it by helping the next.

>   **AUDREY**
>   (laying a hand on his arm)
>   Thank goodness the world is still full of
>   kind people. What you are doing here makes me
>   feel so terribly useless and unimportant...

Her voice catching, **AUDREY** steps to one side to compose herself.

>   **AUDREY**
>   (to **ROB**)
>   I'm not sure...I can take this...

>   **NURSE**
>   (pointing to a tent)
>   Would you like a moment? In there?

A hand pressed to her belly, **AUDREY** almost stumbles out of the range of the cameras.

>   **AUDREY**
>   (from within)
>   Oh, Robby, I fear that I won't ever be
>   able to recover from this trip...

SOMALIA, ABOUT WHICH SHE LATER said that there was "no place worse on Earth," was where my mother found herself unable to pretend anymore. The Academy Award–winning actress and virtuoso of make-believe could not fake her responses on this, her last trip. To truly know Audrey Hepburn is to live that experience in what none of us realized were the waning days of her life. It is the key to unlocking her soul.

In many ways, the physical and emotional hunger that haunted her after a childhood under Nazi occupation is what shaped her—and will shape this book. At the outbreak of the Second World War, my Belgian-born mother was a schoolgirl in Kent, England. Believing the family homeland in neutral Holland would be safer, her baroness mother flew her to Amsterdam on one of the last passenger planes out.

When the Nazis invaded six months later and half starved the population to feed their own people, my teenage mother nearly died. "In Arnhem we lived on a watery broth and flour made from tulip bulbs," she told me. "We were cold and hungry, living in the basement to avoid the shelling by the Allies in what turned into a major battle between good and evil."

By the time she was liberated, not long before her sixteenth birthday in May 1945, my mother was in such poor health through malnourishment and jaundice that doctors said she was weeks from dying. "I was so hungry, I lay in bed reading the same books over and over or simply sleeping. I was too tired to walk and too weak to seek food for the rest of the family as I had done in the beginning," she later said. Her immune system was compromised for life, even though she built up her stamina over the years by living and eating healthily.

It is very typical of my mother that when she was first approached by a diplomat cousin forty years later to appear at a UNICEF fundraising concert in Macao, China, at a time when she was withdrawing from her acting career, she immediately agreed. She'd attended countless charity events in her lifetime and often donated her appearance fees to organizations caring for veterans and victims of famine and war.

Witnessing how comfortable she was speaking about the plight of children after the concert, Jim Grant, UNICEF's executive director at the time, quickly realized the potential she had to highlight the plight of the world's most beleaguered children. When he asked her if she might consider becoming an ambassador, she jumped at the chance, describing it as "an honor and a privilege." It was, she said, a relief to finally do something to help. With me and my younger brother flown from the nest, she welcomed the fresh challenge. "I have cared for you and Luca all these years," she told me. "Now it is time to care for the world's children."

Brought up in a noble family long devoted to good deeds, Mum had been connected to humanitarian relief work conceptually and spiritually since she was small. An overriding sense of obligation—noblesse oblige—was a family philosophy handed down through the generations from our Dutch ancestors. "Throughout my childhood, every member of my family was doing something to help others," she said. It was especially evinced by their involvement in the Resistance during the Second World War, helping raise money for those with nothing and sheltering a British airman even as my mother ferried secret messages to those in hiding.

My mother not only took the family's ethical credo to heart but ended up pushing it to the extreme in a way that carried her right through to war-torn Africa five decades later. What especially inspired her was her experience of receiving charitable aid as a teenager. "After liberation, I was one of the lucky recipients of the food and medicine that the UNRRA and the Red Cross brought into the country," she said, always careful to add, "although my case can in no way be compared to that of the children of Africa."

Driven by this overwhelming moral obligation to use her fame for good, Mum was the first celebrity to put herself on the front line for UNICEF, traveling to conflict zones and regions hit by famine and civil war. She took on what she considered the most important role of her life, even though she knew it would take a heavy toll. "I've always had very deep feelings about children and about their suffering," she admitted. "I've sat in front of the television so often and seen photographs and been frustrated by articles... so pent up with the feeling...

that we can't do anything." She added that she'd "go to the moon" to help the children of the world if she thought it could make a difference.

By the end of her five years as the agency's highest-profile Goodwill Ambassador, she'd been to some of the world's most wretched and dangerous places, including Ethiopia, Bangladesh, and Sudan. Nothing, however, prepared her for the scenes of misery and deprivation that awaited her on her last mission—to Somalia.

Having spent several grueling days flying all over that ravaged country at enormous personal risk, my mother had already experienced the horrors of war-ravaged cities like Mogadishu and Kismayo. But the sight of the smallest and weakest "snuffed out like candles" in Baidoa gave her fresh nightmares that robbed her of her sleep. Within days, the sixty-three-year-old whose life had been a three-act play of heartache, war, and triumph cut an increasingly frail figure. I never forgot the impact that visit had on a woman who knew what it was like to face death.

After her first few missions to Africa and to Central and South America, among other places, she returned home exhausted but generally uplifted. "I gasped at the beauty of the people in Ethiopia, which has a very old culture and is the cradle of humanity," she told reporters. "They were very beautiful, proud, and dignified, patient, gentle, and hardworking. They are easy to communicate with because even though they don't know the language, they smile, and they touch, and they talk with their eyes."

Although she witnessed thousands seriously ill or dying from malnutrition or disease and others going blind from vitamin deficiency, she also saw how ravaged communities sprang back to life once wells were dug, livestock replaced, trees planted, and seeds sown. Children came alive, clamoring around her noisily and behaving exactly as children should. "[This type of aid] is called long-term aid because these things help people in the long term," she explained. "And it is highly successful."

She was also deeply moved by the devotion of those working tirelessly to feed, educate, and distribute supplies to those most in need. "UNICEF is a loving arm that reaches around the world for every child," she declared. "These are countries too poor to help themselves, but the [people] are eager to be independent and...help themselves. It doesn't bear thinking about what will happen to them if they don't get the assistance they need."

Somalia was a very different experience, however. With the added complication of feuding warlords, there was little beauty or hope in most of the towns she visited, and what aid was able to get through was often too little, too late. Field officer Ian McLeod, who accompanied her at Baidoa, said, "She appeared before [the Somalians] as an elegant white lady with a smile that beamed kindness. She didn't speak their language, but her face and gestures gave such an obvious psychological boost to so many. They may not have known who she was, but it was clear to them by her aura that she was someone special who was bringing them some hope."

As my mother walked among them, she could see and feel the anguish of mothers, also in pitiful condition, who knew they could do nothing to save their children. To ensure that she'd get the maximum publicity for the unfolding disaster, she was accompanied by a crew filming her every move. It was a presence she almost forgot about as her maternal instincts took over, and it was only when the director asked her to do something specific for the camera that she took note of it.

"She was uncomfortable then," Ian McLeod recalled. "She told me that it seemed so wrong to be filming the plight of human beings in such a situation, but she knew that the only way she could make a difference to their lives and to those of hundreds of thousands of other women and children across Somalia was to try to raise as much awareness as possible. Filming was a necessary evil to meet this goal." Nevertheless, she refused to pose for pictures if it would be disrespectful to the dignity of those suffering. The photographers were permitted to take shots of her only as she moved around clusters of people or tried to help in some small way.

I was aware of my mother's discomfort at being filmed in such places. She felt what she called a "curious embarrassment" whenever she first arrived, as if she were intruding and shouldn't be there—like the feeling of walking into a room where someone is dying. One picture from Somalia perfectly captures her agony for me. In her arms she carries a child of indeterminate age and gender. Draped in nothing more than rags and with a medical wristband wrapped around their spindly wrist, they peer out through hollow eyes at a world they cannot begin to comprehend. The image is painful enough for anyone, but the expression on my mother's face is what haunts me. So much anger that the world allows this—time and again.

Another image from Somalia was burned into her memory. It was the sight of a little blind girl dressed in a scrap of hospital gown feeling her way around the perimeter of the Baidoa camp. Unable to go any farther when she reached an open gate, the child faltered as if waiting for help crossing it while a swarm of flies buzzed around her nose and mouth.

To my mother, that orphan represented everything tragic about the plight of a child who'd been abandoned by the world. Crouching down beside her and taking her tiny hand, my mother tried to comfort her and help her find her way, but the girl's smile had long ago been lost. Her expressionless face illustrated her crushing sense of having been expended, disregarded like so many thousands of other children. Her milky eyes, robbed of their sight purely by malnutrition, spoke of a silence of the soul.

One of the things that pained my mother most in the "slice of hell" of the Somali camps was that so many of the children who'd beaten the odds to make it there had—like that little girl—completely shut down emotionally and lost the ability to smile. This was especially heartbreaking for a woman whose smile could light up a room and who used it to devastating effect, on- and off-screen.

There wasn't even the smallest flicker of a reaction from this traumatized innocent. "There was nothing, Seanie," she told me. "Nothing at all. I couldn't stand it." She knew that the child—like so many of the "discarded orphan wretches" she encountered—would likely be dead within weeks. It was no wonder that my mother had to slip into a tent occasionally to escape the cameras, dropping the public mask that she'd long hidden behind. Collapsing in on herself in an intensely private outpouring of rage and distress, she railed at the betrayal after being promised as a child by the grown-ups around her that a holocaust of this magnitude would never happen again.

The breaking of that promise was the reason why she chose to give back in what she called her second and most important vocation, which preoccupied her far more than her film career had. It was never about her legacy or what others might think of her. She had always thought of others before herself, and these final years of her life were no exception. "This is what is real and meaningful," she'd say. "I finally feel as if I am doing something of value and importance."

Rob Wolders, my mother's partner of thirteen years, who was by her side through every UNICEF tour, was the one into whose arms she collapsed in Baidoa. Someone who had also been half starved by the Nazis in Holland, he could do nothing but try to comfort the woman on an unstoppable mission to try to heal the world. He said later, "Audrey had a love for people that goes beyond sympathy. It is perhaps more than empathy. An ability to project her imagination so that she could actually feel what others are feeling." He added that although people tend to think of Mum as a film star first and a humanitarian second, those who knew her well understood that the two roles were "intertwined and inseparable."

I would go further, because I came to think of her work for the children as being like a drug she became addicted to. This was a concern for me, as I knew what she was like once she became passionate about something. I worried for her safety—and her health. "Don't overdo it,"

I'd warn. "You'll only wear yourself out." She'd smile and nod, but after a few risk-free missions she began to press UNICEF to be sent to the most lawless places, those where no other celebrity was going or that she feared had been overlooked by the media. Even though each trip was risky and arduous, and she'd set off with a heavy heart knowing she'd witness something devastating, she still volunteered.

"It is in those far-flung places where children have been forgotten that I can do the most, Sean," she insisted. "I have to go. No one else will." With typical humility, she continually described it as a "bonus and a blessing" to be "one of those lucky people who can help a little bit."

What is astonishing to many is that even though my mother was paid only a token American dollar a year for her UNICEF work, she still bought her own airline tickets or sought sponsorship to be able to witness unspeakable horror. She felt it would be morally wrong to fly first-class to a disaster zone, so she booked economy flights and stayed in modest hotels or in the camps themselves, alongside staff. Day after day, she pushed aside her own physical and emotional suffering to comfort grieving mothers and clasp the hands of the dying. "The best thing to hold on to in life is each other," she once said, and the woman famous for her viselike hugs with everyone she met longed to embrace those for whom kindness and compassion were a distant memory.

Then, when she reached a ravaged country and saw the vastness of the tragedy, becoming not only marked but angered by it, she wanted to go back again and again, while there was still time to save people. She couldn't tear herself away. "Thousands of children are dying every day," she'd rail. "How can I stay home playing with the dogs and deadheading my roses when there is still so much work to do?"

I came to realize that my mother was a lioness, although she wasn't born that way. A strange mix of resilience and vulnerability, she was soft and strong at the same time and had the gentlest of hearts. Some have described her as "an iron fist in a velvet glove," and it's true she never flinched from doing what was right. She always went the extra mile for everyone but herself. From cooking to gardening, acting to her charity work, she was the kind of person who would see things through to the end.

I'd be among the first to stress that she wasn't a saint, however. She wouldn't have liked that description at all. She was just a regular person, as she'd been throughout her life, regardless of how famous she became. But one thing her work with UNICEF did was give the world confirmation that the girl it had first fallen in love with at the movies and had been rooting for ever since really was as beautiful inside as out.

———◆———

ON HER FINAL AND MOST harrowing mission, to Somalia, the face of the woman who was as close to royalty as Hollywood would ever know became increasingly pinched. She was painfully thin and existing on little sleep, her eyes ringed by dark circles after years of flying around the globe to—as she put it—"see, feel, return, and tell" the world what was desperately needed.

Few but she knew, as she uncomplainingly kept up her grueling schedule, that she was in great physical pain. All of us, including her, assumed she'd picked up a stomach bug and that she'd feel better once she returned home to her regular healthy vices—chocolate, a few cigarettes, and the occasional scotch.

UNICEF field officer Ian McLeod was aware of the mental toll the work was taking on my mother, but he also knew how determined she was to continue. "I don't believe she or Rob knew how ill she was," he said. "If they had, I'm absolutely positive that he and her family would have tried to stop her from going, although I'm sure her strong will would have prevailed anyway."

My mother's devoted protector-cum-housekeeper-cum-driver, Giovanna, who'd been with her since the 1960s, was also appalled by what her employer was putting herself through. Taking one look at my mother's ashen face when she walked through the door after yet another long journey back to her Swiss home, she'd insist, "La signora needs to rest." Giovanna, a kindhearted Sardinian, helped my mother through so much and had long been a human litmus paper for whatever was happening in her life. Mum used to tell her, "Husbands may come and go, but you and I will always be there for each other." And they really were, working together in the kitchen or the garden, sharing their secrets and fears in a relationship that was far deeper than just that of employer and employee. Dear Giovanna lived for only a few years beyond the woman she'd devoted so much of her life to.

The Christmas before Mum flew to Mogadishu in 1992, Giovanna and I were equally worried, and after we shared our concerns, I told my mother, "You look exhausted. Can't you slow down these missions just a bit? I know I can't ask you to stop, but do you have to go away again so soon?"

She gave me a tired smile and patted my face. "I'm fine, Seanie," she said. "I'm tough, remember? Just this one more trip." She insisted that the children of Somalia had to come first. She then agreed to everything that UNICEF asked of her, even though she admitted to having had what she called "an overdose of suffering."

Proud as I am of my mother's charity work, I am sad that it made her so grave in her final years that she nearly lost her own smile. I am also in no doubt that all of it contributed to her premature death. And this last trip was the beginning of the end. It was as if chunks of her soul started to fall away. In Somalia, she found herself staring into the abyss. She was a natural empath, and her skill as an actress meant she had the ability to imagine herself in another's shoes, so the sights she saw there had such an emotional impact that she could physically feel the Somalians' pain.

When she returned home and I called her from California, as I did at least once a week, I could hear something in her voice that I'd never heard before, and I felt a chilling dark cloud. She told me, "I've been to hell, Sean. We have to do all we can to stop Somalia falling off the edge of the Earth." When I asked her to tell me more, she said she'd explain when she came to Los Angeles, but I sensed that the damage had already been done.

Of the many flashbacks she'd had to her own childhood, the worst were to what it felt like physically to almost starve to death. That was something she never forgot. In a painfully slow and insidious process, as a teenager she lost a dangerous amount of weight, her legs started to swell, and her body began to shut down. Finally, anemic and without any energy, she felt a terrible fatigue set in until she could no longer get out of bed. It was, she said, a gnawing hunger that consumed not just her body but also her mind. She saw that same hunger in the eyes of the dying in Africa.

The Audrey people think they know isn't the one we knew, or even the one who ended up doing all she did for UNICEF, sacrificing her health and her happiness for the children of the world. Behind the glamour and the smile was a Cinderella figure who had picked herself up from the ashes of war to become one of the world's most celebrated faces. Everything she'd experienced in her early life made her who she was and informed all her choices. To really know her is to appreciate that the true Audrey Hepburn was forged by hardship and heartbreak. Ever the pragmatist, toward the end she recognized that there was a strange kind of poetry in that.

---◆---

2.

Love does not terrify me, but the going away of it does. I have been made terribly aware of how everything can be wrenched away from you and your life torn apart. —AH

INT. A DARKENED BEDROOM, BRUSSELS, BELGIUM, 1935

A six-year-old girl sits beside the bed where her mother, **BARONESS ELLA VAN HEEMSTRA**, lies curled into a fetal position, dabbing her eyes with an embroidered handkerchief.

The heavy brocade curtains are drawn, and the large, high-ceilinged bedroom is in semidarkness. The atmosphere is somber.

      AUDREY
   (tugging at the velvet bedspread with tiny
       fingers)
   Mother, tell me again what
    happened the day I died.

ELLA

(groaning)

I don't feel like it today. Besides, you've heard that story a hundred times.

AUDREY

Please, Mama. Just once more?

ELLA

(sighing and pulling herself up a little on her pillows)

You were born on May 4, 1929, and you died a few weeks later. Your heart stopped in the middle of a whooping cough spasm, and you turned blue.

AUDREY

(eyes wide)

Oh, Mummy! And you saved me?

ELLA

Me and Jesus Christ. It was he who told me to pick you up and spank you. That's when you cried out and took a breath. He gave you another chance at life.

AUDREY

Was Daddy there too?

ELLA

(giving a sigh)

No, Audrey. He was away.

> **AUDREY**
> Like now?

> **ELLA**
> (nodding tearfully)
> Like now.

> **AUDREY**
> Where's Daddy gone?

> **ELLA**
> (her face crumpling)
> On another of his trips.

> **AUDREY**
> But when will he come back?

> **ELLA**
> (her voice catching)
> I don't think he will, Audrey. Not this time. You'll have to be a good girl and help me. We're on our own now.

AUDREY frowns and clambers onto the bed to half sit on her mother's lap. Staring into the face of the thirty-five-year-old baroness, she traces the tracks of her tears with tiny fingers.

> **AUDREY**
> (her expression pensive)
> Doesn't Daddy love us?

ELLA

Of course he loves you. You will always be his little Monkey Puzzle. But he's not here anymore. He's living in another country now.

AUDREY

Why?

ELLA

(sniffing)
Because he doesn't want to be here.

AUDREY

But why?

ELLA

You wouldn't understand. And now we're going away too. We're going to stay with your aunt Miesje, your uncle Otto, and your grandparents. You like it there. It's the place where you climbed trees with your half brothers.

AUDREY

Is Daddy coming?

ELLA

(dabbing her eyes)
He'll write...but no, we shan't be together like before.

AUDREY

Why?

                        ELLA
                     (impatient)
     Stop asking so many questions, please, Audrey.
      It's terribly tiresome. Just do as I say.

                       AUDREY
           (a tear rolling down her cheek)
                     I miss him.

                        ELLA
                  (closing her eyes)
                     Don't cry.

                       AUDREY
                      (wailing)
          But how will Daddy find us if we
           go away? Please, Mummy, no!

                        ELLA
    Stop that nonsense! You'll make your face uglier
     and bring on your asthma. I've asked Greta to
     start packing your things, so go and help her.

                       AUDREY
                 (her face crumpling)
       But I don't want my nanny, Mummy. I want you.

                        ELLA
                   Audrey, please!

Bewildered and afraid, **AUDREY** climbs down but
hesitates by the side of the bed. Seeing her

mother roll on her side and pull the bedspread up to her neck, she shuffles mournfully from the room, closing the door carefully behind her.

The day forty-six-year-old Joseph Hepburn-Ruston walked out on his wife and young daughter, abandoning them for good, was one that was seared into my mother's memory. By her own admission, she was devastated. Her father's absence made her insecure for life, shaping almost every decision she made, especially when it came to men.

"One day he just went out and never came back," she recounted. "I was destroyed at the time. I cried for days and days. I'm not afraid to say that something of that feeling stayed with me through my own relationships. When I fell in love and married, I lived in constant fear of being left. I was terrified that something would take him away from me."

What she frequently described as the tragedy of her childhood left a deep and enduring scar. She dearly missed the man whose loss created a different kind of hunger in her. For the rest of her life she carried the sadness of his abandonment, even though she was not naturally a sad person at all.

To my six-year-old mother, the Anglo-Irish Joe Ruston she so worshipped was a heroic, almost mythical figure. Yet he was a flawed individual and someone I would describe as an emotional paraplegic. Working infrequently, he was a suave, pipe-smoking divorcé in a cravat, with no money but grand aspirations.

He first met my divorced grandmother, Baroness Ella van Heemstra, in the Dutch East Indies, where she had been living with her previous husband and their two young boys. The baroness was certainly a force to be reckoned with. Born into aristocracy but not great wealth,

Ella had longed to train as an opera singer when she was a teenager, but her parents had deemed that an unsuitable occupation for a young lady of her position. Although she had an allowance, she still needed to be careful, finding part-time jobs and seeking out reasonable, inexpensive accommodation.

What Ella lacked in love she made up for in common sense, teaching her children the true meaning of resilience and that their home was wherever they were living at the time. She was a formidable role model who instilled in them the importance of manners and decorum and the value of hard work. They were lessons my mother adhered to her entire life.

Joseph Ruston, by contrast, was far from hardworking. Instead, he prided himself on speaking multiple languages, flying gliders, and being an excellent horseman. The handsome playboy, who was eleven years Ella's senior, swept the twenty-six-year-old off her feet, but once he became her second husband, he proved to be a spendthrift who lived way beyond her inherited means. It was he who'd decided to add the name Hepburn to his own in the hope of giving himself a hint of the nobility he craved. He did it after he discovered that the Hepburns in his family had a spurious link to the 4th Earl of Bothwell, third husband of Mary, Queen of Scots. It created a unique surname for his and Ella's only child, who was christened Audrey Kathleen Ruston, later adding Hepburn, a name she then shortened to simply Audrey Hepburn.

When she was small, my mother believed that they, like many daughters and fathers, had a special bond and loved that her dad made up a nickname for her, Monkey Puzzle. Her half brothers were never given such a privilege. While her mother was typical of noblewomen of her era, unable or unwilling to show affection, reserved, and often judgmental, her father was playful and fun.

Despite his many failings, she had fond memories of the early years she spent with him and recalled him taking her gliding and horseback riding, which they may have done when they visited his relatives in England before the war. Going up in a glider with him was especially thrilling to her, and she remembered how windy yet peaceful it was, as if she were really flying like a bird. One of her treasured photos of the two of them together shows him lying in the long grass beside her, smiling into the camera. That was something her buttoned-up mother would never have done.

My grandfather was undoubtedly a complicated man. Restless and never ideal husband material, Joe Ruston spent increasing amounts of time away. Ella stayed home to care for the children but accompanied him on his travels in support of Europe's growing fascist movement. In an era when it was fashionable among aristocrats to support nationalist politicians who were promising economic revival after the First World War, the couple became members of the British Union of Fascists, led by Sir Oswald Mosley. They not only befriended the controversial socialite Unity Mitford but traveled with her to Germany, where they met Chancellor Adolf Hitler and had their photograph taken with him, unaware of his plans for war or the annihilation of Europe's Jews.

In 1935 Ella even wrote an article praising the spirit and health of the Germans she'd encountered, stating, "To watch their boundless enthusiasm as they march past in endless formations, hailing their beloved Führer Adolf Hitler, is one of the most inspirational sights on earth. Hitler has a magnetic and most charming personality, which fully reflects the spiritual aspirations of this mighty people.... Well may Adolf Hitler be proud of the rebirth of this great country and of the rejuvenation of the German spirit. The Germany of today is a most pleasant country and the Germans, under Nazi rule, a splendid example, to the white races of the world."

As a little girl, my mother was oblivious to her parents' politics, but to the end of her days, their prewar allegiance to fascism was a source of shame and embarrassment to her. Even though she appreciated that they were young and foolish and caught up in a wave of political fervor, their views still seemed misguided. Some might say that a desire to make up for them contributed to her determination to do good.

My grandparents were both strong-willed, and their tempestuous marriage resulted in arguments that brought on headaches and asthma attacks in their only child. Curled up in her bedroom, whenever she heard them shouting, my mother would bite her fingernails or eat some of the Belgian chocolate her nanny gave her to calm her down. All her life she'd nibble on a small square of dark chocolate to help chase away her blues.

The bickering continued whenever her father was home, and it became increasingly clear that he found her mother impossible to live with. Personally, I'm not surprised. Ella was like a one-woman panzer division and seemed to have a constant need to criticize the people she loved, which made for an uncomfortable atmosphere. I know Mum witnessed many of their rows, but I got the impression she wasn't home for the one that signaled the end of the marriage. Nevertheless, Joseph Ruston's abrupt departure from their Brussels home after what was only ever described to her as a "scene" still came as a seismic shift. The reasons behind it were never made clear, and there has been speculation that her parents may have objected to his spending and his fascist politics, which Ella had also adopted, and given him no choice but to leave. I suspect he walked out because he'd had enough.

Whatever the reason, his sudden disappearance from the lives of my mother and grandmother shattered them both equally. "It was the most traumatic event of my life," she later said. It was even more distressing for them when he left the country and moved to London to become a fundraiser for the fascists. The idea of him never coming back not only devastated my mother but turned my grandmother's hair white virtually overnight.

Mum had always thought of Ella as indomitable, so seeing her collapse in on her grief was earth-shattering. "I saw her endless tears and was terrified, worrying what would happen to me," she said. "I didn't think her crying would ever stop." Having witnessed her mother's pain, she was afraid to leave her side for a time, so worried was she about what she might do. All that she had known and trusted was pulled out from under her at the tender age of six.

The reasons for the marital rift never mattered to her; she simply wanted her daddy back. "I think it is hard sometimes for children who are dumped," she said later. "I don't care who they are. It tortures a child beyond measure. They don't know what the problem was. Children need two parents for their equilibrium in life." It was an emotional equilibrium she spent the rest of her life searching for.

Although my mother rarely talked about her father, his disappearance from her life certainly left her with abandonment issues and exacerbated her anxiety. However, I don't believe that single event alone is responsible for all her insecurities. I think they were the result of a complex interplay of factors. Although she was incredibly strong in many regards, I'm not sure she was ever truly secure at her core.

Even when she was in her sixties, after years of being famous, I watched her nerves almost get the better of her whenever she had to return to the spotlight. "I don't think your insecurity ever disappears," she once said. "Sometimes I think the more successful you become, the less secure you feel. This is kind of frightening."

THE DELICATE BALANCE OF HER childhood was tipped still further when, not long after her father walked out, she was uprooted from Brussels and taken to stay with my grandmother's family at the thatched Villa Roestenburg, their comfortable home in Oosterbeek, near Arnhem, in Holland. Owned by Ella's father, Baron Aarnoud van Heemstra, a former governor-general of Suriname, it had been familiar to Mum all her life, as it was where her parents had dropped her whenever they went traveling.

With her half brothers Ian and Alex, my mother took full advantage of the wooded parkland adjacent to the property, where she enjoyed being a tomboy, running free, climbing trees, and relishing the outdoor life that had been denied her in Brussels. Their only restriction was their Calvinist grandparents' insistence that she and her brothers go to church every Sunday, join in with the family's daily prayers, and say grace at meals.

Despite the loss of her father, my mother was happy in Holland surrounded by her family, so the decision by her mother to send her to a small private school in the village of Elham in Kent, England, came as yet another upheaval in her young life. With her brothers living with relatives in The Hague and her grandparents remaining in Holland, she would be left alone on the other side of the North Sea. The shock of that remained with her always. "My mother and I became closer after my father left," she told me. "So to be separated from her, too, was extremely painful."

Ella's motives for sending her daughter to England in 1935 were many. As part of her divorce, she was negotiating visiting rights with Joseph and so thought it best that my mother move closer to London, where he was living. It was one of the few things the couple agreed on, as Joseph Ruston had long wanted their daughter to be raised as the British child her passport declared her to be because of his Anglo-Irish heritage and to learn the language of her ancestors. "And my mother thought it was right for me to speak English, being brought up as an English child."

Ella also hoped the move might improve my mother's health, as Elham was only eight miles from the port of Folkestone, and sea air was thought to be beneficial for childhood asthma, which Mum eventually grew out of.

Enrolled at the village school run by spinster sisters named Rigden, the six-year-old who became known locally as "Little Audrey" and spoke only French to begin with was set to work studying English, elocution, and manners. Initially, the baroness remained in the village, too, lodging in a former pub that was now a guesthouse owned by Edward Butcher, a retired miner, coal merchant, and haulage contractor, and his wife Evelyn, who'd worked as a domestic servant. Ella and Joseph had previously stayed there on vacation.

My grandmother was encouraging about my mother's new life but frequently missing as she traveled back and forth between England and continental Europe despite the growing political unrest. Still allied to fascism, she continued to promote Hitler's plans for economic recovery after the First World War and returned more than once to Germany. She didn't have a lot of money, and her journeys to visit her daughter by train and boat would have taken a day or two and been costly, so she may have stayed away out of necessity. She probably wanted to toughen my mother up, too, as she was such a sensitive child.

In anticipation of how she might feel, the baroness is said to have written her a poem in which she described Mum as a "free spirit" and hoped she'd prepared her for being on her own. I never set eyes on this poem and heard about it only recently, when it appeared in another unauthorized biography. If it really existed, I can only imagine it was something my mother may have kept for a while and then lost in the war. She certainly never mentioned it.

Either way, no amount of poetry could compensate for my mother's unhappy first few months in England, during which her father didn't even visit. "He never made the effort to see me, but maybe he didn't want to," she said years later, with evident sorrow. She told us how hurtful she found it to see other children with their fathers, all the while wishing her own daddy were around so she could feel similarly loved. For a long time, she didn't know if he was dead or alive, but she prayed he was still out there somewhere. She dreamed of being reunited with him one day but almost gave up hope of that ever happening. Mum was the first to admit that losing him gave her complexes she was never quite able to shake. As she once admitted in a television interview, "I was born with an enormous need for affection, and a terrible need to give it."

The sad thing is that she found out years later he had written several letters but her mother had kept them from her. Because Mum never replied, Ruston eventually gave up. This may well have been the reason he never visited. Mum didn't even find out about the missing letters until after he'd died, and she resented Ella bitterly for never telling her about them.

SPEAKING ONLY A LITTLE ENGLISH, my mother undoubtedly found her first few months in Kent difficult. Elham was small, pretty, and traditionally English, with a village shop, a bakery, a tearoom, two pubs, a watchmaker, a church, and a school. One of fourteen students, all British, Mum had no choice but to learn the language quickly and adapt to her strange new life. "I liked the children and my teachers," she said later, adding that music, history, and astronomy had been her favorite subjects, "but I never liked the process of learning. I was very restless and could never sit still for hours on end."

In time, however, she settled, later insisting that her crash course in how to be independent was character building. She made friends, gained weight and height, joined the local Brownie troop, played with her hosts' pet dog and a neighbor's daughter, and studied with the four daughters of the local vicar. Despite her secret sadness, over the next few years in that warm and welcoming community she did so well with her studies that she achieved a mention on the honor roll. She graduated effortlessly to the local secondary school.

Desperately wanting someone on whom to shower love, my mother dreamed of having children of her own when she grew up. Soppy about babies, she'd stop passing mothers in the street to coo over their infants, lifting them out of their strollers for a cuddle. From as far back as she could remember, she'd imagined herself a mother, and later made a firm resolve never to let her own children feel as unwanted or unloved as she did. It was a promise she kept.

Her baroness mother was largely unsympathetic to her daughter's initial misery at being left in England and, on her few visits, told her to stop feeling sorry for herself. Once or twice, she sent for her to join her and her half brothers on vacation in Europe. In a photograph of Mum, age nine, at an airfield near Rome in 1938, she is dressed in a helmet and jumpsuit, smiling into the camera after a gravity-defying flight in a biplane. She fed on the memories of these visits when she was left to fend for herself again in England.

"It was frowned upon to bother others with your feelings," my mother later explained, adding that Ella had a stock response to any complaints. "She reiterated that no one was interested in me, so I should just get on with it." This maxim helped mold Mum into someone who was unfailingly polite, humble, and selfless. Her Edwardian mother also told her never to show off or make a spectacle of herself, and that, too, stuck for life. My grandmother even told her once she was an established star that, considering she had "no talent" and wasn't interesting, she'd done surprisingly well for herself. It was the latest in a lifetime of put-downs that led my mother to doubt herself constantly. Unable to appreciate her own worth, she was grateful and surprised whenever people paid her a compliment. She never saw herself as particularly beautiful, talented, or lovely in any way, which of course only made her even more so.

Alone in Kent, where some of the villagers began to refer affectionately to their European misfit as "the girl with the saucer eyes," she channeled her innermost feelings into reading, listening to music, and drawing. Sketching constantly, she drew flowers, favorite scenes from nursery rhymes, animals, and children—always children. It was also in Elham that she first developed an emotional connection with English literature and especially the works of Rudyard Kipling, which she was introduced to by her half brother Ian.

The highlight of her school life, however, was the weekly dance lessons given by a young ballerina at the village's Fellowship Hall. These rekindled a love of ballet that had first been sparked by performances she'd seen in Brussels as a little girl. Dancing gave her a taste of what it meant to perform. "I fell in love with dance," she later admitted, starry-eyed. "I loved it, just loved it." In physical movement, she could finally express herself without the need for language, and that helped her through her darker moments. It was also the start of a lifelong passion. Even in her final years she admitted to being "fanatic" about becoming a dancer, adding, "That is still my dream, to be a prima ballerina in a tutu and dance one day at Covent Garden. I wanted that more than anything in the world."

The only problem was that Mum thought she was too tall and not shapely enough to make it to a stage. She often made fun of her own looks. I remember her describing herself as flat chested and lanky, "with never enough up top," adding that her feet were too big, her face too wide, her nose bumpy, and one of her teeth crooked. Envious of small girls with "pretty shoulders and pretty little feet," as she admitted to one interviewer, "you could even say that I hated myself at certain periods. I was too fat or maybe too tall or just plain too ugly. I couldn't seem to handle any of my problems or cope with people I met." Hearing that from someone who went on to be considered one of the world's most stunning women is a reminder that none of us are ever entirely happy with the way we look.

Mum had enough self-worth, however, to resist later studio suggestions that she change her name or have her nose or tooth fixed. Famously, when one director asked her if she'd wear false boobs, she replied, "But I am!" Her resistance to the pressure they must have placed her under bears testament to her strength of character and the fact that she took her mother's advice and simply got on with her life, doing her best with what she had.

With the baroness abroad much of the time, my mother spent most of her school holidays in the Kent countryside with the Butchers, who had taken her in to earn some extra money. A loving and kind couple in their fifties, they were people Mum grew to adore. Mrs. Butcher taught her baking and the names of flowers, while Mr. Butcher tended his vegetable plot, which sparked a lifelong passion in my mother for growing things. Aside from having lots of children, it was her dream to one day have a cutting garden and an orchard and to make jam just as they did.

She also became "potty" about dogs and so loved the Butchers' little terrier that she kept a framed photo of it on her dressing table her entire life. She once said, "I think an animal, especially a dog, is possibly the purest companionship you can have. No person and few children, unless they're still infants, are as unpremeditated or as undemanding. They only ask to survive—to eat. They are totally dependent on you and therefore completely vulnerable. And this complete vulnerability is what enables you to open your heart completely, which you rarely do to a human being. Except perhaps children."

Feeling things so deeply, my mother grew into a perfectionist and a people-pleaser who was determined to become the best pupil, the best dancer, the best member of her local Brownie pack—anything so as not to disappoint. Being good enough was, she later said, her "greatest anguish." Unfailingly courteous, thoughtful, and kind, she felt a constant need to be loved that stemmed from her sense that she must have done something wrong for her father not to have stayed. And I think that need to be perfect began for her in England, where she waited so patiently for her daddy to return and rescue her. A truly gentle heart, she just wanted to love and to be loved. The best-kept secret about

Audrey Hepburn is that, alongside the sweetness of her, there was a great deal of sadness.

AFTER A YEAR OR SO in England, everything changed for Mum. Happier and more settled, she became an accomplished dancer and was fluent in English, with the elegantly clipped diction she'd be known for. With audible hints of her international background, her accent had a unique and endearing quality.

She'd have happily remained in Britain forever but for the chilling events in Europe that were about to change her life and the lives of millions. After the Nazis partially annexed and then invaded Czechoslovakia between 1938 and 1939, causing fears of further incursions, a conflicted Ella remained with her family in Arnhem. When Poland was invaded that September and Britain and France declared war on Germany, she realized that her ten-year-old daughter could accidentally end up at the center of a bitter conflict started by the very dictator the baroness had once written so glowingly about. Kent, in the south of England with its many seaports and airfields, would be especially vulnerable.

Panicking, Ella applied for legal and consular permission to evacuate my mother to Holland, a country many expected to remain neutral, as it had in the previous war. Without much thought for what impact it might have on an already insecure ten-year-old to be uprooted from her contented little world, arrangements were made for her immediate departure, although that was no mean feat.

Three weeks after war broke out, a passenger flight from Malmö to Amsterdam came under fire over the North Sea from a German fighter that mistook it for an Allied warplane. The bullets that peppered its fuselage killed one passenger and terrified the rest. To prevent that happening again, many commercial flights to Europe were grounded or instructed to fly unusually low so as not to be mistaken for enemy aircraft. The few Dutch planes still flying were painted bright orange, with the airline's name, "KLM," or "HOLLAND" added prominently in black lettering on each side as an added precaution.

In the autumn of 1939, Mrs. Butcher was instructed to escort my bewildered mother to London's Gatwick Airport so she could fly to Amsterdam and be reunited with her family. At the departure gate, my mother bid a tearful farewell to the woman who'd cared for her for the previous three and a half years. In gale-force winds, however, the plane skidded off the runway during takeoff and got stuck in wet clay, so she was ferried back to Kent.

Two days later, it was a rare encounter with her father that heralded my mother's final departure from the country she'd grown to love. As she explained later, "There were still a few Dutch planes that were allowed to fly, and somehow my mother contacted my father and asked him to meet me in London." After Mrs. Butcher put her on a train, my grandfather collected Mum from Charing Cross railway station and escorted her to an Art Deco airport near Shoreham-by-Sea in West Sussex, where she boarded one of KLM's vividly colored planes. My mother never spoke of that brief reunion with her father, but I know she'd have been proud to show off her English and tell him how she felt more British than Dutch. I'm also sure that she hoped seeing him again might rekindle their relationship. Sadly, it wasn't to be. "That was the last time that I saw my father in decades," she said later.

I've long thought that moment must have been a bit like the final scene in the film *Casablanca*. Only it was she who was leaving her beloved daddy behind this time, and they were soon to be parted by war, possibly forever. My mother would have been happy and sad at the same time. It must have been so poignant.

Not only was my grandfather about to be arrested and interned in Britain as a Nazi sympathizer, first in London and then in a detention camp on the remote Isle of Man, but—to her mind—he appeared to have given up on being her daddy completely. Little did either of them know, as his little Monkey Puzzle waved him goodbye through the window of her departing plane, that she was headed straight into the eye of the storm. "Having him cut off from me was terribly awful," she would say of that separation. It remained her gravest loss.

———◆———

3.

There is probably nothing in the world as determined as a child with a dream, and I wanted to dance more than I feared the Germans. —AH

INT. SCHOUWBURG THEATER, ARNHEM, HOLLAND, May 1940

A few days after her eleventh birthday, **AUDREY** waits in the wings of the city's Schouwburg Theater, wearing a floor-length white taffeta dress. It has a Peter Pan collar and a single black button and bow. The fabric rustles when she moves. In her arms, she holds a bouquet of red roses and tulips almost as big as she is.

She turns to glance nervously at her mother, **BARONESS ELLA VAN HEEMSTRA**, who stands ramrod straight behind her. When the baroness gives no reaction, **AUDREY** stares back at the corps de ballet of the Sadler's Wells Ballet, led by its principal dancer, **MARGOT FONTEYN**, who performs a grand jeté as **AUDREY** gasps.

When their performance ends, the thirty dancers line up at the front of the stage to take their bows, along with their director, **NINETTE DE VALOIS**. Clapping, **AUDREY**'s mother, **ELLA**, steps center stage to thank them first in English, then in Dutch.

                  ELLA
           (smiling at the audience)
As the daughter of Baron Aarnoud van Heemstra, the esteemed former burgomaster of Arnhem, I know I speak for everyone when I offer heartfelt thanks to Sadler's Wells for its marvelous performance here tonight as part of their goodwill tour of France, Belgium, and Holland. It is through the arts that connections between sympathetic nations are strengthened, and we are delighted to welcome you here. I would now like to present the company's director with a small token of our appreciation.

She signals to **AUDREY** to step forward. With practiced steps, the girl who has only just turned eleven wears the smile she's rehearsed and glides across the stage to place the flowers in the arms of **NINETTE DE VALOIS** before giving a deep curtsy. With a nervous smile at the audience, **AUDREY** steps backward, almost tripping over her dress.

ELLA
It is now my great pleasure to invite
the entire company for a supper reception,
where our most eminent citizens will
be waiting.

Whispered murmuring breaks out among the dancers. In the orchestra pit, members of the city's philharmonic hastily pack away their instruments, and at the rear of the auditorium, scores of people start hurrying home.

NINETTE DE VALOIS
(looking at her cast)
I'm afraid that buses are waiting to drive
us to The Hague to catch our flight. As
I'm sure you appreciate, time is of the
essence, and the British consul has strongly
advised us to fly back to London tonight.

ELLA
I assure you that we have allowed
enough time for all that.

She pauses to give the director a smile.

ELLA
You are, after all, here to promote
international solidarity.

NINETTE DE VALOIS stares at the baroness. With a slight nod, she claps her hands together and with purposeful steps ushers her company off the stage while giving orders.

NINETTE DE VALOIS
Get everything ready for departure
in under an hour.

STAGE MANAGER
But we'll never be able to pack it in time!

NINETTE DE VALOIS
Then leave it behind.

Visibly shocked, the **STAGE MANAGER** sighs before yelling instructions to his men.

ELLA
(shepherding the director off the stage)
This way. Now, I must ask what it was like
to train under the great Diaghilev.

AUDREY wanders onto the stage as dancers, musicians, and crew run right and left, scooping up clothes, instruments, and props. Spotting **MARGOT FONTEYN** sitting on the floor untying the ribbons of her toe shoes, she wanders over bashfully.

AUDREY
(staring into the face of the raven-haired
soloist with striking eye makeup)
Oh, but you were marvelous!

> **MARGOT FONTEYN**
> Thank you, my dear...
> (after a beat)
> And so were you. I love your dress.

> **AUDREY**
> (touching the taffeta in wonder)
> Mummy had it made specially.
> (looking up and blurting suddenly)
> One day I hope to be a prima ballerina just like you!

> **MARGOT FONTEYN**
> (standing, shoes in hand)
> If you truly want that, you must work jolly hard to achieve it. I wish you the best of luck.

She pats **AUDREY**'s head and hurries offstage.

Standing alone by the footlights, **AUDREY** faces the empty auditorium. Gazing out into the darkened space, she places her feet in fourth position and smooths down her dress. After doing a plié, she spins away from her supporting leg to complete a perfect pirouette.

Smiling, she can almost hear the applause and gives her deepest curtsy before arching gracefully forward to pick up a single tulip fallen from the bouquet.

———◆———

On May 11, 1940, the day after that magical night watching the Sadler's Wells Ballet that galvanized my mother's determination to become a professional dancer, she was woken by the throbbing of approaching aircraft rattling her windowpanes.

My grandmother rushed into her bedroom in the center of Arnhem that Saturday morning, threw open the curtains, and cried, "Get up. War has begun!" The eight-month so-called Phoney War, with only a few skirmishes and no major offensives, was over, and the military action they'd all feared had begun. The pair of them gazed skyward to see formation after formation of German warplanes flying overhead.

My mother's immediate fear was that the aircraft were heading for Britain, where her father could be in danger, but having flown 150 kilometers west of Arnhem, the heavily laden Heinkel aircraft turned back over the North Sea to launch surprise firebomb attacks on The Hague, Amsterdam, Rotterdam, and the northern port of Den Helder. In what proved to be the start of a mass invasion, thousands of Dutch civilians were left dead, wounded, or homeless. The nation was in shock.

Under such intense bombardment and with little military capability of their own, the Dutch had no choice but to surrender within days, their precious neutrality lost. To the relief of many and the dismay of some, Queen Wilhelmina and her senior officials fled to London to establish a government-in-exile. My mother, my grandmother, and almost nine million other defenseless citizens were left at the mercy of the enemy.

When news came on that first afternoon that German paratroopers were on the outskirts of Arnhem, a fresh wave of fear rippled through its picturesque streets and leafy parks. Although martial law had been imposed in Holland three weeks earlier and all men over the age of eighteen had been enlisted—including my mother's half brother Alex—the possibility of Germany invading still felt unlikely. It was only when the Dutch army dug antitank trenches and blocked roads into the city using barbed wire and felled trees that the threat began to feel real. Even though Czechoslovakia, Poland, Denmark, and Norway had all been occupied, many—including Ella—had believed Holland would remain independent. Then air-raid sirens began to wail, and instructions came that everyone should close their shutters and remain in their homes.

As a single mother responsible for eleven-year-old Audrey and the younger of her two sons, Ian, all of them now living in a first-floor apartment on the Arnhem street of Jansbinnensingel, a few miles from her family home, Ella must have shuddered at the thought of what lay ahead. My mother had been enrolled in the local school for only a few months when the Germans invaded, so her education was once again interrupted by war. Far more dangerously, she hadn't yet mastered the Dutch language. Speaking mainly English and having a British name in a place where Nazis were patrolling the streets placed her in great peril. Not that she understood that yet. She was still just trying to do her best.

"It was a traumatic experience being in this huge place with nobody knowing a word of what I was saying," she later recalled of her first few weeks in school. "Every time I opened my mouth, everybody roared with laughter." Not only was she unable to make herself understood, she missed her Kent friends and especially her ballet dancing. As was her way, however, she dried her tears and made the best of things—until the Germans arrived on her doorstep.

She and my grandmother watched from their window as streams of refugees fleeing from the unfolding conflict trudged past, carrying children and animals. It was clear that Western Europe was lost. Once word came over the radio that France, Belgium, and Luxembourg had all been breached, Ella knew her hope of being spared from war was futile.

My mother had very clear memories of that day. "We were told to stay indoors. We were being invaded. 'Close your curtains, do not even peer out of the windows,' they said." There was a risk that anyone doing so might be mistaken for a member of the Resistance and shot. Too curious to obey, she peered out anyway to see German tanks rolling in, followed by hundreds of soldiers in gray uniforms, their weapons raised, marching past "for hours." Typically of my mother, she noted how "spick-and-span" they all looked, even as they overran her city.

The events of that pivotal week were to change the course of her history irrevocably. The memory of the occupation was, she later admitted, the "second-worst memory I have after my father's disappearance." Only a few months after she'd been plucked from the relative safety of Kent, she found herself surrounded by a conquering German army. For the next five years, almost to the day, she and her family lived under Nazi occupation with dire consequences for them all.

Fearing that my mother's name alone could place her in danger of being identified as English or, mistakenly, as Jewish, my grandmother declared that her daughter was "Edda van Heemstra," altering one of her own old documents to create a credible forgery. She added loops to the two *l*'s of Ella to make *d*'s and changed the birth date and the photograph. My mother was under strict instructions to answer only to her new name from that day on and never to speak English in case she was overheard. The fear of being interned by the Germans as the only British member of her family was considerable, and her experiences in Arnhem shaped the rest of her life. "The occupation gave me both fresh anxiety and a deep appreciation for the liberties we had lost."

After the initial shock of invasion, however, life returned to a strange kind of ordinary for the Dutch as the Germans lulled the people they'd referred to as their "cousins" into a false sense of security. Aside from the ubiquitous swastika flags and the mangled remains of the city's main bridge, which Dutch soldiers had destroyed to thwart the enemy advance, normal life continued. Then things began to change. Street names were switched to German, a curfew was imposed, and there was rationing for civilians to ensure the invading forces were fed first. Meanwhile, my mother still attended school each day, and my grandmother worked in a hospital that also treated German soldiers.

When Mum's half brother Alex returned from the front, everyone was relieved, but he immediately went into hiding to avoid being taken for slave labor or forcibly conscripted into the Wehrmacht. Although he and my mother had never been that close, she was still worried for his safety as yet another significant man in her life vanished. The family believed that the younger brother, Ian, wouldn't be at risk, as he was under eighteen, so for the next year of occupation he and my mother became closer still, spending their weekends and school holidays with their recently widowed sixty-eight-year-old grandfather, Baron Aarnoud van Heemstra, at his rented residence in the nearby Huis Zypendaal.

The redbrick regency manor in the north of the city was where the baron had taken a few rooms after selling the family villa following the death of his wife in 1939. My mother's aunt, Countess Miesje, and her husband, Count Otto, also rented rooms in the picture-postcard manor. Set in landscaped parkland with a small lake, Zypendaal was a haven where Mum could breathe, climb trees, and dance freely around the sweeping lawns. That vast outdoor space was a place she cherished her whole life and longed one day to re-create for herself.

Being there must have been a dream come true for a little girl who in the space of a few years had lost all contact with her father, moved countries twice, had to learn to speak Dutch and English fluently, and witnessed the invasion of her ancestral homeland. Her grandmother had died shortly before the invasion, her oldest brother had evaporated, and her other brother was in constant danger of being taken. All this had happened before she was twelve.

Each new shock piled up on the last, creating layer upon layer of trauma that gave her an emotional depth beyond her years. With her unique insight, not one of her experiences would be forgotten, but, true to her family ethos, she tried to brave each bombshell and "get on with it."

As it had been in England, ballet became my mother's salvation. To help quell her daughter's growing anxiety about the war, Ella enrolled her at Arnhem's conservatory of music so she could continue with her classes. Her teacher was a former professional ballerina named Winja Marova who spent the entire war hiding her Jewish identity from the Nazis. This courageous woman immediately spotted her new pupil's potential and noted that whenever my mother was on the stage, people were mesmerized. "A flame lit the audience," she declared.

Mum didn't just want to dance, she wanted to be Margot Fonteyn, Anna Pavlova, or Isadora Duncan. She kept an old black-and-white photograph of Margot as Odette in *Swan Lake* until her dying day. I found it in her belongings. In Arnhem she choreographed all her own performances, dancing tirelessly to the music of an old gramophone even though she still didn't think she was good enough or pretty enough to make something of herself. But as her dance tutor recognized early on, she had something else—a kind of star quality that was hers and hers alone. That was what everyone who ever saw her perform came to appreciate too.

Perhaps due to her natural shyness or because she hadn't yet mastered the language, my mother remained a largely solitary child who was happier listening to music, reading, or drawing women in various outfits than trying to make friends. She also played with the many cats that inhabited the manor, preferring animals to dolls.

She found affection in two new father figures, her cigar-smoking grandfather, "Opa" Aarnoud, and her kindly uncle, "Oom" Otto, Count van Limburg Stirum, who helped restore her faith in men. But when Otto, a public prosecutor, was one of five innocent men arrested by the

Nazis and later executed in retribution for an attack on a freight train in Rotterdam that they'd had nothing to do with, the shock was seismic. One by one, the men in her life were being taken from her. Of this latest blow, she said afterward, "If you've lost someone you love very much, in the beginning you can't bear it, but as the years go by the pain of losing them is what reminds you so vividly of them.... My experiences and the people I lost in the war remain so vivid for me because of the pain."

Once America joined the war in 1941 and the Nazis invaded Russia on the eastern front, they began to systematically bleed Holland dry of its provisions, crops, and livestock to feed German soldiers or send food home to German families. In Arnhem, as elsewhere, it became harder to get even the most basic provisions. Before too long, real hunger began to bite, and my mother and her family were among the millions who craved all those things they'd previously taken for granted, such as coffee, quality bread, butter, cheese, sugar, and chocolate. In Mum's case, especially chocolate.

Although there was a thriving black market, prices were exorbitant and there was little left to pay for anything, as citizens had been forced to hand over their valuables and assets to the Germans, including cash and property. The family lost almost everything they owned overnight. My grandmother managed to keep back a little jewelry, which she used to barter for staples, insisting that "a pearl necklace can't feed any of us," but when the last of her pearls were gone and winter came, the van Heemstras began to suffer genuine hardship. With fuel in short supply or cut off completely, they joined those scavenging for coal and wood, chopping down trees in the town's parks, sawing up picket fences, and even dismantling parts of shell-damaged houses.

For the hundred thousand or so Jews in Arnhem, many of whom had fled to Holland from Germany to escape the restrictions of the virulently antisemitic Nuremberg Laws, life became untenable. After being forced to register and wear yellow stars, many Jews started to be sent away, first to a transit camp at Westerbork and then to unknown destinations. Thousands were kept hidden by brave Dutch citizens, but the unlucky ones were rounded up and deported. More than once, my mother was at the railway station with my grandmother when she saw those poor people being roughly loaded onto trains. As a frightened teenager, she gazed upon the faces of terrified families crammed into open cars, not knowing where they were being sent. Those scenes broke her heart.

She later recalled, "It was the worst kind of horror.... I saw families with little children, with babies, herded into meat wagons—trains of big wooden vans with just a little slit open at the top and all those faces peering out at you. And on the platform were soldiers herding more Jewish families with their poor little bundles and small children."

Still only a child herself, she was told by her mother that they were being sent to "special camps" in the countryside, a concept she found impossible to understand. Watching boys and girls her own age being mistreated, she was particularly struck by a little girl in a bright-red coat, amid all the grayness, stepping onto a train with her parents. Although my mother didn't know that the family were likely being sent to their deaths, the sight of that child's pale, terrified face never left her, and she spoke of that moment her whole life.

It was the color of the girl's coat that especially stood out and made it all real, especially as she knew that the child could so easily have been her. While working with Steven Spielberg on her final film, *Always*, she told him about that moment. When his film *Schindler's List* was released nine months after my mother died, there was an almost identical scene featuring a little girl in a vibrant red coat among a sea of people, all depicted in black-and-white film. I thought that was such a nice touch—a tribute to what Mum witnessed and a way of memorializing all those children who didn't make it.

The sight of a frightened child wasn't the only horror awaiting her, however. One day, searching with her mother for whatever food they could find in the town center, my mother heard bloodcurdling screams coming from the upper floors of a former bank that had been taken over by the Gestapo, the German secret police. When she asked my grandmother who was making those terrible sounds, she was told that the place was a prison where people were tortured. She couldn't get that thought out of her head. Another time, she was in town when German soldiers suddenly closed the street, pushed her and other passersby to one side, and made them watch as they put several young men up against a wall and shot them dead. My mother had a photographic memory, and such images haunted her for life.

As long as she could keep dancing, she was able to dispel these ghosts a little through the rigors of daily training. The same applied to spending time at the manor with her beloved grandfather, so when that privilege was denied, she was shattered. After the execution of her uncle Otto and the repeated attention of senior Nazis who wanted to requisition the manor for themselves, his widow, Miesje, and my great-grandfather decided to leave Zypendaal and move to a detached villa they owned in the tree-lined district of Velp—the same suburb where Ella had been born.

Velp was several miles farther from my mother's ballet school and from the city's cultural activities that the family so enjoyed, but when those events were dominated by the kind of Nazi sympathizers Ella had now turned her back on, having lost all faith in Hitler and his party, she too moved to Velp with her two remaining children. In that house full of fearful adults, my mother entered what would normally have been an exciting adolescence with "no parties, no radio, and no new books." She had never felt more isolated.

"I was growing up with people much older than myself," she later described. "I had been cut off from the world of youngsters my age because the war made me a prisoner, and not just physically but mentally." Taken from all she'd grown accustomed to, she withdrew still further into herself, becoming, in her own words, "a rather moody child...quiet and reticent...I liked to be by myself a great deal." Even the almost daily sight of Allied planes flying overhead on their way to bomb Germany didn't convince her that the war would end soon, with another winter to be endured.

It was her baroness mother who kept her going. My grandmother knew that dancing was the only thing that would keep her introspective daughter from giving up hope. In fact, my mother danced so obsessively that she wore out pairs of her precious ballet shoes and had to patch them with felt or try to find replacements on the black market. Sometimes she was so hungry that she barely had the energy to dance, but she did it anyway.

Ella may have been unable to show my mother affection, but as someone who'd been forbidden by her own family from pursuing a stage career, she was determined that not even war would destroy her daughter's dream. She helped organize several events at the Schouwburg Theater in which my mother featured prominently, performances that meant the world to her.

To dance on the very stage where she'd delivered flowers to the director of the Sadler's Wells Ballet was one of the highlights of my mother's years under Nazi occupation. She still choreographed her own performances based on her favorite ballets, and she became a self-taught seamstress, helping her mother fashion costumes from whatever scraps of material they could find, including old curtains.

Perhaps one of the most important things she was learning from my grandmother was resilience in the face of adversity. Ella and her stoic aunt Miesje were the latest in a long line of independent women who inspired her to seek her own path in life. They included dancers like Anna Pavlova, Ninette de Valois, the elfin Margot Fonteyn, and her ballet tutor Winja Marova, who she only later discovered had been hiding her identity in plain sight.

As GERMAN RESTRICTIONS ON EVERYDAY Dutch life tightened and my mother felt herself shrinking inside her clothes, she began to suffer the effects of malnutrition. Pale and thin, she was permanently tired and hungry. A greater danger than starvation was the proximity of senior Nazis who started to requisition many of the grander houses in Velp and evict their occupants. The van Heemstra family somehow managed to remain in their villa, but the Germans insisted on setting up a radio monitoring station in the attic, which meant soldiers were passing through daily.

With rumors of local women being snatched for the "entertainment" of German officers and enlisted men, Ella was so fearful for her daughter's safety that she considered moving away. My mother, too, understood the risks and said later, "I didn't know if I would just disappear, as had so many young girls and women...or if I would be taken...to help clean the building or serve at a military kitchen. All I knew was that I was...terrified."

With a nearby Luftwaffe base a key Allied bombing target, their suburban sanctuary was disturbed daily by the boom of antiaircraft fire. There were several near misses, too, as unintended bombs leveled neighboring properties. British and American crews who parachuted from burning planes were either rounded up by the Germans or spirited to safety by members of the Resistance, who were already hiding Jews and teenage boys at risk of being sent to work for the Reich.

Then, one day in 1943, my mother looked on in horror as the Germans came for Ian and marched him away. Along with hundreds of other men and teenage boys, her half brother was sent to work as a slave laborer in Berlin, and his family had no idea if they'd ever see him again. From then on, she fretted not only that her father might be killed in a bombing raid on England but also that Ian would be in similar danger in Germany. It's hard to imagine what that must have felt like for a nervous teenager who'd already lost so much.

Skin and bone as she underwent a growth spurt that had her

towering over her classmates, especially when in toe shoes, Mum was forced to give up her training for a while and rest. But without the freedom of expression that dance gave her, she felt even more trapped, and she couldn't keep away long. For a few Dutch guilders, she started giving ballet lessons in Velp when she wasn't working for a doctor at the local hospital. She soon discovered that it was a secret headquarters of the Resistance and a refuge for hidden Jews.

Embracing the spirit of resistance, she danced in invitation-only soirees to help lift morale and raise money for the hundreds of men, women, and children in hiding from the Nazis. Known as zwarte avonden, or black evenings, these risky musical events featuring several brave performers were held in the homes of sympathetic locals who posted guards, closed windows, and drew their blackout curtains. When each show ended, people dropped money into a hat passed around the room and were instructed not to applaud for fear of drawing the attention of German soldiers.

Instead of clapping, the audience just smiled in the dark. That expression—*smiling in the dark*—came to have such resonance for my mother, and it became a maxim for us all to live by and an example to follow. My mother recalled those blacked-out nights with great fondness. Pretending to be Margot Fonteyn or one of her other heroines, she pirouetted around the room in her homemade tutu and tried to forget the misery of occupation. "The best audiences I ever had never even made a single sound at the end of my performance," she said, claiming that her "humble" and "amateurish attempts" at dancing were also her way of making some kind of contribution to those living under oppression.

As she spoke perfect English and had already proved her loyalty to the Resistance, the leaders began to give her more responsibility, instructing her to distribute an underground pamphlet listing secret events and to pass messages to those in hiding. The hope was that she, a pretty young girl on foot or on a bicycle, was unlikely to be stopped and searched. My mother was initially told that she'd be delivering billets-doux to loved ones. Caught up in the romance of that, she took them gladly, putting the folded letters under the insoles of her shoes before setting off—an innocent teenager on an errand. It occurred to her only after the war that the messages had been secret instructions from the Resistance relating to sabotage or escape for which she could have been arrested, tortured, and executed.

After she delivered one such message to a downed British airman hiding in a forest on the outskirts of town, my mother's heart clenched when she spotted two members of the Nazis' so-called Green Police approaching. With an outward calm that belied her inner turmoil, she stooped to pick a bunch of wildflowers. When the officers gruffly demanded her ID papers, she gave them her prettiest smile and, with the grace of a dancer, presented them with her posy as stylishly as she'd presented a bouquet to Ninette de Valois. The unexpected gesture won the soldiers over, and they waved her on.

She put herself in danger yet again that year when another British plane was shot down over Arnhem on its way to a bombing raid. Max Court, a twenty-two-year-old wireless operator from Tonbridge in Kent, managed to parachute into the grounds of a large property on the outskirts of Velp. Once he was discovered by the owner, who had a policy of handing any captured Allied airmen over to the Germans, my mother was fetched because she spoke English.

The fourteen-year-old girl whom Max later described as "beautiful with a lovely personality" explained that he would be taken as a prisoner of war. Accepting his fate, Max handed her his gold signet ring, which he feared would be taken from him by the Germans. "I promise to give it back to you after the war," she told him solemnly, and for the next four years she wore it on a chain around her neck.

As was my mother's way, after the war she played down her Resistance role, saying, "Every loyal Dutch schoolgirl and -boy did a little bit to help. Many were much more courageous than I was." And she was right. Huge risks were taken by the few who used illegal wireless sets to listen to Queen Wilhelmina and her government-in-exile broadcast messages to their beleaguered nation on the program *Radio Oranje*. These messages were quickly spread by word of mouth to boost morale.

Mum always said that *occupation* was too small a word to describe life under Nazi control. It didn't cover what felt to her like an eternity of enslavement and constant danger after the Germans arrived to pillage their country. All sense of normality melted away. She could no longer go to school or see her friends.

"The things I saw during the occupation made me very realistic about life," she said, adding, "Don't discount anything awful you hear or read about the Nazis. It's worse than you could ever imagine. I came out of the war thankful to be alive, aware that human relationships are the most important thing of all, far more than wealth, food, luxury, careers, or anything you can mention." She added that her family got through the war only by imagining that it would be over any day—"Next week, six months, next year.... Had we known that we were going to be occupied for five years, we might have all shot ourselves."

———◆———

IN THE SUMMER OF 1944, the family heard some thrilling news—Allied soldiers had landed in Normandy. Along with the rest of the country, my jubilant mother imagined imminent liberation. "After living long months and years under the Germans, you dreamed what would happen if you ever got out," she would recall. "You swore you would never complain about anything again."

Sadly, nothing changed, and with no Allied intervention to save them, the restrictions on food and fuel only tightened. The family began to suffer serious hunger then and lived on boiled vegetables, wild mushrooms, and crackers—until they ran out. They went to bed early every night, as the electricity was patchy and lamp oil and candles were precious. Once the nights started to draw in, they were permanently cold and hungry.

With so many German soldiers battling the Allies, the Nazis were desperate for manpower, so more men, women, and teenagers from the occupied territories were taken and sent east. One day it was almost my mother's turn. As she rounded a corner in Arnhem after another futile search for food, she was apprehended by a German officer who already had a group of teenage girls lined up against a wall.

Mum said she knew that any moment a truck would arrive to take them away to work—or worse—so when the soldier was momentarily distracted, she made a run for it. Fleeing into the warren of streets and alleyways she knew so well, the terrified teenager hid in the basement of a bombed-out building, her heart pounding as her ears strained for the sounds of her pursuers. "The only thing I remember for certain is that, over and over and over, I kept saying to myself in Dutch, 'Our Father who art in heaven…'" She was too scared to move until—under the cloak of darkness—she crept out and made her way home to her mother, who was beside herself with worry.

Scared of being caught again, she didn't venture out for weeks, and, while trapped inside dark, airless rooms, she developed jaundice, anemia, and a form of rheumatism. The doctor prescribed rest and a diet of red meat and leafy greens for her recovery, but there was no meat, and the only vegetable anyone could get was endive, a salad leaf she came to hate but bravely ate in the dishes she made for us when we were children.

Worse was to come when, in September 1944, the Allies launched a massive offensive code-named Operation Market Garden to secure the main bridges between Holland and Germany. Arnhem was targeted as a major hub of the retreating Wehrmacht thanks to its bridge across the Rhine offering a direct escape route.

As bombs began to rain down on the city, the theater of war landed right on the family's doorstep. Seeing the unprecedented mass of three thousand aircraft headed their way and hearing the start of what would become a relentless bombardment that virtually flattened Arnhem, they sought shelter in their basement for the worst early weeks, huddled together on mattresses with almost nothing to eat or drink.

All my mother could see of the world outside was a slice of blue sky through a small window as they heard German V-1 rockets being launched nearby. Night and day they felt the bone-rattling crump of exploding shells and listened to the constant rat-tat-tat of antiaircraft fire. "I knew the cold clutch of human terror all through my teens," she later remembered. "I saw it, felt it, heard it—and it never goes away. You see, it wasn't just a nightmare: I was there, and it all happened."

Still, she sought the positives in their situation, and the family rallied together and did what they could to keep their spirits up. "We needed each other so badly that we were kind, we hid each other, we gave each other something to eat." She told me how they decorated their temporary basement home with furniture and art from their living room and entertained themselves with music and songs by candlelight. They swapped books and read pages aloud—anything to keep their minds off what was happening. They even shared memories of their favorite meals, although the thought only made them hungrier still.

Crowded into that limited space, huddled with the others around a candle or small fire, Mum learned lessons in humanity that she never forgot, and there was something unexpected too. "It was not all misery," she recalled. "In many ways it was quite a wonderful period.... The circumstances brought family and friends closer. You ate the last potatoes together."

She was especially grateful for her grandfather Aarnoud, a man I sadly never met, who stepped into the role of father and gave her the affection she'd craved. The two of them would sit doing old crosswords together by the light of a single oil lamp, or she'd draw sketches of her mother reading, or sunny depictions of happier times, including ladies in gowns and a seaside Punch-and-Judy show—pictures I still possess.

My mother said that during those dark days her relatives were marvelous. She spoke of how much she admired their innate resilience as well as the gallows humor with which they joked about everything from their lack of food to the Germans who marched in and out of their home. Although they were in such a dire situation, the family comic gene is a strong one, and they found amusement in some of what was happening and did their best to keep up morale. Very often laughter was all they had as they waited for the war to end, and, knowing how my mother loved to pull silly faces and strike amusing poses, I am sure she helped lift the mood. She always said that, in many ways, she wouldn't have missed what she called those "delicate, precious years" because she learned so much about human nature. They were lessons she put to good use throughout her life.

When the battle for Arnhem finally ended in a bitter Allied defeat on September 26, 1944, with thousands dead, the Germans took swift revenge on all those who had assisted the Allied advance. The entire country was punished by a brutal blockade that prevented vital transports of food getting through. When Arnhem's remaining citizens were forcibly evacuated, thousands of homeless people took to the streets with what little they had, many of them traipsing through Velp on their way west.

"I feel sick when I remember the scenes," my mother said. "It was human misery at its starkest—masses of refugees on the move, some carrying their dead, babies born on the roadside, hundreds collapsing of hunger." As ever more evacuees arrived and several were sheltered in the van Heemstra villa, people slept on the floor or in chairs until the Germans ordered them all out.

What the Nazis didn't know was that the family was also sheltering an escaped British Army major right under their noses—in their basement. He was a decorated officer named Tony Deane-Drummond, famous for two previous daring wartime escapes. When the Resistance finally arranged for his evacuation, my grandmother opened an old bottle of champagne for his send-off. He made it back to Britain to rise to the rank of major general and become one of the chief architects of the modern Special Air Service (SAS), but he never forgot the family's kindness—and courage.

IN WHAT WAS TO PROVE the last and most challenging months of the war in Holland, Velp was under near-constant attack, and many of the houses surrounding my grandfather's were set alight or blown to pieces. Parts of their own villa were badly damaged too. Mum said they never knew how much of their own property was still left standing above them until they peered out between raids. Still working in the hospital when she could, she continued to help deal with the wounded and was especially good at comforting children grieving the loss of parents or siblings.

Then winter returned, and with nothing growing and all train traffic stopped, the few supplies of food left dwindled. The family had no heat and no electricity. Their only light and warmth came from a small fire they burned in the cellar, kindled with whatever wood they could forage. Praying for liberation after five years of oppression, the family sat around and made up stories, entertaining each other any way they could to take their minds off what Mum would later call their "horrible life."

There was little left in the few remaining shops, and their daily rations amounted to less than five hundred calories. They didn't know it yet, but the beleaguered Dutch were heading for what became known as the Hongerwinter, the famine of the 1944 to 1945 winter that killed at least twenty thousand people and left thousands close to death. To make matters worse, a tuberculosis epidemic swept through the weakest, killing hundreds more.

My mother became highly anemic and had asthma, painful joints, and swollen legs, all from long-term malnutrition. The swelling was called edema, and she found out later that she could have died had the swelling traveled up her legs and reached her heart. As she told a reporter after the war, "Five years of malnutrition is no joke."

Although she was often too weak even to enjoy the solace of dance, she continued delivering vital drugs and the Resistance bulletin to those still sheltering in their suburb. She even handed out festive gifts to Velp's children for Sinterklaas, the traditional Saint Nicholas Eve, taking them from a secret stash of toys the Resistance had discovered, hoarded by the Germans to send to families back home.

With nothing growing in the winter, the family was living on stored turnips and a kind of bread made from tulip bulb flour. Local soup kitchens served a watery broth made of cabbage and carrots, while others distributed whatever food they could find and tried to get milk to the youngest children. There was no sugar, candy, or wheat. Candles and matches cost many guilders, and meat was nonexistent.

Most of the family pets had been killed and eaten, so they also lived on leftover dog biscuits and a kind of green bread made from dried pea flour, as well as maggoty sugar beets and sour potatoes. These were turned into a stew called hutspot, or a porridge-like mash known as stamppot. Some in Holland resorted to eating grass, but I don't think things got quite that bad in Velp, although my mother did fill herself up with cups of hot water.

Whenever they became desperate, one member of the family would volunteer to hike to an outlying farm and trade cash, gold, jewelry—anything of value—for a few eggs or some bread. There was a story of one local farmer who traded his supplies for so much art, antiques, and jewelry that he hid it all in an underground bunker for fear of the Germans discovering his stash. When he went to recover his loot after the war, the bunker was waterlogged and almost everything spoiled.

The longest the beleaguered family went without food was over

Christmas 1944. To trick their grumbling bellies into feeling full, they drank plenty of water or sipped thin vegetable broth. Age fifteen, my mother remained in bed to conserve energy and read a well-thumbed copy of Tolstoy's *War and Peace* several times over until she became too tired even to read. "I'd heard one could sleep and forget hunger," she later said. "So perhaps I could sleep all through Christmas. I'd try." By the third day, there wasn't any broth left or even a slice of green bread, which is when her aunt instructed her to stay in bed and sleep.

"I was very sick but didn't realize it. My mother often looked at me and said, 'You look so pale.' I thought she was just fussing, but now I understand how she must have felt." Despite the bleakness of their situation, she never lost hope entirely and still believed in the power of prayer. Incredibly, her prayers were answered when salvation arrived in the form of a Christmas miracle. "That very night, a member of the underground brought us food." There was flour, jam, oatmeal, and cans of butter. "And potatoes—the most wonderful and beautiful thing I ever saw."

Venturing out between air raids for some fresh air and to assess the damage to their neighborhood, my mother continued to search for food and fuel. One day she found herself in the middle of a convoy of German tanks just at the moment when a squadron of British Spitfires homed in from above, opening fire. Sheltering under one of the tanks, her hands over her ears, she found it ironic that she was saved from the strafing of Allied bullets by the armor of an enemy war machine.

In another rare moment of madness, pale as a ghost from being trapped inside for years, she risked venturing outside once more to soak up some sun in the garden of the villa and feel the warmth on her bones. As she told a reporter years later, she'd almost dropped off to sleep when the earth shuddered beneath her, and she fell off her seat. Expecting to be "blown to oblivion," she dug into the earth with her nails in fear as fragments of shell whizzed past her and gravel peppered her skin like buckshot. What she didn't reveal was that a small piece of shrapnel embedded itself in her neck and had to be removed. The story came to light only in 1990, when she went to Ecuador for UNICEF and struck up a friendship with her interpreter there, an American named Gary Stahl.

"We chatted about lots of things over whisky in a bar one night and I asked how she managed to maintain her amazing posture even during long car journeys on terrible roads," he remembered. "I told her, 'I understand on a movie set you have to hold yourself in a certain way, but you are like that all the time!' That's when she told me that not long before the war ended, she was hit by a piece of shrapnel. 'There was an incident,' she admitted. 'It left me so I can't bend my neck in the ways other people can.' She looked at me then as if she regretted confiding in me and added, 'Promise not to tell anyone as long as I'm alive!' She didn't want anyone feeling sorry for her or taking pity, so I kept my promise. She was an amazing woman and so humble."

I had never heard that part of the story and didn't know about the secret memento of war she carried, but it made perfect sense. She always held her head and neck in a certain way, even when playing with us at home. Everyone thought she'd learned her deportment from being a dancer, but there may have been more to her poise than she allowed even us to know.

One morning not long afterward, in April 1945, the explosions and shelling she'd grown so accustomed to in Velp stopped abruptly. As my fifteen-year-old mother and her family crept cautiously out of their basement, they were amazed to hear English voices and even distant singing. Instead of the familiar smell of cordite, she caught a whiff of real cigarettes, which she thought was the most wonderful scent in the world after years of those around her smoking stinky ersatz roll-ups made from the leaves of local trees. This new and distinctive aroma could mean only one thing: liberation.

"That was the day I learned that freedom has a bouquet, a perfume all its own—the smell of English tobacco and petrol," she said later, inhaling the memory as if smelling a favorite rose. When the family opened the front door and peered cautiously out, they found themselves surrounded by Canadian soldiers aiming their weapons at them. One, who had orders to investigate the radio station in their attic, politely apologized for disturbing them. My mother laughed and "screamed with happiness" before telling their liberator, "You can go right on disturbing us." Surprised to hear her speak, the soldiers gave a cheer for liberating "the only English girl for miles."

Having been given her first cigarette and five bars of chocolate, she made herself violently unwell by choking on the smoke and gorging on the sweets along with a tin of condensed milk, but it all felt worthwhile. The war was finally over, and she celebrated her sixteenth birthday three days before peace was formally declared. Even though she was very weak, their salvation was enough to make my mother dance because, as she later put it, "Life began again."

◆

4.

I came out of the war thankful to be alive, aware that human relationships are the most important thing of all.—AH

INT. A LARGE SCHOOL CLASSROOM, VELP, HOLLAND, May 1945

AUDREY, sixteen, wearing a sunflower-yellow cotton dress that's too big for her and tied at the waist with some cord, stares wide-eyed at the clothes stuffed into the crates stacked haphazardly on the floor of her old school classroom.

Her jaw dropping, she watches as women and children rummage frenziedly through the dresses, blouses, trousers, and coats donated to those who survived the Hunger Winter. Behind her, her mother, **ELLA VAN HEEMSTRA**, stands equally agog until she snaps herself out of it and pushes her daughter forward.

ELLA
Don't be shy, Audrey. Go and pick out something
to wear for the summer.
You'll need skirts and cardigans,
a couple of dresses, some new
shoes—definitely shoes.

AUDREY
But who sent all this, Mummy? I don't
understand.

ELLA
Americans, mostly. Although things have
come from all over. Now stop dawdling or
all the good clothes will be gone.

AUDREY takes a few steps into the room and wanders to a box spilling over with garments as her mother starts on an adjacent crate. Reaching for a strip of green fabric, **AUDREY** pulls out a large square scarf that was stuffed into the pocket of a thick woolen coat she'd have died for the previous winter.

ELLA, draping dresses over her forearm, sees what **AUDREY** is holding between her hands and gasps.

ELLA
Let me see that. Goodness, that's silk. It's
Dior! Well done, Audrey. Keep going.

AUDREY
But why have people given away
things that look so new?

ELLA
Well, they might seem new to us, but others might think they were too last season. People know we have nothing here, and they want to help. It's called humanity.

ELLA lays the dresses she is holding on her crate and takes the scarf from **AUDREY**'s hands.

ELLA
Here, let me show you what you can do with this. You can wear it around your head and tie it under your chin, or throw it around your shoulders like this, tying it in a loose knot at the front. Voilà. Now, where's a belt? Ah, yes, here, look. This is genuine leather. Slip off that old cord and replace it with this. Quickly now.

AUDREY undoes the cord and allows her mother to fasten her dress with the narrow belt. Tugging on **AUDREY**'s shabby dress to pull out the wrinkles, she turns her to face a mirror in the corner of the room.

AUDREY
(gasping)
Why, I look completely different!

Turning, she runs her fingers through her hair and gazes in wonder.

ELLA

What did I tell you? You can wear the same old dress every day, but with a different scarf or a clever piece of jewelry, people forget about the dress and start noticing how stylish you are.

AUDREY

It's like magic! And I feel different, Mummy. I really do.
(smiling shyly)
I feel a bit like my old self again.

ELLA

In the right clothes you can be anything you want to be. Remember that, Audrey, and never underestimate the power of quality fabric or a simple line. Look how that scarf brings out your eyes! For an ugly duckling who's as thin as a reed, you could almost pass for attractive.

ELLA turns back to her crate to slap the hand of a young woman about to help herself to the dresses she's set aside.

ELLA
(hissing)
Oh, no you don't, missy! Pick your own things.

AUDREY, holding out the hem of her dress and curtseying balletically in the mirror, stares at her gaunt features before giving her reflection a resolute nod.

AUDREY
(whispering)
One day the ugly duckling saw his own reflection in the water and realized that he had grown up to be a beautiful swan...

AUDREY turns back to the box with sudden enthusiasm, her fingers reaching in as her face breaks into a smile.

THE INDIVIDUALITY THAT MY MOTHER was known for was first forged by her wartime experiences. The teenager who'd had to give up her dream of becoming a prima ballerina was forced to reinvent herself, even though that fantasy had helped sustain her throughout wartime when food couldn't.

After liberation, she and her mother found themselves in a dramatic change of circumstances with all their valuables lost and their money stolen and had to do whatever they could to get by. They survived initially on charitable relief—food and clothing provided by the United Nations Relief and Rehabilitation Administration (UNRRA).

"I remember lots of flour and butter and oatmeal, and all the things that really feed a child and that we hadn't seen in ages. It was everything we dreamed of." Her first proper meal in years was sugary porridge with condensed milk. She ate so much of it, she became "deadly ill," as she wasn't used to absorbing food, let alone anything rich. But that first cigarette sparked a lifelong addiction that often surprised those who had imagined her to be unsullied by such habits.

Once peace was declared, my mother was desperate to go to the movies—an everyday experience that had been denied her for years. With the local cinema leveled by shelling, innovative Canadian troops erected a screen across a narrow street and set up a projector and chairs in the town square. One of the first films she saw was *Spellbound*, starring Gregory Peck, but she was also crazy about Gary Cooper in *For Whom the Bell Tolls*. She loved the musical *Top Hat*, starring Fred Astaire, for its dance routines and fell for another heartthrob of the era named James Stewart. Sitting in the dark, staring up at the silver screen, she could never have imagined that one day, she'd get to star alongside most of them.

Her mother the baroness, who also had two sons to feed after they'd returned from slave labor and being in hiding, survived the war with barely a cent but somehow managed to scrape enough together from friends and family to take her daughter to Amsterdam to resume her ballet training. She knew it would be the best way for her to recover her physical and spiritual health. The two boys remained behind to continue their education while my mother and grandmother lived in a single room in a house shared with other tenants.

It was while they were living there in 1946 that a woman who lived on the same floor knocked on their door. She was an editor at a publishing house who had a first draft of a book she thought my seventeen-year-old mother might be interested in.

"My publishers are releasing it soon but asked me to canvass for opinions and, knowing how much Audrey loves to read, I thought she could give us some insight into the mind of a teenage girl caught up in war," she told Ella. "It's called *Het Achterhuis, The Secret Annex*, and is a diary written by a hidden Jewish girl named Anne Frank."

Neither she nor my grandmother imagined the devastating effect reading Anne's diary would have on my mother, who immediately identified deeply with the dead girl and her wartime experiences. Sobbing into her pillow for days, she was reprimanded by her mother for her unseemly histrionics, even though Ella appreciated that the similarities between the two girls' lives were uncanny.

For my mother, Anne felt like a soul sister. They were almost the same age, and both had lived in fear of the Nazis for years while dreaming of success, marriage, and children after the war. "She wrote about everything I experienced and felt," Mum told me. "Like me, she lost her freedom and spent years staring at four walls feeling wretched and with very little to do. Everything she wrote about nature and life and love was all that I experienced. She even reported on the shooting of innocent hostages, including my uncle Otto. It was like having the war played back to me."

From the day my mother finished reading the diary, she never stopped thinking about the girl with an overwhelming desire to survive who had perished in the Holocaust with almost her entire family. Mum's natural ability to empathize deeply began and ended with Anne Frank in many ways. The shadow of the dead girl followed her throughout her life, and she drew inspiration from Anne Frank's words, especially during her UNICEF years.

As my mother herself admitted, "War left me with a deep knowledge of human suffering which I expect many other young people never know about. The things I saw during the occupation made me very realistic about life, and I've been that way ever since."

My daughter, Emma, has learned a lot about the grandmother she sadly never met and said of the war, "I think her reaction to the trauma of wartime was to be in a constant state of gratitude—she carried the great responsibility and privilege that comes with having survived the unsurvivable. Today we might call this 'survivor's guilt,' but I think ultimately it led to her never taking a single day, a gift from life, or a measure of success for granted. She wanted to live up to the chance she had been given."

Insisting that she had been merely "the right girl in the right place at the right time," my mother put her success down to luck. After almost dying as a baby, she was fortunate enough to survive the war when people around her died of starvation or were blown to bits. Then she won a scholarship to study with the Ballet Rambert in London and lived under the roof of its founder, Madame Marie Rambert. After a year of trying to get back to her previous form, she learned that after the privations of the Hunger Winter she had neither the stamina nor sufficient technique to become the prima ballerina she longed to be.

Marie Rambert broke the news to her that although my mother had the dedication and self-discipline, she would never make it to the top because of malnutrition and the years of training and muscle development that she'd missed. Her ballet mistress kindly offered her the chance to teach, but that wasn't what my mother wanted, and she left her generous tutelage.

"I was absolutely crushed," she explained. "I just wanted to vanish then because my dream had died." It was only later that she accepted the news had been a lucky break because if she hadn't been told the truth, she might have carried on trying rather than finding an alternative way to earn a living. Instead, she kept looking for another way into the spotlight.

Hoping to cheer her up, that Christmas my grandmother took my mother back to Kent to visit old friends from before the war. Once there, they were sad to discover that Mr. Butcher, their kind host, had died in 1945 at the age of sixty-two. They spent some time with his widow, Evelyn, and their little dog before moving on to a task that my mother had waited several years to complete.

Max Court, the downed airman she had been a translator for in Velp, had eventually returned to his family in Tonbridge after two years in a POW camp. He was astonished to hear from my teenage mother that she was in the area and wished to return his gold ring. Delighted to be reunited with it—and his young savior—he took her to a New Year's Eve dance with his girlfriend. The story made the local newspaper, and, when asked why she was there, my mother replied simply, "Why, I promised to give Max back his ring!"

WITH HER CAREER PLAN DASHED and no money, Mum took the only work she could find in London—as a chorus girl in cabaret shows, where she showed early promise despite not having a clue what to do at first. "I was the tense, rigid girl trained for ballet who had to watch everyone else." Once she got the hang of it, though, she recalled those days as some of the best of her life. "I *loved* being in the chorus," she declared. "Dancing and being one of the girls was so much fun. I never wanted our time together to end."

The British comedian Bob Monkhouse, who later became a joke writer for the likes of Jack Benny and Bob Hope, knew her as a twenty-year-old dancer in a 1950 West End revue called *Sauce Piquante*. Their costars included the comedians Norman Wisdom and Tommy Cooper. When Monkhouse first met my mother and asked about her accent, she grinned and told him, "I'm half Irish, half Dutch, and I was born in Belgium. If I was a dog, I'd be in a hell of a mess!" He later said the other girls in the chorus line loved my mother because of her sweetness and had a lot of fun with her backstage, where she'd adopted a stray cat. But they were also jealous of how much attention she attracted from the audience, even though she was the worst dancer. One told Monkhouse, "They can't take their eyes off that face! Those eyes! That bloody smile! She's a darling girl but, honestly, I could just murder that Audrey Hepburn."

Monkhouse, who went on to have a small part alongside Mum in one of her earliest roles, in the film *Secret People*, had a theory about how she seemed to affect people so profoundly. "She had an air of defenselessness; of helplessness," he wrote in his memoir *Crying with Laughter*. "When people sense this, they respond to it immediately.... I think everyone in the audience thought, *I want to look after little Audrey.* She seemed to be too pretty; too unaware of the dangers of life."

I was touched to read a letter from an admirer who'd seen one of my mother's West End shows. It was something my mother had kept for more than forty years and that I found in her personal effects. It speaks volumes that it was from a WWII serviceman, because her whole life after the war, she gravitated toward those who'd served or had experienced war.

Captain Roger Marley, who was in the Parachute Regiment, wrote: "You will, I hope, forgive a stranger for writing to you. I have read that you were at Arnhem on 17th of September when we landed by parachute. Had I known you were there I would have fought until I was killed to get you out because, if you will excuse me for saying it, you are by far the most attractive girl I have ever seen. Don't worry, I am no 'wolf.' I have an attractive wife and a fine child, but the fact remains had I known you were at Arnhem on that day I should not now be alive to write to you. In conclusion, I do hope you will have all the luck and success you deserve. I apologize for the fact that we only fought for nine days. We did our best."

Instead of taking up with a soldier, however, my mother began her first romantic relationship when she met the Belgian singer Marcel Le Bon, who sang his way through *Sauce Piquante*. The crooner, three years her senior, promised to take her on a nightclub tour with him. My grandmother thoroughly disapproved, of course, and was delighted when the tour never happened because of a lack of funding and the pair split up.

At the suggestion of her fellow chorus girls, who were far more experienced at finding ways to make money, Mum auditioned for a few bit parts in some B movies because she needed the cash. "Acting paid three pounds more than ballet jobs," she explained, ever the pragmatist. My financially destitute grandmother, who—along with her family—had lost almost everything in the war, joined her from Holland and found work as a concierge at an apartment building in London in return for a small flat and a meager wage. Scrubbing the stairs, supervising workmen, and delivering the mail, she did whatever she could to make ends meet while my mother fell into acting.

She appeared for a few seconds in the 1951 movie *The Lavender Hill Mob*, wearing a pale couture dress with a black belt and gloves as she kissed the cheek of the film's British star, Alec Guinness, in thanks for a gift. Despite the brevity of her performance, she made an immediate impression. "She only had half a line to say, and I don't think she even said it in any particular or interesting way," Guinness reported later. "But her fawn-like beauty and presence were remarkable."

PART OF WHAT MADE HER so remarkable for the times was her distinctive personal style, which spoke volumes about the chic individualist she'd become. Prior to movie budgets and high fashion, her postwar look and mode of dress were entirely original. Cutting her hair short for simplicity, the shy, skinny teenager whose dresses hung off her was a perfect package of imperfections.

A refugee with a childlike enthusiasm for pretty things, she owned only a skirt, a blouse or two, and one good dress—all made by her on a little sewing machine. Taking her mother's advice, she'd jazz up her outfits with a beret and one of the many silk scarves she'd been collecting since the war.

Malnourished and without funds, she chose clothes that suited her body—and her purse—like many women of her era, who exercised far more caution than women do today when it came to buying clothes. Most invested in a few signature pieces rather than filling their closets with cheaper items they hardly ever wore. And my mother's outfits, such as a turtleneck sweater and slacks, were opposite to what everyone else was wearing. She might add subtle embellishments like a sprig of heather or a pinched-in belt, but never to excess, impressing everyone she met with her innate élan by creating a great look out of very little.

On her size 8½ feet she wore the ballet flats she'd always felt most comfortable in, which had the added advantage of detracting from the fact that she was taller than most girls her age. With her dancer's posture and European sophistication, she was able to carry it off. Whenever she could get hold of some special item of clothing from a thrift store or a friend, she loved the way it made her feel. Simply wearing something silky against her skin or feeling the soft touch of cashmere gave her a little more faith in herself.

"There is something magical about a beautifully made dress," she once said, "and no substitute for exquisite detail, a perfect fit, a fine fabric. You can wear it season after season with a confident feeling of being well dressed." From an early age, she came to value the confidence good clothing gave her. It was a kind of armor.

Her look and her screen presence were enough to get her noticed in the industry, and before long she was signed by the British television and movie company ABC for the princely sum of fifty pounds per week, around $1,500 in today's money. She could hardly believe it and, with customary humility, later said, "I probably hold the distinction of being one movie star who, by all laws of logic, should never have made it. At each stage of my career, I lacked the experience."

She also lacked experience in love, but when she began to mix in new social circles during the summer of 1950, at the age of twenty-one, she met a statuesque Englishman named James Hanson. Drawn to elfin actresses, the six-foot-four son of a wealthy Yorkshire hauler had already dated the actress Jean Simmons, who had a similar appearance to my mother. During the war, Hanson had served with the Duke of Wellington's Regiment, which had taken part in Operation Manna, in which more than three thousand sorties by the Royal Air Force dropped 6,684 tons of food to the starving population of Holland, including my mother's family.

From the day in April 1945 when, as a teenager, she'd emerged from the family cellar to find smiling Allied soldiers bringing freedom and chocolate, Mum had felt a deep affinity with and gratitude toward those who served to help liberate people like her. Now she was dating one of those handsome ex-servicemen. Seven years her senior and an accomplished sportsman, pilot, and sailor, Hanson was the kind of playboy and businessman that her father, Joseph Ruston, had always aspired to be. The comparison can't have been lost on her, especially as she'd built up her absentee dad to be a vaguely heroic character in her mind and not at all like the scoundrel Ella painted him to be, forbidding her to try to make any contact.

I don't think it's true that my mother was looking for father figures all her life, as some have suggested. But, having grown up surrounded by adults, she certainly gravitated toward men who were more mature. A former army officer who was tall, accomplished, and dashing would have been perfect husband material, and I'm certain my grandmother approved.

The handsome young couple were first introduced at Les Ambassadeurs Club in London, and my mother later described their meeting as "love at first sight." Hanson said years later, "Everybody saw in her this wonderful life and brightness and terrific strength of character. She was a very strong young woman." When he proposed a few months later, my mother happily accepted. For someone who'd once believed she was too ugly ever to find a husband, James Hanson was almost too good to be true. She even had her mother's blessing, proven by the fact that Ella did the unthinkable and served the couple breakfast in bed one morning when Hanson stayed overnight.

Having given up the rigors of daily ballet training, Mum didn't imagine that her part-time acting would interfere too much with the business of being married to an international businessman with apartments in New York and London. Besides, James Hanson was generally supportive and assured her that she could still do "one movie or play a year" after they were married.

"James is being wonderfully understanding," she told reporters fascinated by the relationship between the scion and his actress girlfriend. "He knows it would be impossible for me to give up my career completely. I just can't. I've worked too long to achieve something." But she also promised that she'd stop working for their first year of marriage just to enjoy being his wife.

Her next role was one she was thrilled about. She was to play the innocent ballet-dancing younger sister to the main character in *Secret People*, a 1952 black-and-white movie about political refugees caught up in acts of terrorism. This first introduced her to the British screenwriter and film director Thorold Dickinson, a compassionate man who quickly put her at ease. If he hadn't done so, she might never have secured her next role—the one that propelled her to stardom.

Although she'd had only a minor part, Dickinson had been immediately impressed by my mother's natural talent. She had what he later called a "silent movie star quality," meaning that her facial expressions and the way she moved her body mattered more than her dialogue. He advised her to connect to the emotions of her character rather than focusing on the acting or the script. "If you get the feeling right, everything else will take care of itself." It was advice she took to heart, and during one scene where her character had to witness a bombing, she broke down in tears, remembering all that she had seen in Arnhem. That was true empathy.

HER NEXT PIECE OF LUCK happened in the autumn of 1951, when Thorold Dickinson was approached by William Wyler, an Oscar-winning director looking for an unknown actress to play opposite the actor Gregory Peck in a new film called *Roman Holiday*. The role was that of a princess who briefly escapes from the rigorous confines of her life, so Wyler wanted someone with a European accent and an air of royalty about her.

The film had been searching for a backer for some time before Paramount took it on, and the sixteen-year-old British actress Elizabeth Taylor and forty-four-year-old Cary Grant were originally suggested for the parts. Grant turned the offer down because he felt he was too old, and Taylor was locked into another studio contract. Then Jean Simmons was suggested, but there was another scheduling clash.

Switching tack and after studying the work of several unknowns, Wyler selected five young women for screen tests to be filmed by Thorold Dickinson on a soundstage at Pinewood Studios on the outskirts of London. The list included my mother, even though she was contractually obliged to star in an Anglo-French production called *Monte Carlo Baby*, to be filmed in Monaco immediately after the screen test. This meant she wouldn't be able to start filming in Italy until the following summer, but that fit with the schedules of the rest of the cast and Wyler himself, who was finishing up the movie *Carrie* with Laurence Olivier and Jennifer Jones.

My mother's memories of her first screen test for a major Hollywood director were vivid. "I was terribly young and terribly new and had no sense about anything," she recalled. Realizing how nervous she was, Thorold reminded her to draw on her own life experiences, especially what she'd lived through in Holland.

After loading the film into the camera and recording the scene she'd rehearsed a dozen times, he kept the camera rolling and began casually chatting with her. "He was fully aware that I was petrified and didn't know how to go about a test," she explained years later. "He asked me questions about myself and what I liked or disliked, and I soon forgot about the camera.... What he did was very good and very clever and very fortunate for me because once I'd played my scene, which I did very badly, he just had me sit and talk to him."

Thorold quizzed her on her life before, during, and after the war. She had already told him how she'd hidden in the basement during air raids, but in response to his gentle questioning, she also told him about her silent candlelit ballet performances to raise money for the Resistance. When he asked what the Germans had thought of them, my mother smiled shyly. "Why, they didn't know about it!" she replied, grinning. Even after she thought the test was over, the camera kept rolling and caught her giggling with relief and asking, "How was it? Was I any good?"

The footage was enough to convince William Wyler that the young unknown Audrey Hepburn was perfect to play the role he had in mind for her. In his letter to Thorold a few weeks later, he wrote: "The test you made is a fine piece of work, and I just wanted to tell you how much we liked it here at the studio. You gave us a good look at the girl's personality and charm, as well as her talent. As a result... a number of the producers at Paramount have expressed interest in casting her."

I don't know if Mum ever bumped into Thorold Dickinson again after that, although I'd love to think so. I was pleased to learn that he became a juror for several film festivals and the first professor of film at London's Slade School of Fine Art. It would have been like her to stay in touch in writing at least, as she ranked him with many of the more famous directors she later worked with and was forever grateful that she'd been fortunate enough to have him by her side for that first test.

Thorold also never forgot that day with my mother at Pinewood. "The minute you saw [her test], you knew she'd get the part," he said. He was right, and my mother counted it as a blessing that only a few years after she'd been saved from starvation by international aid, she had begun what she always referred to as her "lovely career." It was a dream come true.

My errant grandfather
Joseph Hepburn-Ruston
(Hepburn family archive)

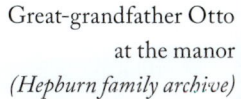

Great-grandfather Otto
at the manor
(Hepburn family archive)

Ella, Baroness van Heemstra
(Hepburn family archive)

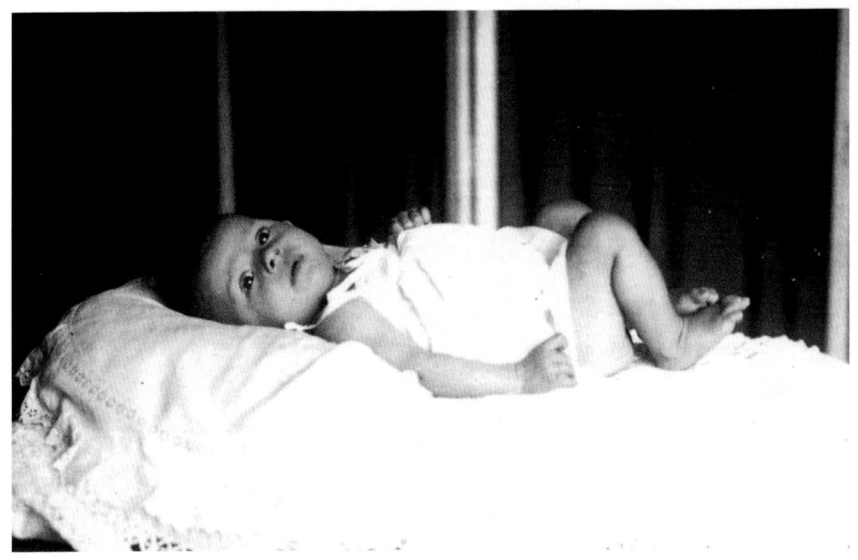
Mum was beautiful even as a baby *(Hepburn family archive)*

Nose in a book, always
(Hepburn family archive)

Her treasured photo of her father before he left *(Hepburn family archive)*

The house in Velp, where my mother lived out the war in the basement *(Hepburn family archive)*

Childhood designs Hubert de Givenchy would have been proud of *(Hepburn family archive)*

Colette, her first lucky charm *(Hepburn family archive)*

The play that made her famous: *Gigi*, New York, 1951 *(Hepburn family archive)*

Checking the costumes for *Sabrina* with Hubert de Givenchy. *(Courtesy of Paramount Pictures)*

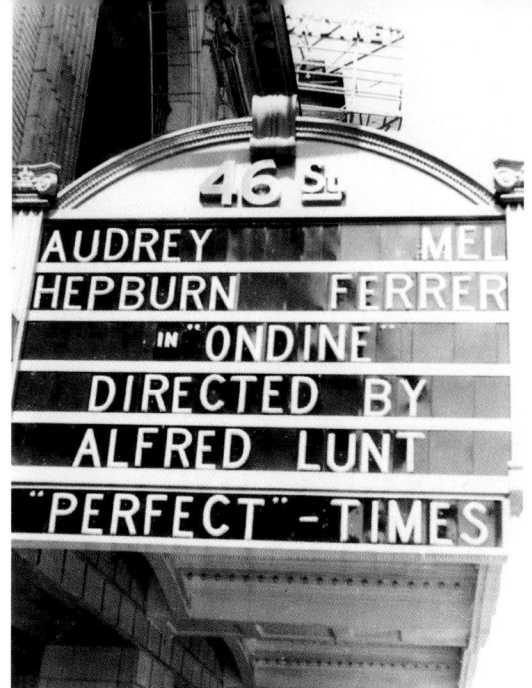

The marquee for *Ondine* with my father *(Hepburn family archive)*

With my grandmother the baroness in London in the late 1950s *(Hepburn family archive)*

Wedding day with Mel, Switzerland, 1954 *(© Ernst Haas / Ernst Haas Estate)*

Leaving the chapel *(© Ernst Haas / Ernst Haas Estate)*

My grandmother admiring my mother's wedding band *(© Ernst Haas / Ernst Haas Estate)*

Winter sleigh ride in St. Moritz
(© Sanford Roth / mptvimages.com)

With Dame Margot Fonteyn, prima ballerina, in Paris *(© Sid Avery / mptvimages.com)*

Arriving at Amsterdam to support BNMO, which helps war veterans and has for more than fifty years awarded a trophy named after her *(Hepburn family archive)*

Dancing with Eddie Fisher and Elizabeth Taylor *(Hepburn family archive)*

Downtime during filming for Mum and Fred Astaire *(Gerard Decaux / Courtesy of Paramount Pictures)*

Montage from *Funny Face* *(© Bill Avery / mptvimages.com)*

Towering over her in more ways than one in the chapel where they were wed
(© Philippe Halsman / Magnum Photos)

With Anne Frank's father, Otto, and his wife Elfriede at Bürgenstock *(Hepburn family archive)*

Our Marbella home—Santa Catalina *(Hepburn family archive)*

Celebrating her Oscar nomination for *The Nun's Story* on the Hassler hotel terrace in Rome *(© Pierluigi Praturlon / Reporters Associati & Archivi—Roma)*

Dad took this one of his pretty wife *(Mel Ferrer / Hepburn family archive)*

Happy at home in Switzerland *(Mel Ferrer / Hepburn family archive)*

Having fun on Lake Lucerne *(Hans Gerber, © Comet Photo AG)*

5.

*Opportunities don't often come along.
When they do, you have to grab them.—AH*

<u>INT. BACKSTAGE AT THE FULTON THEATRE, NEW YORK,
December 1951</u>

Twenty-two-year-old **AUDREY** beams into the camera
as her fingers play with her wig, which exactly
matches the color of her own short hair and gives
the impression of far longer tresses. Dressed
in the navy-blue nautical dress that defines her
role as Gigi, she is sitting in her dressing
room.

Behind her is a rack of outfits she'll change into
during the two-act adaptation of the novel by
Colette. In front of her is a five-man film crew
for CBS recording an episode of the popular TV
series *We the People*.

AUDREY

This is a wonderful Christmas for me. Miraculously, I'm in New York. On Broadway! I can hardly believe it. I never thought I'd land here with a face like mine. What luck!
(after a beat)
Now, the Christmas I want to tell you about is one that took place here... (she points to a photograph of a town pinned to her mirror) in Arnhem...

DIRECTOR

Cut!

AUDREY

Oh, did I do something wrong?

DIRECTOR

No, sweetheart, that's fine. It's just that if you're gonna talk about living under Nazi occupation, you shouldn't look quite so happy about it.

AUDREY

(laughing)
Oh, but I am so terribly happy! We were saved from starvation that December. It was our Christmas miracle. And then the war ended... on my birthday... and liberation was so exciting because everything was new. Suddenly we could do everything we longed to do. We ate jam and chocolate and danced in the streets! The feeling of being free again has never

really left me. It made everything bad that happened before disappear, don't you see?

DIRECTOR
(scratching his head)
Yeah, well, I guess so.

AUDREY
(breathlessly)
And here I am just a few years later doing something I could never have imagined in a million years. I wanted to be a ballet dancer, not an actress. And now I'm on Broadway and engaged to be married and about to star in a Hollywood movie even though I have little experience and don't even look right. It's all happened so terribly fast.

DIRECTOR
Well, maybe we should get some footage of you saying all that.

AUDREY
(grinning)
Yes, of course.

DIRECTOR
Okay, roll!

AUDREY
Where would you like me to start?

DIRECTOR
How about on the day your luck changed?

AUDREY
Very well. That would be in Monaco shortly after I'd been accepted for my first major Hollywood film even though I was about to star in a comedy, *Monte Carlo Baby*. One morning I was on the beach there when I spotted an old lady staring at me. She was in a wheelchair and had a cloud of bright-red hair. I waved and smiled but she didn't wave back. Then a day later, I was about to do my scene in the Hôtel de Paris when the same old lady was wheeled into view and looked at me in that strange way again. I couldn't understand what she found so fascinating.

DIRECTOR
Go on.

AUDREY
Well, I didn't know it then, but she was the famous author Colette, and she turned to her husband and cried, "*Voilà!* There is my Gigi!" She knew nothing about me but decided there and then that I should be the star of her Broadway play! Can you believe it?

DIRECTOR
Cut!
(after a beat)

That's great, Audrey. Thanks. That's
much more in the festive spirit. So this
all happened at Christmas, right?

AUDREY
(laughing)
No, not at all! It was a beautifully
warm and sunny September day.

DIRECTOR
(crestfallen)
Oh. Well, this episode has a Christmas
theme, so let's take a break and go from
the top on your first story.
Okay, kiddo?

The **DIRECTOR** steps away, and a makeup girl steps in to powder **AUDREY**'s face as she sits patiently, eyes closed.

MAKEUP GIRL
(dabbing gloss onto **AUDREY**'s lips)
Were you really discovered like that?

AUDREY
(opening her eyes and beaming)
I was.

MAKEUP GIRL
Gosh. I've always wanted to go to
Europe—especially Paris.

AUDREY

(sighing)

Oh, you must. It's such a marvelous, romantic place. They call it the City of Light.

MAKEUP GIRL

(stopping and staring into Audrey's eyes)

I can't imagine what it's like to have your life—traveling, being onstage, meeting famous people.

AUDREY

(taking her by the hand)

But you don't understand! I can't imagine it either. I'd failed as a ballerina and became a chorus girl, working like an idiot doing twelve performances a week before a floor show in a nightclub. Anything to earn a buck. I'd never spoken a word onstage, but here I am. Colette was desperate for someone to play Gigi, and I just happened to be standing right in front of her.

MAKEUP GIRL

(sucking air through her teeth)

Gee. But you seem so natural. Like you've been acting your whole life.

AUDREY

(thoughtfully)

In a way, I suppose I have. All I know is that I'm going to make the most of my big break and pray that it lasts until the end of the run, so wish me luck!

My mother always insisted that she could never have achieved such success without a long list of people whom she considered lucky charms, including the celebrated French author Colette.

She dearly loved the eccentric grande dame crippled by rheumatism, who adored her in turn, having spotted her when she was desperate to find a young woman to play the lead in a Broadway adaptation of her bestselling novel. Not only did my mother look perfect for the part, but Colette also noted how others also recognized something special in this pixie of a girl. Another factor was that the screwball comedy she was starring in was being filmed in French and English, a breeze for my bilingual mother—a fact that further impressed.

A bisexual feminist who'd risked staying in Paris during the Nazi occupation of the Second World War despite having a Jewish husband, Colette was in her late seventies—the final years of her life—when she decided my mother was "the one." Despite her insistence, Mum never quite understood why anyone should think such a skinny survivor of war capable of being a star. As someone who'd previously spoken only a few lines of dialogue, she initially thanked the author profusely before adding that she couldn't possibly take the role because, as she had also told Thorold Dickinson, "I can't act!"

Colette refused to accept my mother's protests and encouraged her to seize the opportunity. "I have every faith in you, my dear," she said. Although Mum was eventually persuaded, she doubted her good fortune almost to the closing night.

There is an endearing photograph of Mum taken at Colette's apartment in Paris's Palais-Royal. Resting her head on the old lady's shoulder as the author reads to her from a memoir, she appears to have fallen under the spell of the vision in polka dot silk. It was a photograph Mum kept her whole life, not least because Colette signed it with the personalized inscription to her that read, "*Trésor que j'ai trouvé sur une plage!*"—"Treasure that I found on a beach!"

Although *Gigi* was a wonderful opportunity, my mother was lonely and nervous in New York and didn't know how she was going to get through each night's performance. Her mother was in London, her fiancé was away on business, and she didn't know anyone in the States. As luck would have it, she found a friend in a young British actor who was staying in the hotel room next door to hers. His name was David Niven.

One night a depressed hotel guest jumped out of his eighteenth-floor window, bouncing off my mother's windowsill as he fell. In shock, she pounded on David's door, not sure if she'd imagined the whole thing because her head was so full of anxiety.

A former soldier who'd risen to the rank of lieutenant-colonel after taking part in the Allied invasion of Normandy, David was almost twenty years older than my mother. Happily married, he was so kind to her that tragic night in Manhattan that they began a friendship that endured until his death from motor neuron disease in the 1980s. He made Switzerland his home in the 1960s, so when she moved there, too, not long afterward, they became neighbors, another happy coincidence. My mother viewed everything that happened to her—even the bad things such as a random suicide by a hotel guest—as good luck. She always said that it is only through our mistakes and our tragedies that we can learn. And, as always, she was right.

Colette was also proved right when *Gigi* became a huge success and my mother won the 1952 Theatre World Award. She was amazed by her sudden change in fortune and told one reporter, "Everything significant in my life has happened gloriously and unexpectedly." Such as James Hanson surprising her on the opening night of *Gigi* in New York with a diamond ring. Happy as she was to be formally engaged, she'd been a relative unknown when she'd first agreed to marry him. Since then, she'd worked in Monaco and been headhunted by one of the world's most famous authors, and she was appearing on Broadway. Before she knew it, she was to star in *Roman Holiday*, and from that day on, her feet would barely touch the ground. Everything seemed to be happening too fast.

Once their engagement was officially announced in *The Times* of London to even more international media interest, a wedding date was set for spring 1952, timed for when the play ended and before she started *Roman Holiday*. Bridesmaids were chosen, a gift list was sent out, and she had fittings for an ivory satin wedding dress made by Italian couturier Zoe Fontana of the famed Sorelle Fontana fashion house. By the time she'd completed more than two hundred performances of *Gigi* and was busy preparing for her role in her first Hollywood movie, however, the ceremony still hadn't taken place, and she persuaded James that it would be far better for her schedule—and her peace of mind—if it was postponed until after the filming was over. He agreed to wait.

ONE OF THE MATTERS FOREMOST in her mind was how she would look on the big screen. Still unsure of herself, she was certain that what she considered her physical flaws would ruin every shot. "I just don't see what all the fuss is about," she'd say, staring into the mirror.

Even when twirling and swirling in the beautiful bridal gown that was being hand-stitched for her, my mother still didn't appreciate that she could wear almost anything and look good. This was a talent recognized early on, however, by Edith Head, the Oscar-winning in-house costume designer for Paramount Pictures. Head oversaw her costumes for *Roman Holiday* and was—in some ways—another fortunate person in her life.

The first time they met, Mum was wearing an elegant dark suit with a white collar and cuffs and a fetching sprig of lily of the valley pinned to her lapel. Head said of her, "She was a little girl with the poise of the duchess of Windsor. If she were not an actress, she'd be a model or designer. As it is, she's all three: a girl way ahead of high fashion, who deliberately looks different from other women, who has dramatized her own slenderness into her chief asset."

Learning to make the most of herself on the hoof, my twenty-two-year-old mother found herself having to adapt to a strange new world of style and design. Paying close attention, she picked up tips from the experts around her, adding to her armory of ways in which to make herself feel more confident and better able to play the role she still couldn't quite believe she'd won.

Despite Mum's lack of confidence, Edith Head declared that she seemed to know what she wanted from the start and wasn't afraid to add her own suggestions to the drawings the studio's designers prepared for her. After looking at them from all angles, she'd scribble "doodles" of wide belts, simpler necklines, or some amusing, whimsical twist. Mum had loved to draw since childhood, when she'd sketched women in grand dresses, so it's no surprise to me that she made her own amendments. She always had such a visual sense of what she liked.

Head may have approved of what my mother added, but she didn't hold back her criticism. While measuring her for costumes, she flatly informed her that her face was too square, her breasts too small, and her collarbones so prominent that they created ugly hollows. Her redeeming feature, Head said, was her waist. She later told the press, "[Audrey] has the slimmest waist since the Civil War—nineteen and a half inches. You could get a dog collar around it." With that in mind, she designed my mother's outfits with skintight bodices to accentuate her hourglass figure and wasp waist.

Her criticism only added to the existing complexes of a woman still struggling to love herself. But what few appreciated was that she'd become the studio's most diligent student, eager to learn what worked for her and what didn't to make the most of her assets and enhance her natural sophistication and style.

The role called for two very different looks for the crown princess trapped in a life of tradition and duty who flees her palace for a day of fun and romance. Cutting both her hair and her psychological ties with her royal life, she forsakes ball gowns for everyday clothes and sets out, hungry for adventure. By the film's end, she makes a grown-up decision to walk away from the love of an American newspaperman and return to the destiny she was born to fulfill.

Overwhelmed, the love interest played by Gregory Peck lets her go, experiencing his own personal transformation from cynical hack to devoted collaborator. But it's the princess who steals every scene. Having realized that she has some agency after all, she accepts her true purpose on her own terms and returns to the traditions and tiaras.

My mother's character needed to look like an ordinary Italian girl, so Edith Head took her shopping. Letting her help choose her own clothes was like giving a child the key to the toy box, and she loved it. Their outings invariably ended with my mother insisting on a post spree "celebration" in a patisserie, where she would devour chocolate pastries with the glee of a toddler. There was only so much she could eat, however, as she had to fit into the costumes she loved. Better still, Paramount had agreed that she could keep her entire wardrobe as an early wedding present once she married James Hanson.

Roman Holiday's director, William Wyler, was another auspicious person in my mother's life. He said of her later, "She had everything I was looking for. She also was very funny. She was absolutely enchanting, and we said, 'That's the girl!'"

A Swiss Jew born in Germany who'd come to Hollywood in his twenties and made several films to aid the European war effort, he was yet another person with a wartime connection with whom my mother felt an instant rapport. When filming started in the summer of 1952, it was Wyler who helped calm her nerves. And it wasn't just stage fright that made her anxious. Italy was in the middle of a bitter political battle between opposing parties, US- and NATO-backed Christian Democrats, and filming in Rome was disrupted on several occasions by street clashes and strikes. Having only recently emerged from war, she was hypersensitive to the tension. When this was combined with the intense summer heat and the added pressure of thousands of excited spectators crowding around every location, she found herself having to do take after take, as Wyler demanded perfection from every scene.

"Don't act, just be," he advised, pointing out that the techniques she'd recently picked up on Broadway weren't subtle enough for film. "He'd been so adorable and very gentle with me," she said later. "Always bringing out the best in me." She added that he believed that only simplicity and truth counted. "It has to come from the inside. You can't fake it. I learned that from him." Wyler learned a lot from Mum, too, describing her at the time as "the spirit of youth," and said that she moved him to tears while he was editing the movie—"crusty veteran that I was." He added, "I knew that very soon the entire world would fall in love with her, as all of us on the picture did."

It wasn't all sweetness and light, however. When Wyler started to lose patience because his star couldn't cry in her big farewell scene, he reprimanded her so severely that it finally triggered the necessary tears. Floundering, my mother turned to someone who could offer her some sage advice—Gregory Peck, the thirty-six-year-old award-winning actor who'd been picked to play the role of the movie's hard-nosed American journalist, Joe Bradley.

Greg was another lucky friend who stood by Mum to the end of her days. By the 1950s he was an international superstar who played the lead in every movie he appeared in, and yet he'd originally started training as a doctor. Born in La Jolla, San Diego, during the First World War, Eldred Gregory Peck was raised by his grandmother after his parents divorced when he was five. After attending a Catholic military school, the six-foot-three student trained to be a doctor but never graduated and tried his hand at acting instead. Often broke and homeless, he tried to enlist during the war but was exempted by a spinal injury he'd suffered, so instead he started to make morale-boosting movies.

For *Roman Holiday*, Gregory Peck was guaranteed solo billing with the option to veto the director's choice of costar. When he was first shown the screen test for "the skinny little dancer from London," he realized that she was such a gift to the camera that she might easily steal the show. When he expressed his concerns, he was advised by William Wyler to meet my mother before deciding and was instantly charmed. Once he saw her act, he said afterward, "Watching her was like watching a flower suddenly come to bloom." He could see straightaway that even though she lacked experience, she had a natural magnetism that drew the eye. She also had an innate understanding of her relationship with the lens and what she needed to do in close-up.

Two weeks into production he called his agent and asked, "What's the billing clause?" The agent said that "Gregory Peck in *Roman Holiday*" would appear above the title, with "Introducing Audrey Hepburn" lower down. Greg told him, "That will not do. You have got to get her name moved up right alongside mine." His agent, Freddie "Mr. Citron," of the famed Chasin-Park-Citron agency, protested, but Greg said, "If Audrey's name is not up there when the movie comes out, I'm going to look like a damn fool. She's going to win the Oscar." The agent didn't like his request, but Greg insisted, and that was the start of a lifelong friendship.

His kindness went far beyond the credits. He showed my mother a great deal of tenderness on set. She'd emerged from Arnhem as an undernourished teenager and had no clue how she'd ended up in a Hollywood movie, so having a kind older actor help her through the process was pivotal. If Greg had been difficult or impatient, things might have turned out very differently.

She had someone else's impatience to deal with when James Hanson unexpectedly flew to Rome and spent weeks hanging around on set, doing whatever he could to support and encourage her. The belief was that they would marry as soon as filming was over. Instead, as soon as the last frame had been captured on celluloid, my mother was summoned back to America for the touring production of *Gigi*. Four months into that tour, she called off their engagement—for her fiancé's sake as much as her own. It was December 1953, by which time the invitations had been sent out and preparations made for a January wedding, including the fattening of fifty chickens for the bridal supper.

"If I get married, I want to be very married," my mother declared in sorrowful statements to the press. "My schedule commits me to a movie here, then back to the stage, then back to Hollywood. [James] would be spending most of his time taking care of business in England and Canada. It would be very difficult for us to lead a normal married life." She convinced Hanson that she'd make a terrible wife, as she was too in love with her work, but she let her dashing fiancé go with considerable regret and even tried unsuccessfully to rekindle their relationship soon afterward.

"It's all very unhappy making," she wrote to her friend Felix Aylmer, an actor forty years her senior who'd given her drama and elocution lessons after the war and become a sounding board. Writing to him of her "heavy heart" after breaking up with James Hanson, she added, "I thought it possible to make our combined lives and careers work out… but I am sure it is the only sensible decision."

Hanson was blindsided and said later, "It was a strange situation… but the fact was Audrey just did not want to get married at the time." He admitted that he loved her very much, adding, "I've not loved very many women in my life in that way." Accepting that his fiancée had been destined to be a star, he added, "It would have been pointless to try to persuade her to do anything else."

The couple spent one last Christmas together before parting amicably. Hanson went on to marry seven years later and had two sons. In 1976 he was knighted for his services to industry, having become one of the wealthiest men in Britain, with a vast empire of businesses. He and Mum stayed in touch, and she invited me to dinner with him and his wife in

London once, where I found him to be perfectly pleasant. A member of my family once suggested that if they'd married, my mother would have been far wealthier, but she ended up comfortably well off anyway, and she would have had a very different life as a "stay at home" housewife.

She was sad that she never got to wear her beautiful wedding dress with its twenty-one-inch waist but insisted that it be gifted to "the most beautiful poor Italian girl" that the designer could find. A farmer's daughter named Amabile Altobella was selected, and she wore it to marry her sweetheart, claiming later that it brought her good luck for what proved to be a long and happy marriage.

GREGORY PECK REMAINED A SHOULDER to cry on throughout that difficult period and jokingly referred to their friendship as *The Greg & Aud Show*. He later claimed that making *Roman Holiday* was "probably the happiest experience I ever had making movies," one in which he'd felt like "the luckiest man in the world." He added, "For six months we believed in the fairy story that she was a princess, and I was the newspaperman. I think we just started believing it, Audrey and I." Mum felt the same and was grateful that he had guided her with "kindness, patience, and humor." Thanks to Greg's support and the expert guidance of William Wyler, my mother became a star almost overnight.

My mother and Greg became so close that she was invited into his inner circle and was delighted to meet his new wife, the respected French journalist known by her maiden name of Veronique Passani, with whom she could chatter away for hours in French. Although the three of them were never able to see each other as often as they'd have liked, as with all true friendships, they always just picked up where they'd left off.

One thing Greg said about Mum really struck a chord with me. He commented that she was "as funny as she is beautiful," making him laugh between scenes, something that I can quite believe. There are only a handful of people left alive who remember how funny she could be, sticking her tongue out, going cross-eyed, grimacing, mimicking voices, and twisting her body into comic poses. This was all designed to defuse a situation or simply make someone smile, as she often said that laughter cured a multitude of ills. Her quick wit and cheeky grin never lost their charm.

Greg's hunch was right about her star quality too. My mother did win an Academy Award for *Roman Holiday*, as well as a BAFTA award and a Golden Globe. Through a combination of luck and talent, the girl who only a few years earlier had rummaged through charity boxes stood before the world in a designer lace gown to accept an Oscar.

Enchanted and delighted, Paramount immediately signed her to a seven-picture contract, and her portrait was featured on the cover of *Time* magazine a few weeks after the movie was released—highly unusual for an unknown. The article read, "Paramount's new star sparkles and glows with the fire of a finely cut diamond." Hollywood finally had its own princess.

———◆———

FORTUNATELY FOR MY MOTHER, SHE was surrounded by people who weren't about to let the crown she'd worked so hard for slip. And one of those key people who came into her life during this period was the Bohemian cinematographer named František Plánička, who had changed his name to Franz Planer.

Born into a wealthy family in 1894 in Czechoslovakia, the fifty-eight-year-old cameraman had already made a name for himself in Europe with his documentary style of filming and clever juxtaposing of light and dark. In 1937 he and his Jewish wife had fled to Hollywood just before Hitler annexed Austria. It was there that director William Wyler first admired Planer's work, sharing his preference for authentic locations rather than phony stage sets. Eager to harness his skills, he hired him for *Roman Holiday*, hoping for some of his magic to rub off.

Much to my mother's delight, the dedicated European who'd first trained as a portrait artist had a deep understanding of how best to capture the angles of the human face. This was important because her lifelong insecurities about being a flat-chested girl with a crooked tooth and wide shoulders were only magnified by the fear of appearing on the silver screen. Being seen from a distance onstage was one thing, but being filmed in close-up so that every blemish showed was quite another. Luckily for her, even though the technology wasn't nearly as good then and the lights were huge and rudimentary, Franz Planer knew exactly how to light her so as not to make her complexion look too sallow.

My mother was a fast learner and came to appreciate what best worked for her, declaring, "Bright colors overpower me and wash me out. Paler ones bring out my eyes and make my hair seem darker." In essence, she was acquiring the one thing that made her such an icon and one of the most photographed people in the world—authenticity and the ability to be entirely herself and comfortable in her own skin. Planer listened patiently to her concerns before working out the best angles at which to film her and the right levels of light to use.

She was so taken by the generosity of his work that she personally requested him on her later films *The Nun's Story*, *Breakfast at Tiffany's*, *The Unforgiven*, and *The Children's Hour*. She was like that. Once she found something that worked, she rarely strayed from it. Few others ever worked with her as much as Franz Planer, and she wasn't the only one who appreciated him. Not only did his peers nominate him for an Oscar for *Roman Holiday*, but the prestigious *Hollywood Reporter* said of his later work with her on *Breakfast at Tiffany's*, "Planer's Technicolor photography is beautifully balanced...whether exteriors or studio shots."

Mum thanked her lucky stars that Franz had been the one looking at her through a lens from her first major role onward. Had anyone less perceptive or sensitive to her needs been in charge of the camera, she feared she might never have made it. Sadly, Franz virtually gave up his camera in 1961 after suffering a stroke. He died two years later, at the age of sixty-eight, having shot over a hundred movies. *The Children's Hour*, a controversial film in which my mother played the object of Shirley MacLaine's secret desires, was Planer's last film, and he never did win an Oscar, despite five nominations and three Golden Globes.

Just as she came to rely on costumes to show off her best features, my mother relied on Franz to paint her with light, so she was doubly devastated when he died. Although she went on to work with other great cinematographers, including Charles Lang, whom she requested twice more after Franz's death, having admired his work on *Sabrina*, it just wasn't the same for her.

She felt much the same about Alberto de Rossi, her makeup stylist, whom she'd also first met on *Roman Holiday*. She claimed the secret of Italian makeup artists was that, while the harsh movie lights required a lot of the foundation known as pancake, they used a "light hand" and gently layered it, giving it a quality that allowed one to go straight to dinner from the set.

She proved this to me one night in Munich, when as a teenager I went to visit her on the set of her film *Bloodline*. When the day's shooting ended, even though she was tired, she was coerced by Terence Young, the director, and Kurt Frings, her agent, into coming to dinner and taking me with them. When someone suggested she might need to stop by her hotel to take her film makeup off, she laughed and said there was no need. And there wasn't. She looked entirely natural the whole evening.

Alberto de Rossi was in high demand with some of the world's greatest stars, including Maria Callas, Claudia Cardinale, Ava Gardner, and Elizabeth Taylor. Born in Rome before the Second World War, he was the son of Camillo de Rossi, Italy's first-ever makeup artist for film. He'd hoped to become a professional painter but was apprenticed to his father as a teenager, learning his craft and especially the use of what he called "color harmony," matching skin tone to different shades and choosing his palette carefully.

The talented artist used his knowledge of color and paintbrushes to great effect, taking note of the light and matching the color of my mother's eyes, the shade of her dress, or the luminosity of a jewel. "[She] has beautiful bone structure that her features need little shading," he said at the time. "She has a very strong jawline, so, in a sense, I reversed her face by emphasizing her temples." He preferred her eyebrows to remain as natural as possible, declaring that "an important face must have eyebrows," and he then further enhanced them, using tinted powder to shape them into wings. About her overall look, he was succinct. "Women have always wanted to imitate her.... They always will."

Mum believed in him completely, saying he was one of the most important men in her life. "I put myself entirely in the hands of my makeup man Alberto, whom I consider a real artist. I let him do what he likes and never look in the mirror all day.... He is one of the dots in my movie contract—I am not filming without him. I even brought poor Alberto to the Congo." He also did her makeup for *War and Peace*, *Charade*, *How to Steal a Million*, and *Two for the Road*, when he wasn't busy elsewhere—creating Elizabeth Taylor's famously striking look in *Cleopatra*, for example.

It was Alberto who created my mother's signature appearance, especially the famous Audrey Hepburn eyes. There was something compelling about them without makeup, but by the time Alberto had finished, the camera—and the audience—were enslaved. Directors and cinematographers deployed them like a secret weapon, doing close-up after close-up as my mother gazed into the camera.

Using simple but clever techniques, Alberto painstakingly drew eyeliner to follow my mother's natural shape and then applied mascara before separating each individual eyelash with a safety pin or tweezers. It was a technique she adopted for the rest of her life, even though it wasn't for the faint of heart. From the earliest age, I can remember how long it took to get her eyes right, as I used to sit under her dressing table caressing her bare feet while she worked on each lash. Once she had finished and was dressed in another beautiful gown for an evening out, she'd often turn to me with feeling and say, "Oh, Seanie, I do so terribly wish that I could stay home and eat in the kitchen with you instead."

That was part of her mystery—the inner struggle between the woman who wanted to be a stay-at-home mum and the Hollywood actress who seemed to sprinkle stardust wherever she went. She never fully appreciated how beautiful she was or how she affected people. Whenever someone paid her a compliment, telling her how lovely she looked, she'd immediately demur and credit the photographer, the lighting designer, or the makeup, especially when they commented on her eyes. "No, no," she'd protest, believing her eyes were too small. "The most beautiful eye makeup perhaps, but all the credit belongs to Alberto."

Theirs was truly a lucky collaboration, and my mother considered herself enormously blessed to have these people in her life. He and his wife, Grazia, a hair stylist, were frequently invited to our home and out to premieres and dinners. They were treated like members of our family, and the feeling was mutual. When I was a boy, Alberto would take me to lunch in Trastevere in Rome and then to soccer matches.

Alberto's death in 1975 hit Mum hard. After twenty years of deep and enduring friendship, she wept when she heard, saying it felt as if she had lost a brother. Without him, she said she'd rather not work again. That's how important he was to her and how much she relied on his expertise to get her ready for all that she had to do. She went on to star in five more films without Alberto's personal touch, but his protégé Nilo Jacoponi stepped ably into his shoes.

Losing Alberto, Colette, and Franz Planer was hard for my mother. Though far stronger than many appreciated, she still needed a protective shield of friendship around her, and they had been some of the most loved.

6.

We all want to be loved, don't we? Everyone looks for a way of finding love. It's a constant search for affection in every walk of life.—AH

INT. HOTEL SUITE, LONDON, ENGLAND, October 1953

A cocktail party in a large hotel suite is in full swing as the host, **GREGORY PECK**, leads a young **AUDREY** to a corner where a tall man is holding court.

MEL FERRER is surrounded by a group of men and women who appear to be enthralled by his conversation.

> **MEL**
> (to the group)
> ...and the amazing thing is that Leslie almost starved to death during the war in France, and yet, just a few years later, she starred in *An American in Paris*, and now she's wowing critics in *Lili*. As the French would say, *incroyable*!

The group collectively agrees as a smiling **GREG** ushers **AUDREY** forward and people nod with recognition.

                GREG
Mel, I'd like to introduce you to the young lady who taught me how to act. Audrey, this is one of my oldest friends, a fine actor and one of the most talented producers in the business—even if he says so himself.

AUDREY shakes his hand.

                MEL
    (kissing her fingertips)
Audrey, I've heard so much about you.

              AUDREY
Oh, I know perfectly well who you are, Mr. Ferrer. I've seen *Lili* three times already, and you were marvelous as the puppeteer.

              GREG
Now now, Audrey, tell him the real reason why you've seen it so often.

AUDREY glances nervously at **GREG**, who at six foot three is the same height as **MEL**.

              GREG
    (laughing)
It's all right, he can handle it.

AUDREY
(reddening)
Well, you see, I do so admire Leslie Caron...
but you really were wonderful too!

GREG gives **MEL** a consoling pat and turns away to chat with his other guests.

MEL
For one so young, Leslie has a rare talent. As do you. I can introduce you to her if you'd like.

AUDREY
Thank you. I'd like that very much. She and I have a lot more in common than people realize.

MEL
(tilting his head, intrigued)
But what about you? Now that your movie is released you should really think about doing another play, you know. I didn't get a chance to see you in *Gigi*, but I read the reviews.

AUDREY
You're too kind. I was so terrified every night that I'm amazed people didn't notice.

MEL
(mesmerized)
Perhaps they did and that's precisely why they loved you.

AUDREY smiles and sips at her martini as she glances around at the famous faces in the room.

> **AUDREY**
> Greg knows marvelous people, doesn't he?

> **MEL**
> (watching her, absent-mindedly)
> You really do have a most compelling way about you.

> **AUDREY**
> (mischievously)
> Oh, come now, Mr. Ferrer. Is that the best you can do?

> **MEL**
> (laughing)
> Did I say that out loud?

They gaze into each other's eyes until **AUDREY** breaks the spell.

> **AUDREY**
> So, what kind of play do you think I should do?

> **MEL**
> Something completely different to *Gigi*. You need to show off your range and prove...

A matronly **WOMAN** steps up to interrupt and take **AUDREY** by the arm.

                    WOMAN
    Audrey, darling. There's someone here
    who's simply dying to meet you.
            (to **MEL**)
    Forgive me if I borrow her?

                    MEL
            (giving a wry smile)
    Of course.
        (to **AUDREY** as she is being led away)
    The play would have to be
    something from left field.

                    AUDREY
    Well, why don't you send me
    something, Mr. Ferrer?

                    MEL
        (beaming a broad grin, which she returns)
    Oh, I will.

LOVE MEANT EVERYTHING TO MY mother. It was the one thing she spent her whole life searching for, especially after her father abandoned her. Desperate for affection, she never found it in her parents, and although she'd had moments of happiness with friends and lovers, they never seemed to last.

Meeting my father at Gregory Peck's party changed all that, although she didn't know it at first. Melchor "Mel" Gastón Ferrer was a very different kind of man from James Hanson. Artistic and ambitious, he was the son of a Cuban doctor who'd died in his early sixties when my father was three years old. Raised in New Jersey by his powerful Catholic mother, Irene, a politician and anti-Prohibition campaigner, he had something in common with Mum in that neither of their mothers knew how to show affection.

Of his three siblings, one sister, Irené, became an eminent cardiologist and the other, Terry, a successful journalist. His brother, José, was a surgeon who was awarded a medal for military service in the Pacific. My father was twenty-two and a Princeton dropout when war broke out. He was saved from military service by a bout of polio that had slightly withered his left arm. After falling in love with acting at summer stock, he worked as a disc jockey and a chorus line dancer and wrote a children's book in Mexico before settling on a theatrical career. After being signed to Columbia Pictures as a director, he worked on several B movies before switching to the stage and appearing on Broadway.

Disinherited and emotionally scarred by his mother, he found solace in playing other men's lives but somehow always needed to be in charge and was better at directing and producing than he was at acting. Married three times (twice to the same woman), he'd had four children and, with the actress Dorothy McGuire, became a cofounder of La Jolla Playhouse in San Diego, which is where he first met local actor Gregory Peck, the playhouse's original founder. The movie *Lili* was one of his first hits and starred the pixie-like French actress Leslie Caron, whom my mother was fascinated by.

A former ballerina, Caron had survived Nazi-occupied Paris during the war, emerging anemic, undernourished, and, along with the rest of her family, destitute. Like Mum, she'd found salvation in dance, and her heroine was the ballerina Anna Pavlova. Having starred in *An American in Paris* alongside Gene Kelly, she was later chosen to take my mother's role as Gigi in the Hollywood musical of the play. The parallels between them were uncanny, and they became friends but never bosom buddies, I don't know why. Maybe they had too much in common, and their wartime experiences may have been too difficult to revisit for both of them.

Fresh from starring with Caron in *Lili*, on the night my father met my mother in 1953, he gave little away about himself (nor that he was married) and focused solely on her. Adopting the role of a paternal producer after their brief but unforgettable conversation, he immediately began searching for a suitable play that he and she could perform together, while my mother prepared for her next film role. Because of their separate shooting schedules, they weren't to see each other again for several months.

IN HIGH DEMAND, MUM WAS contracted to star in *Sabrina* with Humphrey Bogart and William Holden, with Billy Wilder directing. For that role, in which she looked her incandescent best, she was once again assigned to chief costumer Edith Head for her outfits. This time, however, she decided to do things differently.

Head went straight to work, drawing designs for my mother to wear based on what she knew had worked for her before. Although my mother had no objection to working with her again, she had her own ideas. Her character was a plain chauffeur's daughter who moves to Paris to escape a broken heart only to return transformed into a swan. She suggested that when Sabrina returns to America, her clothes should be her first-ever haute couture outfits, designed in Paris by a real French couturier—the kind normally only available to the European elite.

She persuaded Billy Wilder that wearing them would not only give the film authenticity but also allow her greater insight into her character's behavior. Her only previous experience of high fashion had been brief, but memorable. In *Monte Carlo Baby* she'd been fitted for dresses made by the Parisian fashion house Christian Dior. The way the garments felt and, more importantly, how they made her feel had had a lasting impact. Up until then she'd had, by her own admission, a couple of dresses, some blouses, and some slacks.

Wilder could hardly refuse his star's request, and after seeking the advice of his wife, an actress and singer also named Audrey, he told my mother to go see the designer Cristóbal Balenciaga in Paris when she was in Europe traveling with the baroness. Her instructions were to say that she wanted the clothes for her own personal wardrobe, or the studio would have to pay more and give him a credit. Balenciaga was too busy and recommended his protégé, Hubert de Givenchy, at his atelier at 8 rue Alfred de Vigny in the 8th arrondissement.

When Givenchy was told that "Miss Hepburn" was coming to see him, he mistakenly believed it was the Hollywood star Katharine Hepburn, so he was astonished by the waif who walked in. "When the door of my studio opened, there stood a young woman—very slim, tall, with doe eyes and short hair, wearing a pair of cigarette pants, a boatneck T-shirt, ballerinas, and a gondolier's hat with a red ribbon that read 'Venezia.' I thought, *This is too much!*" She reminded him, he said, of a fragile doe with beautiful big eyes.

Like every other designer in the city, Givenchy was putting together a collection for his first Paris fashion show and didn't have enough staff or hours in the day. He politely informed the virtual unknown, whose film *Roman Holiday* hadn't been released yet in France, that he couldn't possibly create anything new for her. My mother gave him that smile that could light up Paris and told him she'd be happy to try something from his existing collection, as long as it had clean lines, was a single color without stripes, and had few embellishments.

Hubert was instantly captivated and amazed at the change in the "little girl" who'd strolled in off the street as she "gave life" to his clothes and moved in them in a way that he had rarely seen. He described the transformation as "unbelievable" and "magic," adding, "Suddenly she felt good. You could feel her excitement and joy." Making a decision that would change both their lives, he decided to help her.

In keeping with her own tastes and instructions to buy only monochrome garments, my mother chose an Oxford gray jacket with a ruffle, a pencil skirt, and a pale-gray turban. She told Hubert that a suit without a hat was like a lamp without a shade. The outfit was for the moment when a sophisticated Sabrina returns from Paris and is unrecognizable. It would be the first time my mother was seen in a Givenchy outfit, but it wouldn't be the last.

Especially popular was her choice of an elegant black satin tea-length dress with bow straps and a plunging back. Hubert later explained, "She wanted a shoulderless evening dress, which she asked me to change to hide the gaps between her collarbones." That so-called *décolleté bateau*, or boatneck, was what became known as the "Sabrina neckline." Copies of the dress were later marketed as "the Sabrina dress" and sold all over the world.

By the time she tried on his stunning off-the-shoulder organdie gown with floral embroidery and a detachable train, the pair of them were in heaven. My mother's dream to be a prima ballerina taking center stage seemed as if it were finally coming true, thanks to Hubert. And he had found his muse.

In studio correspondence after my mother returned with her handpicked selection, it was stated that Wilder and Edith Head both "agreed with Hepburn" about her choices, an astonishing concession for a young starlet who was making only her second film. My mother had learned to navigate the labyrinth of a male-dominated industry and had the studio eating out of her hand.

Having almost dismissed her at first, Givenchy even agreed later that Paramount's in-house costumers could alter the organdie gown from black with white embroidery to white with black stitching to be more in keeping with a summer party. For the next forty years, Hubert remained my mother's designer of choice, even though she repeatedly altered his work. "Audrey would remove everything from the dresses: bows, ornaments, belts—everything which was not essential," he later said. "And in the end, she was right."

My mother favored simplicity and said, "He kept the spare style that I love. What is more beautiful than a simple sheath made in an extraordinary way with special fabric and just two earrings?" Their friendship was forged from a shared love of beautiful things, but it deepened as they realized that they were kindred spirits in other ways too.

A handsome French count who was six foot six, Hubert had set up his own fashion house in 1952—the same year she got her big break in *Roman Holiday*. He was twenty-four. Like my mother, he came from an aristocratic family, but the similarities didn't end there. When he was small, he had lost his marquis father, who died of pneumonia at age forty-two after being gassed in the First World War.

Like Mum, Hubert wasn't yet a teenager when war broke out. His widowed mother, Béatrice, signed up as a nurse, as my mother and grandmother had, and worked in the military hospital in medieval Beauvais, seventy-five kilometers north of Paris. As the Germans closed in, she refused to abandon the wounded and flee to Brittany with the rest of her family. Instead, she stayed and put Hubert and his brother to work distributing soup to the injured and to refugees. It was only when the Germans encircled their town before burning it to the ground that they left, managing to get on the last train out.

"It felt like a modern version of *Gone with the Wind*," he later said. "The three of us took the last train leaving Beauvais in an atmosphere of indescribable panic because the enemy was arriving...we left all our belongings behind." Placing her children with her sister, his mother returned to her unit. Like Mum, Hubert had also lost a favorite relative during the war—his grandmother—and witnessed death and destruction. "Daily life...became dramatic," he said. "The villages were successively occupied by the Germans, who shot the inhabitants at random.... The brutality no longer knew any limits." And just like my mother, he added, "I will never forget these terrible images."

Bonded by war, they had a friendship cemented for life. Their "special love affair" was so deep they joked that it could easily have ended in marriage if Hubert hadn't been gay. My mother was extremely loyal to the people she loved, and when Givenchy was never even credited on *Sabrina*, she was furious on his behalf.

He later admitted that he, too, was upset, and that a credit at that early stage in his career would have been enormously helpful. The fact that Edith Head went on to win her seventh Oscar for the costumes in *Sabrina* only hurt him more. From then on, my mother insisted that Hubert be properly credited in every movie she had him design for her, starting with her next for Paramount, *Funny Face* with Fred Astaire—another story about a Cinderella character who undergoes a dramatic transformation.

It is astonishing to think that she was only twenty-five years old and on her third movie yet dictating what the studio needed to do to keep her happy. She realized, in her own quiet way, that her wardrobe was such an inherent part of each story that it could almost be defined as one of its characters.

Hubert may have towered over my mother physically, but psychologically he knelt at her feet, describing her as a myth that existed. As my mother said, "We discovered each other. There are few people that I love more. He is the single person I know with the greatest integrity." Even after she died, he said, "In every collection a part of my heart, my pencil, my design goes to Audrey."

BILLY WILDER HAD BEEN INSTRUMENTAL in bringing them together, and my mother always felt blessed to have been put in the hands of yet another great European director. Born Shmuel Vilder, he'd been a close friend of director Fred Zinnemann, a fellow Austrian, and had fled to America when Hitler came to power. Several members of his family perished, and in 1945 he returned to Germany with the US Army to make a film designed to educate German citizens about Nazi atrocities.

The Oscar-winning director of *Sunset Boulevard* and *Stalag 17*, Wilder became a precious friend to my mother and was her favorite person to sit next to at a dinner table. She loved to be with people who made her throw back her head and laugh with abandon. The cigar-smoking Billy had great wit and charm and told the funniest stories—with a strong German accent—so he made her laugh more than anyone else. One of his favorite lines was, "What's wrong with the French? They have money that crumbles in your hand and toilet paper you can't tear." Or he'd claim he'd deliberately shoot a few scenes out of focus on the off chance that he'd win a foreign film award. "A director must be a policeman, a midwife, a psychoanalyst, a sycophant, and a bastard," he declared, although for my mother he was more like a gentle father figure.

Wilder certainly took a paternal interest in my mother, claiming that she was born with what he called an "extra element"—a special ingredient that transforms someone from a mere mortal into a star. She also worked extremely hard at pleasing him and everyone else around her, partly as a way of countering her deep-rooted imposter syndrome. As she said in one interview, "If you want to get psychological, you can say my determination... stems from underlying feelings of insecurity and inferiority. I found the only way to get the better of them was by putting my foot down, by adopting a forceful, concentrated drive."

On film sets and in the theater, she would rise between four and five in the morning to be sure to turn up early or on time, never late, and always fully rehearsed. A true pro, she knew all her lines and memorized the name of everyone working on the film, from the director to the runners. With the instructions of her mother echoing in her ears, she behaved impeccably and even baked the crew brownies.

One member of the cast who fell under my mother's spell was the actor William Holden, one of her costars in *Sabrina*, with whom she began a brief but intense affair. "You have to be a little bit in love with your leading man and vice versa," she confessed later. "If you're going to portray love, you have to feel it. You can't do it any other way, but you don't carry it beyond the set." Holden was not only married with three children, he'd also had a vasectomy, which was a deal-breaker for a woman desperate to have children of her own. When filming ended, their relationship did, too, even though Holden had fallen hard for the woman eleven years his junior and carried a torch for her for years, describing her as the greatest love of his life.

My mother was recovering from that heartbreak when my father, Mel Ferrer, came back into her life, having finally found what he thought would be the perfect vehicle for them both on Broadway. It was the 1938 play *Ondine* by the French dramatist Jean Giraudoux. Based on a German fable, it tells the story of a teenage water sprite named Ondine who falls in love with Hans, a medieval knight-errant, to be played by my dad.

This appealed to the little girl in my mother, who'd loved fairy tales and used to draw princesses and fairies, and she immediately agreed to do it. With her name attached, Dad had no problem getting the financial backing for a Broadway production, and the couple started dating soon afterward.

Although he never received the kind of recognition he longed for as an actor, my father was gaining a reputation as a producer. Nevertheless, my grandmother suspected that the man who was twelve years older than my mother secretly hoped that his patchy career would be boosted by his connection with the new hot star of the season. Even the press suggested it once their relationship became public, claiming he was a Svengali to my mother's ingenue and was benefiting from her fame, but I don't think it's that simple. They genuinely loved each other, and he wanted to help her. Like most of the men in her life, he fell under the misapprehension that she was helpless.

The problem was that my father was a neurotic perfectionist and famously controlling when it came to any productions he was associated with, even when he wasn't directly involved as producer or director. Every night after the rehearsals for *Ondine*, he'd spend hours coaching her further in the Greenwich Village apartment they shared, often undermining instructions the director, Alfred Lunt, had given her. This created tension between the two men and placed my mother in an unenviable position, especially as she was falling in love with my dad.

My grandmother Ella, who frequently attended rehearsals and witnessed my mother's discomfort at my father's interference, was openly scathing in her description of him in a letter to Felix Aylmer, who'd become a family friend. The baroness wrote, "That frog-faced delinquent with the spindly legs has caused sufficient havoc to last a long time and I believe that Audrey is getting rather sick of the neurotic side to him!"

Wearing pixie ears, a blond wig, and flimsy costumes—one of which was little more than a fishing net over a "nude" body stocking with strategically placed seaweed—my mother gave an opening performance in February 1954 that was described by one critic as "pulsing... all grace and enchantment." Dad must have done something right. The "magical" production won the New York Drama Critics Award, and my mother won the coveted Tony Award for Best Performance by a Leading Actress in a Play just a few days after accepting her Oscar for *Roman Holiday*. That must have been quite a week.

Although my father's performance in *Ondine* went unrewarded, by the time the play ended, the couple were engaged to be married. Dad gave Mum the affectionate nickname of Acorn because of the shape of her hair and head. The girl who'd only ever been dubbed Monkey Puzzle before—by a father who considered his daughter something of an enigma—was delighted with her new moniker. In return, she called her new beau Melly. She loved how romantic and chivalrous he was with her and was delighted at the success of the play. Here was a well-educated man who not only supported and understood her career but was helping her develop it, unlike James Hanson, who'd wanted a more traditional wife.

She also loved being part of my father's family and became good friends with his sister-in-law Mary. And she was impressed by how passionate Dad was about music as he exposed her to the vibrant nightlife of New York. It was he who introduced her to bossa nova and jazz, which she came to adore, especially the music of Louis Armstrong and Dave Brubeck. The early 1950s were wonderfully exciting years for her, and my father played a major part. Most importantly of all, he helped her break free from her mother at last and make her own way in the world with the support of those she'd curated with care.

Rob Wolders, with whom Mum had her last and longest partnership, later agreed that my father had done a lot of good things for her. "Audrey could not live without trusting herself to someone, to put herself in someone else's hands," he stated. "She did some of her best work when married to Mel."

THE TRUE MEANING OF LOVE for my mother wasn't just about romance or fashion, but also about friendship. Female friendship was terribly important to her, especially in the cutthroat entertainment business, and one important connection at that time was with the British actress Deborah Kerr. The pair first met when they shared the 1953/54 award for Best Actress of the Broadway Season in a poll of New York drama critics.

Deborah was starring in *Tea and Sympathy* at a nearby Broadway theater, and the pair would grab lunch together and visit each other backstage. Mum once told me that Deborah's final words in her play created one of the most profound moments of acting she had ever witnessed. The closing line went, "Years from now when you talk about this—and you will—be kind." That was something she wished for herself and others too.

The daughter of a Royal Air Force pilot who'd lost a leg at the Battle of the Somme, Deborah Kerr had been married to an English Spitfire pilot who had been awarded a Distinguished Flying Cross for his action in the Battle of Britain. Her second husband was a German-Jewish novelist and screenwriter whose parents had emigrated to America before the war. When the couple married in Klosters, Switzerland, a week after I was born, my mother's gift was a pink wedding gown made by Givenchy with a matching organdie jacket.

Like Mum, Deborah had originally trained as a ballet dancer and lived through wartime privations, in Britain. Six years older than Mum, she'd toured Holland, France, and Belgium with ENSA, the entertainment service for troops on the front lines. She and my mother had both fallen into acting by chance and bonded over their shared experiences, supporting each other throughout their lifetimes. Deborah went on to be Oscar nominated for *From Here to Eternity* and later starred with Yul Brynner in *The King and I*. She ended up living not too far from my mother in Switzerland and then in Marbella, Spain, right next to where my parents built a charming beach house for the winter.

As she said years later, "To the world [our friendship] may not have seemed that constant or deep an association, but we became very close even though we didn't see each other much. I couldn't say, 'She was my best friend in my whole life.' Yet in a way, perhaps she was."

Another good friend was the French model and comedic actress Capucine, better known as Cap, who also lived in Switzerland and—coincidentally—once had an affair with William Holden. She and my mother first met through Hubert de Givenchy and stayed friends until Capucine jumped to her death from her eighth-floor apartment window at the age of sixty-two. Her suicide reduced my mother to tears for days. She had done her best to support her reclusive friend through years of depression and was the reluctant executor of Cap's will, having prayed that she would never have to carry out that task.

It's hard for people today to imagine what it was like for a woman in the theater and film industry in the fifties, especially those who'd just lived through a war that must have felt like the end of all they'd known. They had been given a chance to take advantage of the shift in power that occurred when men went to the front. Yet afterward, they still found themselves in a male-dominated world, which meant they had to work twice as hard to prove themselves. Then, once they reached a certain age, especially in the entertainment industry, they were discarded like yesterday's news.

It is still incredible to me how hard Mum had to work to achieve all she did in those early years. Less than a decade after she'd almost starved to death, she was a full-time actress locked into a seven-movie contract. She was allowed time off between films only to star in plays, as if that constituted a break. But the industry was fickle, and women had little agency of their own, so she was pushed to do more and more. By her mid-twenties, she was exhausted from working flat out since her teens with few or no breaks.

Her appetite had long been affected by stress, and even though *Roman Holiday* and *Ondine* had both been very successful, the play had to be cut short by five weeks when she lost too much weight, became anemic, and was too weak to continue. Her health had been precarious since the Hunger Winter, and when her childhood asthma returned, it further compromised her immune system.

While my father was working on a movie of his own, and with reporters and autograph hunters hounding my mother, Dad sent her to Switzerland for some cleaner air in the peace of the mountains. She found peace in the seclusion of a private resort in the mountaintop town of Bürgenstock, overlooking Lake Lucerne. It was so beautiful that before too long she'd persuaded my father (whom she also affectionately called Melchior after one of the three Magi) that it was the perfect place to hold their wedding. The ceremony was planned for later that year in a small thirteenth-century Protestant chapel, to be followed by lunch with a few close friends. The couple wanted Gregory Peck to be their best man, but much to their disappointment, he was in the middle of filming three movies back-to-back and was locked into his schedule, so Fritz Frey, the owner of the resort, gallantly stepped in.

My mother wrote to her old acting coach Felix Aylmer in her signature turquoise ink and invited him to join them: "How dearly we would love you to be with us on our wedding day... and how very much it matters to me. Please come. We will have the car take you up to our mountain peak for a gathering in our chalet of our nearest and dearest.... We want to keep it a dark secret in order to have it without the press."

That didn't work out quite the way she'd planned, as reporters got wind of the ceremony anyway and began to swarm the area like locusts. Managing to avoid them, on September 24, 1954, my parents were married by the mayor of Lucerne in a civil ceremony in the parlor of his home in the village of Buochs. The following day they repeated their vows at a religious ceremony in Bürgenstock's little chapel. The service was presided over by Pastor Maurice Eindiguer, another man who was to become a close friend. With so many reporters clamoring at the door, the couple selected a single journalist and one photographer—the legendary Ernst Haas—to enter the chapel and later posed for photos outside.

My father wore a tailored navy-blue suit while my mother had on a stunning Pierre Balmain organdie dress with a high neck and puff sleeves, and long white gloves. A delicate crown of white roses nestled in her hair, and on her feet were a pair of white stilettos.

The sixty or so guests included my grandmother Ella, who swallowed her dislike of my father to attend, along with Ella's friends the former British ambassador Sir Nevile Bland and Freddy Heineken, the Dutch brewing heir who was later kidnapped and chained to a wall for three weeks in what proved to be one of a spate of high-profile kidnappings that would have an impact on us all. My father's children and his sister were also at the wedding, as was Richard Mealand, head of Paramount's London studios. James Hanson, whom Mum had remained friends with, was invited but sent his regrets.

My parents stayed in Bürgenstock for a private honeymoon before escaping from the press and heading to the secluded Villa La Vigna (also known as Villa Rolli after the owner, a government adviser). It was a beautiful farmhouse in a vineyard in the Alban Hills near Cecchina outside Rome, close to where Dad was finishing up his Italian film *Proibito*. Once married, my parents began to lead what my mother described as "a gypsy life," traveling the world for work, much as she had done all her life. From the day her father walked out she'd been itinerant, moving from Belgium to Arnhem, Velp to Amsterdam, London to New York and Los Angeles.

In the first ten years of their marriage Mum starred in twelve movies and my father in more than twenty films, television shows, and plays. Work and play took them to Italy and Africa, America, France, Spain, Belgium, Holland, and Mexico. If they weren't in rental properties or staying with friends, they gravitated to the Hotel Hassler in Rome, the Connaught in London, or the Hôtel Raphael in Paris, their favorite of all hotels, not least because the staff understood my mother's obsessive need to create a comfortable environment in their suite—long before feng shui became trendy.

Frequently thanking Dad for "taking her off the shelf" and eager to prove herself the ideal 1950s wife despite such a busy career, she became a mistress of logistical organization, ensuring that her husband was looked after, fed, and clothed, even when she was away filming. "I have to be sure that my home and my family life are run as smoothly as they can," she told friends. Wherever they traveled, she surrounded them with their own silverware and bed linen, even packing their favorite records to dance to. Large items of furniture were sent ahead by ship or plane, and everything else was transported in large trunks, all of it listed in a complex filing system she developed, and catalogued in a binder by their loyal assistant Margaret Brown.

Mum was determined that, even though they switched locations so often, she would instantly be able to lay her hands on my father's best suit, her Limoges ashtray, or—later—my favorite sweater in one of the umpteen methodically packed and numbered cases. It was, I now realize, one way of showing love and of staying in control of a crazy, vagabond life.

Whenever they had any downtime, they would return to a small property they rented in Bürgenstock. Villa Bethania was the one place where she could pad around barefoot without makeup, doing all the chores and cooking herself, as if she were an ordinary housewife. The days there were some of the happiest of her marriage.

───── ♦ ─────

It was at Villa Bethania one chilly day in 1957, however, that she had one of her most moving encounters. Otto Frank, the father of Anne Frank—whose diary had almost broken my mother as a teenager—asked permission to visit with his wife. For several years Mum had felt an intense personal connection to Anne Frank, but when her wartime diary was published in Holland, it became an international bestseller. My mother's "sister of the soul" became public property almost overnight.

Anne's diary was published in America just as Mum was about to start filming *Roman Holiday*, and before she knew it, the annotated manuscript she'd read in the privacy of her little room in Amsterdam became one of the world's most inspirational books. It would go on to sell more than thirty million copies.

With such huge public interest and plans to turn the address of Anne's secret annex into a museum, it was only a matter of time before someone decided to create a movie out of it. The Academy Award–winning director George Stevens was signed up to oversee the making of *The Diary of Anne Frank*, so all 20th Century Fox had to do was find its star. Who better to play her than someone who'd gone through similar wartime experiences less than a hundred miles away—"the other Dutch girl," as my mum was sometimes called.

Her gut reaction was no, but she reluctantly agreed to reread the diary and think about it. As she had feared, she found the experience as devastating as the first time as it triggered memories that were never far from the surface. She had to go to bed for a day to recover. "I was quite destroyed by it again.... There were floods of tears. I became hysterical...I couldn't deal with it." It brought back all her nightmares. "It's never the same dream, but it's always about German soldiers. I had them all the time after the war." She told me later that even as an adult she sometimes felt she had the mentality of a twelve-year-old in arrested development and was not at all worldly.

Revisiting her years under occupation, she couldn't help but compare her own experiences to Anne's and ponder how differently things had ended for them. It was hard to fathom how and why such a beautiful soul, who had written such profound words, could end up dead while my mother survived. She was unable to put herself through that harrowing period of her life again and felt it would be morally wrong to ride on Anne's coattails and enrich herself in any way on the tragedy of her family.

Then she received the letter that almost persuaded her to change her mind, even though she'd said no and was exhausted after shooting two films without a break. They were *War and Peace*—in which she played Natasha to my father's Andrei—and, later, *Funny Face* with Fred Astaire. It was while filming *War and Peace* that my mother was delighted to find out that she was pregnant with my father's child six months after they'd wed, but then she lost the baby early in the pregnancy. It was March 1955, and she was twenty-five years old. Dad's solution was to distract her with work and not give her too much time to dwell on her heartbreaking loss.

While resting in the mountains to recover her health after *Funny Face* wrapped, she finally agreed to meet Otto Frank and his second wife, Elfriede, known as Fritzi, who made the journey from Holland. The meeting was arranged by the ever-persuasive Oscar-winning director George Stevens, who was still hopeful that Audrey might accept the part of Anne Frank. The director had a deep personal interest in the story, having enlisted during the war. After serving in the Middle East, he was put in charge of a film unit, where he catalogued pivotal events such as the Normandy landings, the liberation of Paris, and the opening of the concentration camp at Dachau.

At Stevens's bidding, Otto Frank arrived in Bürgenstock with Fritzi, another survivor of the Holocaust, whose first husband, Erich, and teenage son, Heinz, had perished but whose daughter, Eva, just two years younger than my mother, had somehow survived. Both Mum and Otto were nervous about their encounter: The sixty-eight-year-old mustachioed German was worried by the idea of asking a famous film star to play his dead daughter, and my mother was afraid to revisit the past. But the proud demeanor and natural serenity of the man who'd lost his entire family to the Nazis impressed her, and she warmed to him immediately. The Franks came for lunch and got on with her so well that they stayed and stayed. Speaking English and Dutch, they all ended up having a lovely day in the mountains above the lake.

My mother was deeply moved by Otto's story and all that he had endured. He and his wife both rolled up their sleeves and showed her their tattoos from Auschwitz. Otto told Mum that he and the director dearly wanted her to take on the role of Anne, believing that no other actress looked more like her or could play her more convincingly. Although she wanted to please them, she just couldn't bring herself to say yes. "I could not have suffered through that again without destroying myself."

In her diary Anne had written to her imaginary friend Kitty, and in trying to explain her refusal, my mother told Otto that in a way Anne felt like her Kitty, they were so similar in age and experience. "I couldn't play my sister's life," she said. "It's too close." Having been completely honest with Otto, she rejected the offer, telling the director that she felt unable to inhabit the role of a fourteen-year-old girl.

Even though she'd said no, the request reminded her that there was no getting away from the comparisons between her and Anne. My mother felt guilty that while she was being a moody teenager in Velp complaining of hunger, Anne had been dying of typhus in Bergen-Belsen, having just watched her sister, Margot, succumb to it. She also couldn't stop imagining the kind of life Anne might have led had she lived, thinking of her at every significant event in her own life.

I remember when she first gave me *The Diary of Anne Frank* to read when I was young and explained how much Anne's story mattered to her. "This was a book that touched me deeply," she said. "I think it will touch you too." I don't think it's too much to say that the injustice of all that Anne was denied in life by hatred and warfare planted the earliest seed of my mother's desire to stand up for children who could no longer speak for themselves.

---◆---

7.

You must learn to bend a little or you'll break...
You must have patience with yourself.—AH

<u>INT. PRETTY WHITE BEDROOM, BEVERLY HILLS, 1959</u>

AUDREY lies in bed propped up on a pillow, her hair neatly pinned back from her face under a white bow. She is wearing a white cotton nightdress and smiling serenely at a middle-aged woman in a nurse's uniform, who is tucking in her sheets.

AUDREY
Oh, Lou. I don't know what I would
have done without you. Thank you,
thank you, thank you...

LOU
No need for thanks, dear. I was
glad to come. How's the pain?

AUDREY
(smiling)
Bearable. It only hurts when I laugh...

LOU
You know the doctor did say it would be safe to take some medication if it gets too much.

AUDREY
(moving slightly and wincing)
I know, but I'm fine.

LOU
You're not. Just very brave. And the most uncomplaining patient I have ever had!

AUDREY
My mother would say I was being stubborn, but she's not the one carrying a longed-for child inside her.

LOU
You know that I wouldn't suggest taking anything if it wasn't safe for the baby. I just hate to see you in so much discomfort.

AUDREY
Oh, but Lou, it's getting better every day, and I'll soon be back on my feet, you'll see.

LOU
Audrey, you broke three vertebrae when that poor horse threw you. It's going to take time and patience to heal.

AUDREY
Not too long, I hope. The director expects me back on set.

LOU
We'll have to see about that. I'm not letting you out of my sight until I'm sure you're quite ready.

AUDREY
(grinning)
Oh, Lou. You must have been the most persuasive of nuns!

LOU
(smiling)
I did my best, with the grace of God.
(pause)
You know, if ever you want to pray, I'd be happy to join you.

AUDREY
(her expression thoughtful)
I pray quietly every day for a healthy baby and a long and happy marriage. I pray for the children of the world and

for its leaders to make wise decisions.
I pray for Mel and for my family. I even pray
for you, Lou, but they're not conventional
prayers, just private thoughts in
my head.

LOU sits gently on the edge of the bed and takes
AUDREY's hand.

LOU
Prayer takes many forms, my dear. And
that sounds like a perfect way to
reach God.

AUDREY smiles and leans back against the pillows, her face pale. **LOU** gets up and fluffs up the pillow around her head.

LOU
Try to get some rest.

AUDREY
I am a little tired. Maybe just twenty
minutes.

LOU
I'll be right here if you need me.

AUDREY
(squeezing her hand)
I bless the day you came into
my life, 'Sister Luke.'

LOU
And I bless this time spent with you,
sister. God works in mysterious ways.

INSTEAD OF PLAYING ANNE FRANK, after *Love in the Afternoon* and the lifeless *Green Mansions* with my father, my mother agreed to take on perhaps her most challenging role, that of Sister Luke in the Warner Bros. movie *The Nun's Story*.

The book the film is based on was recommended to her by several friends who suggested she consider the role. One was Gary Cooper, who thought Mum would be perfect to play the nun. The actor she called Coop had starred alongside her in *Love in the Afternoon*—which fulfilled yet another of her teenage dreams. He liked the story so much he sent a copy to director Fred Zinnemann and suggested her for the role even though he knew how taxing it would be, given her past.

A fictional retelling of the true story of missionary nun Marie Louise "Lou" Habets, the script follows the character as her passion for medicine leads her to join a convent with the hope of working in a mission hospital in the Belgian Congo. Once there, she struggles with her religious duties and is drawn to a mercurial doctor who works her to exhaustion. When she contracts tuberculosis, she returns to Europe shortly before war breaks out.

After she learns that her beloved father, a surgeon, has been gunned down by the Germans while treating refugees, she is so overcome by grief and thoughts of revenge that she can no longer sustain her vows. The film ends poignantly with her slipping back into her civilian clothes and leaving the cloister, stepping silently out onto the street. "I love the part," my mother told one interviewer during a break in filming. "It's a terribly good part, although a terribly difficult one—for me, anyway."

When the real Lou Habets lost her father to a German bullet, she abandoned the holy order to work as a nurse for the Resistance. She cared for men wounded in the Battle of the Bulge and the carpet-bombing of Antwerp, only 150 kilometers from where my mother and grandmother were also helping in a Resistance hospital. When the war ended, she joined UNRRA (which later evolved into UNICEF) to distribute food and help to millions of starving and displaced persons, so her story had deep resonance for my mother.

Lou Habets emigrated to America with the help of a fellow aid worker, Kathryn Hulme, a former journalist and the woman who became her lifelong partner. While Lou worked in a Los Angeles hospital, Hulme went on to write the novel on which the movie *The Nun's Story* was based.

It was my father who encouraged Mum to say yes to the movie. Dad may have been a rather wooden actor, but he was well read, was fluent in four languages, and instinctively knew the value of good material. He also recognized the benefit to her career of the dramatic shift from a frivolous romantic comedy with Gary Cooper.

Zinnemann was delighted when she agreed, describing my mother as "delicate but with a hint of iron." Before accepting the part, she had only one condition. Dad had bought her a Yorkshire terrier, whom she'd named Mr. Famous, and she insisted the dog accompany her to the Belgian Congo. Although my mother was as far removed from a demanding Hollywood star as you could imagine, in a foreign land without my father to support her, she needed the companionship of what would now be called a therapy pet, her adored reminder of home.

The studio quickly appreciated that Mr. Famous was much more than that. He was my mother's surrogate baby who traveled everywhere with her, enjoyed morsels of the finest tidbits in restaurants, and underwent grooming rituals that rivaled her own. He'd even made a brief appearance in *Love in the Afternoon*. Executives agreed to get special permits for him to travel to Africa with the rest of the cast, accepting that the lengthy paperwork was a small price to pay to keep their star happy.

Besides, they had far bigger concerns, as there were worries that the story of a nun giving up her calling might upset the Catholic Church and cause problems at the box office. Encouraged by Zinnemann, a man whose own parents had perished in the Holocaust, my mother consulted the real Sister Luke on how best to dramatize her character's struggles with her conscience.

Taking her research further, my mother and her fellow "nuns" spent time embedded in two Assumptionist convents in Paris and Brussels. They slept in cells, often rising with the sisters at 4:00 a.m. for morning prayers on a cold stone floor before a day of duty and what Mum referred to as the Grand Silence. She learned how to walk, how to keep her hands clasped or in her pockets, and to close every door behind her. She emerged—according to Zinnemann—"excited" about what she'd learned but "purple with cold."

Writing a long letter to my father about the experience from Belgium, she said her "cubby hole" was tiny, with a washbasin and mirror, a small hospital bed—too short for her—and a chemical heater that smelled very strongly but failed to warm the room. "I cannot tell you how bitterly cold it was...it was a little while before I did peel off my clothes...I crawled shaking into bed having filled my little Swiss plastic hot water bottle with the hot water I have been given to wash myself." As requested, one of the sisters woke her early, and she was in the chapel by 6:15 for a service that lasted until 8:30. "Two hours in the chapel had frozen me and the icy cold floors seem to have penetrated my very bones—Fred arrived around 4 o'clock and I told him I felt I should not stay another night as I knew my resistance was running low and I might easily catch a cold....It wasn't long before I was back in the Raphael and soaking in a hot bath."

Staying out of the sun to keep her skin alabaster white, and forgoing her love of music, my mother also lived for a while on a frugal convent diet as part of her preparations for the role. As with all her films and her later work for UNICEF, the woman who considered herself uneducated after being denied schooling because of war researched everything most diligently. To really feel the character she was playing, she'd try to get under her skin and take note of the details that could legitimize every scene. Hers was a spontaneous adherence to Method acting, but she had never been formally trained, so this was something she did instinctively.

The studio also arranged for her to witness surgery as her character would have to in the film, and she spent time in both a laboratory and an asylum so that those scenes would be authentic. "After looking inside an insane asylum... and watching operations, I felt very enriched," she said afterward. "I developed a new kind of inner peacefulness. A calmness. Things that once seemed so important weren't important any longer." Zinnemann was immediately impressed with her work ethic and found her completely believable in the role. She fulfilled his desire for Sister Luke to be someone with a "human spirit that could not be broken" despite the many challenges she faced.

My mother would have felt a strong connection with a plot that showed that it was OK to have doubts about belief and to choose to change one's ideology, just as her own mother had with fascism. As someone who had witnessed the danger of entrenched ideas in the 1930s and '40s, she was against any kind of ideology. Although she had been baptized a Protestant, she did not believe in God in any conventional way, and her faith was more in tune with the natural world. The miracle of life was enough for her.

One of her great heroes was the German humanitarian, philosopher, and mission doctor Albert Schweitzer, winner of the Nobel Peace Prize for his philosophy that humans should devote a part of their lives to others. "Any religion or philosophy which is not based on a respect for life is not a true religion or philosophy," he wrote. She found her research into his life especially helpful for her role, as he'd lived and worked in African mission hospitals for years and the parallels with Sister Luke's life were useful. Before she left America, she told reporters that she very much hoped she might meet the philosopher one day, but their paths never crossed.

In her letters to my father, Mum also explained how she'd been taken to meetings with the film's ecclesiastical adviser, Father Leo Lunders, who came from the same order that Lou Habets had joined. The studio had arranged these meetings as part of its charm offensive, not realizing that my mother had strong views and was determined to express them.

"Their greatest fear is that we wish to give a generalization of life in the convents as being detrimental," she wrote. "I explained to [Father Lunders] how I understood the point of view of the Order and how their purpose was usually a good one but that nevertheless their purpose limited and checked Sister Luke in her wish to give and serve lovingly and without limits.... I know that Lou is today tragically sad at not having succeeded, nevertheless the way the story is told now she is a marvelous and determined woman, not obstinate (perhaps headstrong), but tremendously forceful in her love of God and her way of serving him.... The coldness she is shown when this honest and courageous woman finally leaves the convent with sorrow in her eyes yet great faith in her heart, should make for an acutely believable finish."

For that scene, incidentally, she had the support of her makeup artist Alberto de Rossi's wife, Grazia, who was indispensable to my mother on *The Nun's Story* and styled her hair, despite it being trapped under a wimple for much of the film. In the moving closing shots, when her character takes off her religious garb and slips back into civilian clothing, Zinnemann wanted her hair to be gray, but she didn't like that idea and asked that Grazia style it so that it looked as if it had been neglected, which worked.

Her hair—and the script—were left largely untouched by the director and the Catholic Church. Zinnemann was openly impressed by the strength of her feeling about how badly the church had treated Marie

Louise Habets but defused the tension with his tongue-in-cheek name for the movie, which made everyone howl with laughter—*Kicking the Habit*.

———◆———

FILMED IN AND AROUND STANLEYVILLE in the Belgian Congo in early 1958 to fulfill the director's determination to use the genuine locations of the book, *The Nun's Story* is set largely in a mission hospital and a leper colony, the kinds of places my mother had only ever read about in Schweitzer's books. Congolese excitement about the film crew's appearance was heightened by the news that many locals would be hired as extras.

The locals were long accustomed to Westerners trying to convert them to Christianity but visibly shaken to see women dressed as nuns sitting around applying makeup during their breaks or my mother smoking her favorite Kent cigarettes. They accepted the jarring spectacle with laughter once someone told them, "They're *American* nuns," to which they replied, "Ah, now we understand." It fit with how they imagined liberal American nuns might behave.

Filming in the Congo with all its heat, humidity, and snakes hiding under breakfast tables wasn't easy for my mother, who was in a heavy nun's habit all day. My father had other concerns about her being there too. Racial tensions in the lead-up to independence from Belgium had led to violence in the Congo, and a curfew barred locals from entering the European quarter, where the cast and crew were staying in a small hotel. Not long after filming ended and the crew flew home, those tensions erupted into riots, in which thousands died, and a massacre in the very location where the movie had been filmed. Sixty of the missionaries, their support staff, and their families were killed, some of whom had appeared alongside my mother. It marked the end of Belgian rule in the Congo.

Dad was understandably worried about my mother's safety—and her health—and he was distressed that his own work commitments prevented him from accompanying the woman he loved. She assured him she would be fine and promised to write every day, which—of course—she did. Those are letters I still have.

Once filming began, she was presented with a pet monkey that was in the script, and the animal lover in her was delighted until it bit her on the arm and the wound became infected. Such was the intensity of interest in her working in such a potentially dangerous place that news reports flashed around the world that she was seriously ill, which caused Dad to panic. Thousands of miles away, he was finishing up on set in LA and spent frantic days trying to get a call through to her in the bush, only to hear her tell him long-distance that the stories were all nonsense. Ever the devoted wife, Mum used up the final few minutes of their eye-wateringly expensive call checking that the complicated domestic arrangements she'd organized for him during her absence were to his liking. Even though she was a busy working actress thousands of miles from home, she was still trying to make sure he was being adequately fed and watered by the cook.

The embellished story about the monkey bite was typical of the kind of fake news her fame generated, which would dog her throughout her life. One of the more farcical untruths claimed that she'd demanded a bidet be shipped out to her Stanleyville bungalow. On hearing that, she laughed and asked, "Where on earth do people imagine it could have been plumbed in?"

The only thing she did ask the studio for, once she began to experience sweltering temperatures of up to 97 degrees Fahrenheit (36 Celsius), was an air conditioner. The studio mistakenly sent a humidifier instead. The locals thought the crew was mad to stay out in such temperatures, but the crew got around the problem by starting work at six in the morning to avoid the fiercest heat and sending for liters of ice water, which Mum decided to dole out personally to everyone, including the locals. Several of the crew noted that she often didn't leave any for herself.

As Zinnemann later said of his leading lady, "She was disciplined, gracious, dedicated, had no ego.... In fact, she behaved like a nun." She was also full of good humor, as always, and tickled by the news that *Sabrina* was premiering in Stanleyville—five years after it was made. Writing to my father, she described how she had been invited to take part in a Q and A afterward, saying, "I gave some very banale [*sic*] answers to some pretty insipid questions, but they were also terribly sweet and seemed so happy with the way things were going that I actually had a good time."

Everywhere she went, my mother gravitated to mothers and children. Early one Sunday she and the rest of the cast, including Edith Evans, Peter Finch, and Peggy Ashcroft, went up the Congo River in the morning mist by steamboat as hippos rose out of the water like monsters. They were headed to a remote leper colony run by an English Baptist minister, where twenty-one leprosy patients were to "graduate" from medical care to return to their villages. My mother and the others had been assured by medical staff that they had little chance of being infected. Any chance of contagion was soon forgotten, however, as Mum homed in on the children of those patients still waiting to be given the all clear. It was only later that she learned the incubation period for the disease is seventeen years.

Touched by the experience, in a letter to my father she wrote, "A little service was held in their chapel which was filled to overflowing with patients and some of their families. A choir consisting of lepers sang English hymns...in their tribal language and some we all sang together each of us in our own language—a most moving experience. At the end, the 21 patients were handed their cards of dismissal, and we all sang a Thanksgiving hymn.... After the service we had lemonade and cakes in the dispensary and were later escorted down to our boat. All the lepers lined the riverbank to wave, clap, and dance us goodbye. All of this and more I will never forget!"

As she had been during the war and its aftermath, she was struck by the selflessness of the people caring for those in need. She noted the serenity of the mission nuns in particular. She often quoted Anne Frank, saying that the wonder of life is that nobody need wait a single minute before doing something good. It was also part of her family's philosophy to practice what she called "that wonderful old-fashioned idea that others come first." She added that the ethos stating that "others matter more than you do" was the one by which she was brought up. It was a principle she wholly embraced, and in the Congo especially.

With hindsight, I think that the poverty and poor health she witnessed there were another important building block in the mind of the future UNICEF Goodwill Ambassador. It would take her almost thirty years, but she finally circled back to Africa to continue what she had seen others beginning.

ONCE FILMING OF *THE NUN'S STORY* switched locations to Rome and Belgium, a very different mood descended on my mother and the rest of the crew. In Bruges and Froyennes, the girl who'd hidden from soldiers in a cellar came the closest she had ever come to physically reliving some of the scenes she'd witnessed in Arnhem. The sight of actors in German uniforms triggered unbidden memories that still haunted her dreams and that she'd feared would bubble up if she agreed to play Anne Frank. "It would be like putting me back into the horrors of that war," she'd said then, yet a few of the Belgian scenes did exactly that. Ever the trouper, she pushed her memories aside and carried on.

When the film premiered internationally in 1959, it was nominated for eight Academy Awards despite its unflinching portrayal of the hardships of religious life. In dealing also with the serious matters of racism, murder, mental health, and the long-term effects of colonialism, it was highly unconventional for the time. My mother accepted this but said that her most profound role to date covered a "sincere and important subject" that meant a great deal to her. "The part was suited to my nature," she added.

As her mother superior points out in the film, the life of a nun is an endless struggle for self-perfection, which was something my mother well understood from what her director described as her own interior voyage of discovery. In letters to Lou Habets, she claimed to have been "altered forever" by the role and to have become "a different person" because of it.

"Delving into the heart and mind of Sister Luke," she wrote, "I have also had to dig deep down in myself. Thereby having done a bit of ploughing of the soul—so to speak—the seeds of all I have experienced have fallen on neatly prepared ground and I hope will result in harvesting a better Audrey."

Years later, her partner Rob Wolders said, "I think she was much more comfortable with Sister Luke than with other parts.... It was the story of a woman who investigated life, who was constantly on a search, as Audrey was."

When *The Nun's Story* premiered in Switzerland in the autumn of 1959, my mother was delighted that the proceeds from the star-studded event were donated to a fund for war refugees. The Actors' Orphanage charity benefited from the London premiere, and in Holland proceeds went to a fund for Dutch war veterans, thanks in part to my grandmother's involvement with the organization. That last arrangement, in a country she had such deep connections to, gave Mum's luminous smile an added gleam of gratitude.

For what proved to be one of her most compellingly personal yet most overlooked roles, she was nominated for her second Academy Award. On the film's sixtieth anniversary in 2020, Warner Bros. described it as having "quite possibly the finest [performance] of [Audrey's] entire career, as an intelligent, empathetic, and strong-willed woman with ambitions beyond the norm."

With minimal makeup and an inability to emote with her body, my mother had only her eyes and the expressions on her face to rely on to portray a complex range of emotions—from her struggles with faith, humility, and obedience to being overcome by grief. A versatile exploration of a woman's inner turmoil during a difficult time, it was a master class in acting from someone who wasn't yet thirty.

WITH STRANGE SYMMETRY, HER FRIENDSHIP with Lou Habets came full circle the year after she'd finished filming *The Nun's Story*. While in Mexico working on her next movie, a Western titled *The Unforgiven* starring Burt Lancaster and directed by John Huston, she discovered that she was pregnant after four years of trying.

Despite the poor timing, she was thrilled, saying, "The one thing I dreamed of in my own life was to have children of my own." Determined to go ahead with the filming, she blossomed on set, spoiled by all those who knew how happy she was at the prospect of being a mother.

Then one day she was accidentally thrown by an Arabian stallion named Diablo while practicing riding bareback, breaking several bones in her back and suffering foot and leg injuries. As her costars and a doctor hurried over to where she lay in agony on the ground, her first thought was for my father. "Please don't tell Mel," she pleaded. "He worries so much."

She was right. My father dropped everything to be with his beloved Acorn and was by her side when the studio flew her back to Los Angeles on a stretcher. During her long recovery at a rented house in Beverly Hills, where she was confined to bed, she was looked after by an exceptional nurse—the real Sister Luke. Lou was as selfless as my mother, and when she heard about the accident she rushed to her side. Under her devoted care, my mother was eventually able to stand and then walk. Lou said that she had never known a patient not once to complain despite refusing pain medication, which she did for fear of harming her unborn child.

Wearing a back brace, my mother returned to Mexico to finish the film, although she had to rest on a special cot between takes. It was only when the movie wrapped and she flew back to my parents' rented chalet in Switzerland to rest that she lost the baby after all. I know that this second loss, at six months—four years after her first miscarriage—was the hardest for her. She was informed that the baby was a little girl, who should have been my older sister. My mother had planned to call her Maria—I think after Marie Louise Habets—so it really felt as if she'd lost a person, not just a fetus, and she carried that pain for the rest of her life. The first miscarriage had been tough enough and a tragedy but had come early in the pregnancy. This second was not just another tragedy but caused her to fear that she'd never be able to have a child at all.

Devastated, my mum told friends, "I blamed God. I blamed myself. I blamed John Huston. I couldn't understand why I couldn't have children." The sadness overwhelmed her for a while, and she lost her appetite for food and for work. "That was the closest I came to feeling like I was going to lose my mind."

Doctors could offer no explanation for her inability to carry a baby to term, although my mother was later told she had what is referred to today as an "incompetent cervix," which can lead to repeated miscarriages. Living in a time when she was expected to get over the death and keep going, she didn't find it easy. It was only when she found out toward the end of 1959 that she was pregnant again—this time with me—that her spirits truly lifted. Her deepest desire, to create a happy family, finally looked to be possible after all.

Even though she went on to star in eight films over the next seven years, including two of her most iconic, *Breakfast at Tiffany's* and

My Fair Lady, family always came first, and she turned down roles if they would mean being separated from her loved ones for any length of time.

True to her promise to make the most of her second chance at life, she walked away from the movie business for a full year to ensure that she didn't lose me, too, and she devoted herself to what mattered to her most—nurturing the kind of loving family life that she had never known.

─── ◆ ───

8.

I always wanted to be a mother and have lots of babies. It's what made my decisions.—AH

INT. A HOTEL ROOM IN NEW YORK, 1960

AUDREY and her husband **MEL** sit by a telephone, waiting to be connected to a call. When it rings, **AUDREY** snatches the receiver and presses it to her ear.

              AUDREY
      Yes, please. Thank you.
            (to **MEL**)
      They're connecting me now.

Listening intently, she stands ramrod straight, her bare feet planted firmly in the white shag carpet as she draws on a cigarette.

              AUDREY
     Gina? Gina, is that you? It's la signora. I'm calling from New York.

She listens carefully, and her face breaks into a huge grin.

AUDREY
Is he there?
(to **MEL**, her hand over the mouthpiece)
She's lifting him out of the cradle now.

Stubbing out her cigarette, she covers her other ear.

AUDREY
Seanie? Sean, darling. It's Mummy!

MEL
And Daddy!

AUDREY
Daddy's here too.

AUDREY squeals with delight, laughing.

AUDREY
Oh, he's gurgling, darling. I think he knows it's us!

MEL scratches his head, nods, and smiles.

AUDREY
Seanie, baby, I miss you sooo much!

MEL

(leaning toward the telephone)

Me too!

AUDREY

We are counting the days until you can join us.

MEL

Ask Gina if he's been good.

AUDREY

Gina? Can you hear me? Has he been good?

AUDREY tilts her head to listen, and a shadow falls across her face.

AUDREY

What? A fever? What do you mean?
Did you call the doctor?
(to **MEL**, her face crumpling)
He has a fever!

MEL

Give me the phone.

AUDREY hands him the telephone, watching his expression.

MEL

What's all this about, Gina? I told you
we shouldn't upset or worry la signora...

AUDREY lights another cigarette, her hand shaking, as she watches and listens.

> MEL
> Yes, yes, all right. And the doctor saw him?

AUDREY jumps up and lets out a small cry.

> AUDREY
> The doctor saw him?

MEL nods.

> MEL
> Yes, I see. And the doctor said
> it was a mild fever?
> (to **AUDREY**)
> Nothing to worry about.
> (into the phone)
> And he gave him some medicine?
> Good. OK. Let the signora say good
> night to him, and we'll call again
> tomorrow.

AUDREY drops her cigarette into the ashtray and takes the phone, cradling it in both hands.

> AUDREY
> (alarmed)
> Sean? Seanie? Are you there, darling?
> (To **MEL**)
> He coughed!

MEL
(shaking his head)
It's a summer cold, that's all. He'll be fine.

AUDREY
Sean? Gina, can you hear me?

She listens and grimaces.

AUDREY
Do you think I should come home?

MEL shakes his head vehemently and gently takes the telephone.

MEL
Gina, we will talk to you tomorrow.

He replaces the receiver in time to catch **AUDREY** as she falls into the armchair, ashen.

AUDREY
I knew I shouldn't have left him! I was afraid
something like this would happen
when I was gone. I want to fly
home and be with him.

MEL
Now, now, Acorn. You're getting all worked
up over nothing. The doctor has examined
him. He gave him something and he'll be
right as rain tomorrow, you'll see.

> **AUDREY**
> Melly...!!!
>
> **MEL**
> Be sensible, darling. You can't shut down the whole production and lay off all the crew just because Sean needed to clear his throat. It would cost a fortune and imagine your embarrassment when you got there and found him all better.
>
> **AUDREY** turns away from him, her face creased in sorrow.
>
> **AUDREY**
> I can't risk it, Mel. You know I wouldn't survive it.
>
> **MEL**
> Nobody is losing anyone. Now let me order you some tea and then I'll run you a bath.
>
> **MEL** caresses her cheek and lifts the phone to dial room service as **AUDREY** wanders to the window and looks out on the bustling streets of Manhattan. Wrapping her arms around herself, she wishes she were back in Bürgenstock holding her infant son.

———◆———

To OUTSIDE EYES, MY FATHER had finally given my mother the one thing she most wanted in the world: a child. They had been married for seven years, and during that time her dreams of starting a big family had been repeatedly crushed.

What few people knew was that he secretly didn't want another child in the first place. Not only did he have four children already, but he had big plans for my mother's acting career—in tandem with his. Taking time off to have babies wasn't part of the plan. What followed was a series of subconscious actions, my mother suspected, to prevent her from keeping the infants she was carrying. Every time she became pregnant, my father would find a reason for them to move, travel, or do something energetic.

It almost became a joke as she'd quip to friends that as soon as any pregnancy test showed a positive result, he'd ask her, "Can you help me with this box of books?" They all thought she was kidding, but she wasn't. With her incompetent cervix, the last thing she needed was to be lifting anything, traveling too much, or moving house. Instead, she was meant to have complete bed rest, especially in the final trimester, so as not to go into labor prematurely. Her theory about all this, she explained to me quite pragmatically later in life, was that his children, although much loved, had been a source of marital anguish for him, especially when he divorced.

By the time I was due, when she was thirty-one years old and terrified that she'd be unable to bear me to term, she was anxious but still bursting with the motherly love she was dying to shower on me. For the final weeks of her pregnancy, she remained in bed in Switzerland. In a letter to her close friend Connie Wald, wife of the producer Jerry Wald, whom she'd first met on the set of *Roman Holiday*, she wrote: "Darling Con... thank you for your dear letter. Youngest Ferrer is due any minute, the house is humming with expectancy and unbelievable joy. The nursery is ready (and a dream all white and palest blue) and so are we. You were the first friend I told my precious secret to. So GLAD. All our love, A."

Despite her concerns, I arrived without any problems, at a healthy nine pounds, on July 17, 1960, in the middle of a summer thunderstorm. The name she chose for me means "gift of God." At first my exhausted mother couldn't allow herself to believe that I was alive—and normal—until the nurses let her hold me. Once she'd done that, she reportedly passed out. When she was feeling stronger, a few days later, she agreed to pose for a series of official photographs, holding me in her arms in her hospital bed as my father leaned in with a fixed grin.

Flowers and telegrams arrived from around the world, sending heartfelt good wishes. They included one from the former actress Grace Kelly, now Princess Grace of Monaco, and one from the director George Cukor, whom she referred to as "Old Uncle." There was another from the actress Sophia Loren and her husband, the Italian film producer Carlo Ponti, whom my parents had gotten to know while filming *War and Peace*. Lauren "Betty" Bacall, the widow of Humphrey Bogart, four months pregnant with her son by Jason Robards at the time, wrote, "Congratulations on the glorious boy. Now you really know what Heaven is like."

Greg and Veronique Peck wrote how "terribly happy" they were for my parents, and her friend the screenwriter Leonard "Lenny" Gershe welcomed me as "Little Funny Face." My favorite telegram came from the actor Raymond Massey and his wife Dorothy. Ray had starred in a failed television production of *Mayerling* with my parents in 1957. The message read: "Congratulations to Sean on his choice of parents, but don't you think 9lbs is over acting?" He had a point.

Back home at Villa Bethania in Bürgenstock, Mum had never been so contented. She settled me into the freshly decorated nursery and spent hours gazing at me in a state of maternal bliss. To ensure my arrival didn't create further tension in her marriage, she insisted that she'd pay for everything I needed throughout my life, including my education, and that I'd never be a financial burden on my father. She kept her word.

Once settled, she wrote to her dear Felix Aylmer, "Sean is truly a dream, and I find it hard to believe he is really ours to keep. I long to show him to you. We all three send all our love and kisses, Audrey." To others, she wrote, "I'm still filled with the wonder of his being, to be able to go out and come back and find that he is still there."

Bowing to the conventions of her tiny village and with a nod to my father's Catholic background, even though he was an agnostic, my mother had me christened at the chapel where my parents had been married. The ceremony was presided over by Pastor Eindiguer, who noted that Mum was "radiant with joy." The photographs prove that. Others noted that I had an excellent pair of lungs, as I bawled throughout the service. As with their wedding, members of the press found out and were waiting en masse outside the chapel. Beaming with happiness regardless, my mother told them she wanted her son to grow up and "play his own small part in making the world a better place." It's telling that while most new mothers can't think beyond the next day, mine was already hoping that my existence would bring something good to the world. I have spent most of my life trying to live up to that hope.

From the day her longed-for child was born, time away from me was agony for her. "Sean is worth much more to me than any film role," she said, perhaps as a defiant swipe at my father. Wherever she could, she took me with her, along with my nanny, Gina Cristoforetti. The middle-aged Gina had been recommended by my mother's influential Italian friends the Rattazzis and coaxed out of her retirement to look after me. She'd agreed as long as I was her last assignment. Trained at a legendary nanny school in Trento, Italy, she always wore a crisp powder-blue uniform with a white apron as she walked me miles in my buggy in the hills and mountains around our home. I loved her to death, and we stayed close until she passed away in her nineties.

THE FIRST BIG TEST FOR my mother in being separated from me came when she began to film *Breakfast at Tiffany's* in New York and Los Angeles. Shooting began in the autumn of 1960, when I was just three months old, and was set to last several months. After much agonizing, it was decided to leave me in Switzerland with Gina and my grandmother, who'd moved into the guest suite temporarily.

Although her part in *Breakfast at Tiffany's* became one of the most defining roles of my mother's career, she very nearly didn't get to play it. Marilyn Monroe was originally cast as novelist Truman Capote's kooky call girl, Holly Golightly, but when she declined to take the role for fear it might injure her reputation, my mother was approached. At first, she too was reluctant to take on the role, worrying that Holly was too controversial. "I hesitated a long time before accepting the part," she said later. "It's very difficult, and I didn't think I was right for it. I have to operate entirely on instinct." She described Holly as "kooky and dizzy, a gay kind of girl."

My father convinced her she needed to break away from being typecast as subordinate to male costars and consider roles that portrayed her as her own woman. Taking the role might be risky for her—and the studio—but would prove that she wasn't a slave to the system, like so many actresses before her, but was prepared to make her own choices.

Director Blake Edwards took credit for finally persuading her to accept, hailing the movie as representing "the dawn of womanhood." He convinced her to think of the character not as a vulnerable woman from a small town but as someone who had reinvented herself as a sophisticated siren who lived by her own code, which Mum could relate to. Holly was less a floozy and more a romantic dreamer, he insisted. That clinched it for the dreamer in my mother. Blake may have finally sealed the deal when he said that Holly had to look fabulous too.

It is true that the underlying story of *Breakfast at Tiffany's* is of a free-spirited, good-hearted girl, but my mother took that premise and elevated it to give it depth and meaning. As with most of her roles, she carefully curated her decisions based on whether they chimed with her own deep beliefs and feelings. The characters she played had not only intelligence and guts but also an attractive hint of vulnerability that warmed the heart. With every part, she managed to somehow truly inhabit the character and shape her to suit who she was inside.

With *Breakfast at Tiffany's*, she used the message of the movie as a symbol for women conquering the world, which she brandished as a flag. The movie became a manifesto for style and sass, showing that even a good girl can have fun and not be punished for it. That film, above all others, was the forerunner to TV shows like *Sex and the City* almost forty years later, whose "girl power" message my mother nailed in 1961. Time and again she makes us want to rescue her characters. But in real life she didn't need saving at all.

As it was a Paramount movie, Edith Head expected to be chief costumer, but instead of relying on her, my mother borrowed the most important pieces from Hubert de Givenchy's collection, including the long black gown that became world famous when paired with a string of costume pearls. In 2006 it achieved the distinction of highest price paid at auction for a dress from a movie when it sold for more than a million dollars.

When filming moved from New York to Paramount Studios in Los Angeles, my father rented an elegant colonial house in Coldwater Canyon. The house was beautiful, but it didn't ease Mum's sadness at being separated from me, and she continued to run up huge telephone bills calling long-distance just so she could hear me gurgling or crying. When I developed more infant ailments, she was beside herself, and it was all my father could do to prevent her from abandoning the set and jumping on the next plane. "It was too great a sacrifice not to be with my son," she told one interviewer afterward. "I suffered so being away from him, and I'd wanted to have him so much."

My mother had insisted on Franz Planer for cinematography because she'd worked so well with him before. Alexandre de Paris was responsible for her iconic beehive hairstyle, and as Alberto de Rossi was tied up on a David Niven movie, she picked Wally Westmore to do her makeup instead. The pair had worked together on *Roman Holiday*, *Sabrina*, and *Funny Face*, so she was confident in his work.

Despite her experience, it was increasingly important to her to have her handpicked vanguard around her, those whose familiar faces made her feel protected and safe. Very few people realized how insecure she secretly was, and the friends she chose to accompany her became a kind of carefully curated family because she needed their love.

It was on *Breakfast* that she began another lifelong and entirely platonic love affair, this time with the thirty-six-year-old composer Enrico "Henry" Mancini, who'd been asked to compose his first film score by the director, Blake Edwards. Born to Italian immigrants, Enrico had fought in the war and, at the age of twenty-one, taken part in the liberation of Mauthausen concentration camp in Austria, one of the most notorious in the Nazi system.

For the movie, he was asked to compose a song for her to sing when homesick for the rural life she'd once known—a concept she could immediately identify with after her happy years in Kent. It took Mancini weeks to come up with the wistful melody for "Moon River" before songwriter Johnny Mercer penned the words. Mancini was thrilled with the end result, which captured some of her character's melancholy sprinkled with just a glimmer of hope. He said, "Though the song went on to be a big hit for Andy Williams and has had over a thousand recordings over the years, no one ever performed it with more honesty, feeling, or understanding than Audrey."

Even though the scene in which she sings it while sitting on a window ledge became one of the most iconic moments of the movie, it almost didn't make it in. The head of the studio, after sitting through an early test screening of the film in San Francisco, apparently cried out in a note-taking session right after it, "And that bloody song has to go!" Mum jumped out of her seat and declared, "Over my dead body!"

She knew it had legs and was deeply invested in it. My father said later that it was the closest he ever saw her come to losing control and that he had to calm her down. Her indignation worked, though, and it was enough to keep the song in, which was just as well because it went on to win two Oscars.

My mother wrote to congratulate Henry Mancini, whom she affectionately called Hank, saying, "A movie without music is a little bit like an aeroplane without fuel. However beautifully the job is done, we are still on the ground and in a world of reality. Your music has lifted us all up and sent us soaring. Everything we cannot say with words or show with action you have expressed for us. You have done this with so much imagination, fun and beauty. You are the hippest of cats—and the most sensitive of composers! Thank you, dear Hank. Lots of love, Audrey."

The pair remained friends to the end, and when I was a young man living in LA, Henry Mancini would pick me up from time to time in his convertible Mercedes and drive me to the Hollywood Bowl to sit in on his rehearsals. Because my mother wanted me to make my own judgments and never made a song and dance about any of her friends being famous, I had no idea of Hank's importance. Nor did I appreciate what I was watching as the only person in the audience. All I knew was that he was a delight to be with.

ONCE THE FILMING OF *BREAKFAST AT TIFFANY'S* was finally over, I was flown in from Switzerland with Gina, my nanny, so I could finally be reunited with my mother. After she'd stopped cuddling and kissing me, she proudly showed me off to her friend Connie Wald, a woman she turned to time and again.

My mother loved Connie more than any other woman in her life, and I grew up thinking of her as a much-loved aunt. She not only admired Connie for being one of Hollywood's most beloved hostesses, a grande dame whose intimate dinner parties were legendary, but she also loved her authenticity and simplicity, which mirrored her own. In letters she wrote to her friend in the seventies, she said, "How blessed I am with a friend like you, I could spend my life with you." She called her "my incomparable Con" and signed off with "love and 'ugs and 'ugs."

Connie, a former model who had grown up in West Virginia, sported a shock of white hair and a ready smile. Dressing casually in chic shift dresses, slacks, and sweaters, often paired with statement jewelry, she was friendly with just about every major star in the Hollywood firmament and loved nothing more than to throw open the doors of her cozy, unpretentious home and invite them in. Always decorated with vases of roses from her garden and with a prevailing scent of home cooking prepared with her own herbs and vegetables, it was a welcome change from the vast, cold mansions of many in her social circle. Friends such as Joan Crawford, Ronald Reagan and his wife Nancy, Clark Gable, Errol Flynn, and Rosalind Russell were among those only too happy to accept invitations to her famous Thanksgiving dinners, for which the beautifully decorated table would be groaning with food.

Connie's husband Jerry dropped dead of a heart attack at the age of fifty when I was two years old, so I have no memory of the Warner Bros. mogul who'd produced films like *Mildred Pierce*, *An Affair to Remember*, and *Key Largo*. People were naturally drawn to his widow. She was always friendly, always laughing, and loved introducing people to each other, often sparking enduring friendships. She had a butler named Charles who was a true pro and knew exactly what everybody drank. His pretty wife helped Connie in the kitchen, where a little ceramic plaque on the wall read "Ristorante Wald."

To her casual Sunday-night suppers Connie invited an interesting mix of classic Hollywood stars, New York friends, European nobility, the kids of friends, and anyone new in town who wanted to be initiated.

She gathered people in and served pasta with her signature sauce made from peppers and sausages, or roast chicken followed by bread pudding and custard. In the old days we'd retire to her living room, which doubled as a projection room where she'd have film screenings organized by one of the dozen or so legendary projectionists in town.

Connie would call one up and say, "I'd love to screen *To Kill a Mockingbird* after supper tomorrow, can you arrange it, please?" The projectionist would then contact the studio and get permission to take the film to the house and show it. The reels were under the projectionists' sole guardianship, but sadly those memorable and exclusive screenings ended because of theft and piracy.

If Mum was in town, she'd almost always stay with Connie, and anyone who wanted to see my mother would have to go through Connie first. The pair of them were happiest staying in and playfully arguing over who was going to cook. Both women liked nothing better than to be in the kitchen, especially if there were children around. One of their favorite television shows was the British Edwardian saga *Upstairs, Downstairs*. It featured a scullery maid called Ruby, a girl put upon by the cook, Mrs. Bridges, and just about everyone else in the house, including the Scottish butler, Hudson. As Mum always insisted on doing the dishes, Connie gave her the nickname Ruby, which stuck forever and became their little joke. Whenever Connie visited us in Switzerland, she'd be equally humble, getting down on her hands and knees in the dirt to help weed the flower beds or plant bulbs.

Aside from the precious time with her dearest friend, my mother didn't spend much time in Los Angeles and would flit in and out of it only when she had to, keeping a low profile. But there was a small coterie of friends she loved to see when she was there, one of whom was her longtime agent, Kurt Frings. A former German boxing champion, Kurt was the nephew of Josef Frings, the archbishop of Cologne, who'd openly defied the Nazis during the war. At Josef's urging, his teenage nephew had fled first to Paris and then to America, where he became a poker-playing pal of director Billy Wilder, who introduced him to my mother.

Becoming an agent almost by chance after his wife Ketti became an award-winning screenwriter, Frings was known for his shrewd advocacy on behalf of a handful of clients, including Elizabeth Taylor, Richard Burton, Lucille Ball, Ringo Starr, and Marlon Brando. Kurt was like an uncle to my mother and someone about whom she cared deeply. Even when he was bedridden after a stroke, she refused to get another agent and would still pay his commissions. She felt the same about her attorney and business manager, Abe Bienstock, whom she loved like a father.

Another friend she looked forward to seeing at Connie's was the actor James Stewart, a regular visitor with his wife, Gloria. Jimmy, as he was known to his friends, was the first major movie star to enlist during WWII, joining the Army Air Corps in 1941 at the age of thirty-two. He quickly rose from private to colonel, winning medals for his service as deputy commander of a bombardment wing based in Britain. After the war, he remained in the Reserves, rising to brigadier general as his star status in Hollywood also rose. He also took part in aerial missions over Vietnam, where his twenty-four-year-old stepson was killed.

My mother never intended to surround herself with those who'd had wartime experiences, but many of the people she was drawn to had served, and Jimmy was something of a personal hero. She deeply admired anyone who'd fought the Nazis, and the fact that he had done so much and put his own life on the line for people like her meant more than words could express.

The statuesque actor was also funny, charming, and loyal, which only added to his appeal. And when Mum found out that after the war he'd initially planned to return home to Pennsylvania and run the family store, she was even more impressed. Here was a person like her for whom acting was something that had happened, rather than something that had been planned.

When the director Frank Capra offered him the starring role of George Bailey in *It's a Wonderful Life*, he took on the one character most people associated with him forevermore, just as Holly Golightly was for my mother. But for all his success, he remained as grounded and loyal as my mother. Like her, he'd known the brutality of war and suffered the consequences. I think that gave them a special bond, as they remained close right to the end. He was one of the last people to visit her before she died. Theirs was a very sweet kind of love.

MY MOTHER LOVED NOTHING MORE than to gather her surrogate family around her, insisting "true friends are the families you can select." It was something she needed increasingly as her marriage to my father began to slowly unravel.

To begin with, she and my dad had been very happy, especially after she bought the house of her dreams two years after I was born. She'd been looking for a place to live that would be kinder than Bürgenstock during the bitter winter months and had a bigger yard, especially for a growing toddler.

On rambling house-hunting trips, my parents would take the train from Lucerne with a packed lunch of tea and sandwiches and hire a car before heading to Lake Geneva. It was on one of those visits that she heard about a house called La Paisible in the tiny village of Tolochenaz and drove over to see it. They didn't have an appointment, and no one was home, so Mum stood on the hood of their rental car to peer over the wall.

The minute she saw the cherry orchard in full blossom and the fields beyond leading to the mountains as a backdrop, she knew she'd found her forever home. The beautiful stone farmhouse with roses round the door was the place that became her sanctuary until the day she died. *Paisible* means "peaceful," and buying it was, she said, one of the best decisions of her life. "There is no place in the world where I feel so much at peace," she declared. Her passion for that house was a love affair all its own.

By establishing a home in Switzerland my mother was rebelling against Hollywood, in her own quiet way. She refused to live in Tinseltown or flaunt her standing in an ostentatious way. Living in the heart of Europe, far from the glitz, she preferred walking her dogs or arranging flowers while listening to jazz to attending galas and premieres. Turning down invitation after invitation, she knew her own mind and resolutely stuck to her own principles about how and where she wanted to be seen. Fame never changed her.

Some of my favorite photos of my mother are family snapshots taken on her Instamatic camera, often catching her without any makeup, in slacks, a T-shirt, and a sweater or in a bikini. Several feature her and Hubert de Givenchy sunbathing in bathing suits on loungers on the terrace, leaning toward each other to chatter away in French. Others show lively dinners with friends like Connie Wald or the actor Yul Brynner and his wife Doris, my mother's neighbors. And—of course— there were roses and dogs in almost every frame. These photos are precious because they remind me of the lovely mum I knew, the woman who never made me feel like the son of a movie star.

Despite decades of gossip that she had an eating disorder because she was so slim, she cooked and baked and ate what she liked but was careful with portions. She started most days with a boiled egg, toast, and jam. She walked every day, setting a punishing pace for those of us trailing behind. "Much better than going to the gym," she'd say. For lunch she'd have a salad or a soup, a sandwich, and a scoop of her favorite vanilla ice cream with maple syrup. She drank the occasional cold beer, and after her daily nap she'd have a square of dark chocolate—her "cure for the blues"—followed by a "finger" of whisky when the sun set. Supper would be a single plate of pasta pomodoro and a salad.

Her homemade flourless chocolate cake was her special treat, and although she did a monthly detox, living on natural yogurt, grated apple, and herbal tea for a day or two, she eschewed all thoughts of fad diets. And any suggestion of plastic surgery was anathema to her, as she honored the history of every line on her face. As she famously once said, citing the quotation, "The beauty of a woman is not in the clothes she wears; it is seen in her eyes—the doorway to her heart."

If proof were needed that she wasn't vain about her looks, it can be found in her exchange with the photographer John Isaac, who took the photo of her in Ethiopia that was her favorite. It shows her carrying a child on her back in the harsh midday sun. When John sent her a proof of the magazine cover it was going to appear on, he asked if she wanted him to "clean up" the lines on her face. She promptly wrote back, "Don't you dare touch my wrinkles. I've earned every single one of them."

Despite my teenage protestations that we needed a better car, she refused to buy anything flashy. Instead, we had a "woody" Mini Countryman and, later, a series of dark-green Volvo station wagons driven by our first gardener, Monsieur Nicole. She chose them because they were the first vehicles built for safety and with seat belts. Frequently encouraged by me and others to upgrade to something more stylish and in keeping with who she was, she wouldn't budge. Her stock response was, "But where would we put the dogs?"

With characteristic decisiveness, she'd given up driving soon after passing her test in 1958, following an incident in which she rear-ended another vehicle. She was driving a hardtop convertible Ford Thunderbird gifted to her by my father, who went ballistic when he heard what she'd done. The accident happened in Beverly Hills while she was on her way to the studio to film William Henry Hudson's *Green Mansions*, a jungle romance he was directing. The other driver was a singer and dancer. After a two-year legal wrangle over the accident, during which time *Green Mansions* bombed and she fell pregnant with me, the injured party took her to court demanding $50,000 (around $500,000 today) in damages. She ended up settling for just over $6,000 after my mother appeared in court to defend herself in person.

Mum was troubled by the whole affair and especially by the need to fly halfway around the world to testify when I was just three months old. She never needed a vehicle much anyway, preferring to stroll to the market or walk the hills, so she sold the car and never sat behind the wheel of one again—unless posing for a movie. Driving wasn't for her, and once she made her mind up about something, that was the end of it. When she later lived in Rome, she told me, "I didn't feel I possessed the necessary aggressiveness to ever become a good driver." While aggression isn't always required to be a good driver, in Rome it's no surprise she felt that way.

In Tolochenaz, she worked hard to create the perfect home for us. Buying or growing vegetables and flowers, she cooked delicious meals and filled her many vases. In the house she'd long dreamed of, she knew exactly how to decorate and where everything should go. All her homes were decorated almost identically in white with simple shapes, a preference she also showed in her choice of monochrome clothing.

Deborah Kerr said of her Swiss haven, "It was charming. Very simple and of course everything in white. Wherever they went, everything was white. I always thought that was so indicative of her. She was trying to recapture the peace that had eluded her childhood."

Being in the mountain air gave my mother a chance to catch her breath for the first time in years. She knew then that it was the place to raise the children she'd always longed for and to find some tranquility in the chaos. She never regretted her decision, especially when she and my father began to drift apart.

Some of my earliest memories are of my parents enjoying evenings of candlelight and soft music. There was always music when my mother was around. I can remember them dancing around the living room in a joyful embrace—Mum barefoot in a long housedress and Dad always elegant.

Suppers were animated affairs during which they discussed every aspect of their work, asking each other for advice on anything from scripts to outfits, directors to cinematographers. It was a true collaboration. For thirteen years they lived and worked together, advised each other, and were parents together. Few normal couples would clock that many hours side by side at work and play over a lengthy marriage, but they crammed it all in over an intense period that ate up their credit much faster.

The chief problem was that my neurotic perfectionist of a father wanted to focus on acting, directing, and producing, and was constantly on the lookout for exciting new projects for them both while, at the same time, being the "heavy" with respect to all the approval aspects of her films. He scoured for them almost as passionately as Mum strove to care for me and lead the simple and anonymous family life she'd always dreamed of. Despite the strong work ethic that had been instilled in her by my grandmother, she even declined to attend the all-important New York premiere of *Breakfast at Tiffany's* in 1961 so she could stay home with me. It was a decision my father strongly disagreed with.

He was truly a type of his generation: self-centered and not at all in tune with the psychology of a relationship. He could also explode into a rage and was brooding at times. Mum once confided in a reporter that my dad could be "very angry at times but knew how to contain himself," which I think was telling. There is no doubt that he'd been pivotal in my mother's life and helped her make decisions ever since she won a Tony for *Ondine*. It was my driven father who knew how important it was for her to stretch herself and never get stuck in the rut of romantic comedies or musicals, and it was he who urged her to keep doing more.

But, painfully aware that his career was never as successful as hers, my father had become increasingly difficult and temperamental, even though he had the capacity for deep and nurturing love. He spent a great deal of time living and working in France and Italy, appearing in movies such as *The Devil and the Ten Commandments* and *Charge of the Black Lancers*. The couple were separated for long periods as Dad pursued his own projects while Mum worked or stayed home with me, and the distance between them became more than just geographical. His Acorn had fallen too far from the tree.

Then he was given a minor role in Darryl Zanuck's adaptation of *The Longest Day*, a movie about the D-Day landings starring an ensemble cast that included Richard Burton, Henry Fonda, Sean Connery, Robert Mitchum, Rod Steiger, and John Wayne. My mother refused to visit Dad on the set in Normandy, France, because she knew seeing soldiers and tanks would only trigger unpleasant memories. She did, however, agree to accompany him to the film's world premiere in the autumn of 1962 in Paris. She had one condition—she also wanted to visit a children's hospital and have him accompany her to the Bal des Petits Lits Blancs or Little White Beds Ball aboard the renovated ocean liner SS *France* to raise money for another children's hospital.

When they arrived at the premiere, however, she was shocked to find Sherman tanks and howitzers lining the route along with hundreds of soldiers in uniform. Wartime searchlights stabbed the night sky, and veterans and military commanders stood to attention as guests arrived, including some who'd overseen the failed operation in Arnhem. My mother was quite unsettled by it all but was somewhat consoled by the knowledge that the proceeds from the glittering event would be going to the Veterans Relief Fund for war widows and orphans, a charity she had special affection for.

The highlight of her evening came when the famed French singer Édith Piaf stood halfway up the Eiffel Tower and sang "Le droit d'aimer"—"The Right to Love." My mother sat spellbound as Piaf sang the words that could have been written for her: "Never will anything or anyone stop me from loving / I have the right to love... and be loved."

For the woman who had become one of the most adored in the world, feeling her marriage slowly wither was intensely saddening. Her love for me and her dream of providing me with an unbroken family life prevented her from giving up on her marriage for a few more years, but I think she must have known in her heart even then that it was over. Once again, she was thinking of others before herself.

MY MOTHER'S REASON FOR STAYING so long, despite her sorrow, was her instinctive desire to save and nurture people. She thought she could heal the hurt of my father's emotional hunger. Demonstrating the resilience that years of rigorous ballet training had taught her, she stuck with him longer than she should have. It was a pattern she was to repeat years later. No matter what life threw at her, she handled each new heartache with grace, to the point that her pain became part of her beauty. Dancers are tough. They have to be.

My parents' last project together happened in 1966 when he produced her fifth Oscar-nominated role in *Wait Until Dark*. In that movie she plays a blind woman whose apartment is invaded by thugs looking for a heroin-stuffed doll hidden there.

Despite the character's inability to see, she manages to dupe them all. It was another part my mother researched fastidiously for, refusing director Terence Young's instruction that she should wear dark glasses, and living in an institute for the blind for weeks to really understand what it was like not to see. *Wait Until Dark* portrays a complex female character struggling against being controlled, one who, when pushed to the limit, chooses to act.

She was like that in her own life, too, because my mother was a born survivor—of a broken marriage, of war, of romantic disappointment, and of the Hollywood system. After everything she had gone through, she'd learned how to draw on her inner strength to survive. Just as several of her characters turn heartache and the manipulation of others to their own advantage, so she took each knock as a way of digging deeper into herself. "Our worst moments in life are often our best teachers," she told me. "Only then can we grow and learn from them."

After the filming of *Wait Until Dark*, which was Mr. and Mrs. Ferrer's swan song, my father finally began to realize that there was little hope for them as a couple. It was a loss he never really got over. Being the Pygmalion of my mother's life had fed his own insecurities for years but made him impossible to live with.

Inspired by her own mother's strength in the face of heartache, my mother had become a self-made, independent woman who was strong enough to defy the old patriarchy but still weak when it came to matters of the heart. In the end, she realized she couldn't save my father, and trying to decide what to do next caused her almost as much distress as she'd felt when her own father left her, adding a new layer as her quest for love continued.

9.

Love is action, it isn't just talk, and it never was.
We are born with the ability to love, yet we have to develop it
like you would any other muscle.—AH

INT. LA PAISIBLE, TOLOCHENAZ, SWITZERLAND, 1966

SEAN, age six, tiptoes along the corridor, keeping close to the wall. Stopping to listen, he freezes before carrying on. Dropping to the floor on his hands and knees as he nears an open doorway, he hesitates again before standing and hurrying on his way, still on tiptoe.

AUDREY, coming up the stairs, sees him through the banister rail and smiles. Putting down the fresh towels she is carrying, she creeps up behind her son. Turning, he jumps at the sight of her, but she grabs him into a hug, laughing.

AUDREY
What are you up to, my darling? Is it a game?
Can Mummy play, too, or is it secret?

SEAN
(staring at his feet)
It's secret.

AUDREY
(folding her legs beneath her and pulling him onto her lap)
That's OK. Secrets can be fun. You know, when I was a little girl, I used to climb trees where no one could find me.

SEAN
(pensive)
Why didn't you want anyone to find you?

AUDREY
I just liked being on my own sometimes. I still do.

SEAN
I like it too.

AUDREY
I know. Would you like to be left alone now so you can carry on with your game?

SEAN
(frowning)
It's not a game, Mummy.

AUDREY
All right, then, what is it?

INTIMATE AUDREY

          SEAN
       I'm being quiet.

         AUDREY
   (suppressing a laugh)
   I see. May I ask why?

SEAN shrugs.

         AUDREY
    Can you tell me?

          SEAN
 (looking along the corridor)
I don't want Daddy to hear me.

         AUDREY
     (frowning)
       Why?

          SEAN
    (hesitating)
   He'll be cross.

         AUDREY
     (wincing)
No, Seanie. Daddy's not cross
     with you.

          SEAN
 (staring at his shoes)
He gets angry with me.

AUDREY

(pulls **SEAN** closer)

No, not with you. Never you.

SEAN

(bottom lip trembling)

He did yesterday.

AUDREY

(her jaw tightening)

Do you know why?

SEAN

I was playing on the stairs, and he said I was making too much noise.

AUDREY

(sighing)

And that's why you're tiptoeing past his office?

SEAN sniffs and nods.

AUDREY

(her eyes sad)

Why don't we go and find the dogs and take them for a nice run in the garden? Would you like that?

SEAN

(his face brightening)

Yes!

AUDREY rises to her feet in a single fluid motion before taking his hand and leading him back down the stairs. As they descend, she glares at the open doorway.

THE DAY MY MOTHER FOUND me tiptoeing past my father's room and speaking in whispers to avoid one of his outbursts was the day she knew that she'd let things go on for too long. It mortified her to think that I was afraid of my own father. I truly believe that this was the moment she decided—if only in her heart—to leave him.

Her procrastination must have been agonizing for her, but the one thing my mother never wanted for me was a broken home. She had known the hurt of that as a little girl, and she continued to cling to her failing marriage for the sake of her only child. She had already been through some of the toughest years of her life. In 1961 her beloved dog, Mr. Famous, was run over and killed on Sunset Boulevard while she was filming *The Children's Hour* with Shirley MacLaine—a loss that shattered her anew. Even though she loved the replacement my father bought her, another Yorkshire terrier they named Assam, she never quite got over the death of her self-styled "surrogate son," who'd died in her arms.

Then in 1964 she had a letter from her mother telling her she'd heard that Joseph Ruston, the father she'd never stopped thinking about since she was small, had died at the age of seventy-five. The news almost broke her. "I was so distraught," she said later. "I realized how much I had always cared. I just couldn't bear the idea that I would never get to see him again." Blaming herself for not making the effort to find him before it was too late, she found herself reliving the grief she'd experienced when she was six years old and he'd walked out of her life.

Seeing how upset she was, my father asked her, "Did it ever occur to you that it's not true, and he may still be alive?" He had come to know his baroness mother-in-law well over the years, and he knew how much she'd derided my grandfather, so he wouldn't have put anything past her if it might keep father and daughter apart. Knowing that Joseph Ruston's absence was a void in Mum's life, he decided to investigate further and, with the help of the Red Cross, discovered that—as he'd suspected—the information she'd been fed was incorrect. Her father was living in a two-room apartment in Ireland and had married a woman thirty years his junior.

My mother would never have made the first move if it weren't for my dad. With her permission, he got in touch with my grandfather, and the three of them agreed to meet at the Shelbourne Hotel in Dublin, Ireland. Joseph knew exactly who my father was and said he'd been following my mother's career. Mum was very nervous about being reunited with the man she'd last seen in 1939 when he put her on a KLM flight that neither one realized was headed directly for war. That had been an extremely traumatic parting for her when she was just ten years old, and now she was an adult, a wife, and a mother—thirty-five years old but feeling like an awkward teenager again.

From the moment she set eyes on her tall, thin father in his well-worn tweed jacket, however, she could tell from his body language that he wasn't going to show her any affection—unlike in her childhood, when he had been funny and kind. She told a friend afterward, "He was so cold. He didn't receive me and that really hurt."

Instead, he mumbled something like "Nice to see you," as if the previous twenty-five years of silence had never even happened. He didn't make one move toward her or even a gesture. His eyes seemed dead, and he didn't attempt to return her hug. Nor did he ever once tell her he was proud of all that she'd achieved. She quickly realized that her father was an emotional invalid. Instead of having the reunion she'd dreamed of, they spent an uncomfortable few hours making small talk about what they'd both been up to in the intervening decades.

Recalling that her father had once been a fine horseman, she told him the story of being thrown by an Arab on the set of *The Unforgiven*. His response was not what she'd expected. "Well, of course you were a fool to ride a gray stallion," he scolded, adding that she should have known the horse would throw her. After it finally came time to say goodbye, my mother turned to my father and said simply, "We can go home now. I never need to see him again." Her dream of a heroic father had withered and died.

Trying to make peace with his aloofness, she gallantly put his attitude down to his upbringing and resolved to stay in touch, by letter at least. After all, she already knew the coldness of a mother who never made a fuss about anything she did and had made peace with that. Even though her father never softened toward her, she continued to send him newsy mail from her travels, signing them variously "Audrey" or "M.P." for Monkey Puzzle, the childhood nickname that he'd given her in the days when he'd seemed affectionate. Drawing a line under their relationship, she chose to forgive him and supported him financially for the rest of his days, sending him $2,000 a month, or more if his wife called to tell her they needed money. (This was something Luca and I continued to do for his widow from time to time.) "It helped me to lay his ghost to rest," she told me.

I only ever met my grandfather once, when I was five years old, when she flew him to Switzerland for a day or two because she wanted him to meet me. One thing that always saddened her was that I never got to know her Dutch grandfather, Baron Aarnoud van Heemstra, who had died at the age of eighty-six, four years before I was born. Her relationship with him had been so important, especially during the war, and she always spoke of him so fondly.

By contrast, she rarely spoke so kindly of Grandfather Joseph, whom I remember as an elegant, stern, impressive figure in tweeds with a matching waistcoat. He seemed somewhat distant with everyone and socially awkward with my parents. It was only later that I came to understand that he had broken her heart early in her life. He broke it further when he remained physically and emotionally unavailable to us both.

When she went to see him on his deathbed in 1980, the ninety-one-year-old didn't offer his only child any kind words of farewell. And he never once apologized for abandoning her. It was only after she left the room upset that he turned to her partner, Robert, and confided that he'd been keeping a scrapbook of my mother's career for years. Mum flew home soon after and didn't return for his funeral.

It was a surprise to us all when, long after my grandmother's death, letters emerged between her and my late grandfather in which they both sang my mother's praises. My mother was touched by their hidden pride but also deeply saddened, asking, "Why couldn't they have just told me?"

DESPITE THIS PERSONAL SORROW, MY mother's career continued its upward trajectory, and she never stopped working, starring in five films in the three years between 1963 and 1966. In a kind of unofficial separation, my father lived largely abroad, starring in and producing the Italian movie *El Greco* as well as appearing in two Spanish movies, including a bullfighting musical made on a shoestring budget. He also had minor roles in *The Fall of the Roman Empire* starring Sophia Loren and *Sex and the Single Girl* with Natalie Wood and Tony Curtis.

Mum meanwhile spent months in France filming *Paris When It Sizzles* with her former lover William Holden, which proved challenging. Difficult to work with and often inebriated, the "Bill" she'd once had feelings for while making *Sabrina* had become someone on a self-destructive path that would end in his premature death. She was saved by the uplifting presence of Noël Coward, whom Mum adored and who she was delighted to discover lived not far from her home in Switzerland. In his diary, Coward wrote of her that she was "unquestionably the nicest and most talented girl in the business" and that she "deluged me with praise and roses." They became friends to the end.

Struggling to enjoy working with Bill Holden, my mother flew home to Switzerland every weekend to be with me, or she had the nanny bring me to the city so we could spend some family time together and do something like visit the circus. As she told a reporter years later, "Working often meant being away for two or three or sometimes up to five months, and that's what I didn't want. I wanted to stay home with my child."

She remained in Paris to film *Charade* with Cary Grant, who became a lifelong friend. Thirty years older than she was, he was reluctant to take the part at first for fear it made him look lecherous, even though in real life he was dating Dyan Cannon, who was even younger than my mother. He had the writer change the storyline so my mother's character chased his, which made the movie funnier and made him appear less unseemly.

Married three times by then, Cary Grant was famously guarded about his personal life, advising my mother that movie stars should remain mysterious and let their work speak for their character. The pair got along so well that he became a frequent dinner guest and, having been sent caviar one New Year's Eve by her business manager Abe Bienstock, who knew she would never spend that kind of money on something so frivolous, Mum served it to Cary and the rest of us with baked potatoes and sour cream, an instant hit.

Cary sensed my mother's secret sadness over everything from her father to her marriage and did what he could to keep her spirits up. "In spite of her fragile appearance, she has great vitality. She's like steel; she bends but never breaks," he said at the time. "We worked well together. She's considerate, always up on her lines, doesn't fuss, and she seems to realize that other people on the site have their troubles too. She mothered the entire company. The day she left we were bereft. We had to stick around and do our fight scenes without her, and we were all furious."

After *Charade*, my mother spent months at the Burbank Studios in California filming *My Fair Lady* before returning to Paris to film *How to Steal a Million* with the British actor Peter O'Toole. She loved the distraction of Peter, who was almost the same age as she was and another "war baby" who'd experienced bombing during the Second World War before being evacuated to a strict Catholic school. The pair had similar senses of humor, which caused problems for the director, her old friend William Wyler, who complained they acted like "laughing gas" on each other, especially when the champagne-drinking O'Toole started playing the fool.

In one scene where the pair were crammed together in a cupboard under the stairs, Peter gave my mother such a fit of the giggles that she had to go and lie down in her dressing room to recover. Wyler, who'd once declared that she "never made a wrong move professionally or personally," was at his wit's end.

My mother had had a soft spot for Willie ever since *Roman Holiday* and described herself as his "baby." *How to Steal a Million* was her third film with him, after *The Children's Hour*, and she loved doing it because Peter taught her how to laugh again and she could stay in Europe with me and my nanny while she worked.

When she found out she was pregnant again by my father after a brief reunion, she prayed it might mean hope for a brighter future for them both, but a month later, at the end of 1965, she miscarried again, this time due to an ectopic pregnancy. At her request, my father wrote to her father and stepmother to tell them the news. No matter how cold Joseph Ruston was to her, she was determined to remain the perfect, dutiful daughter. Dad wrote, "Audrey lost the little baby we were expecting—approximately in her tenth week. However, she is

Greeting director William Wyler as Gary Cooper looks on *(© Al St. Hilaire / mptvimages.com)*

Animals galore at Gary Cooper's ranch in Santa Monica *(Hepburn family archive)*

Keeping warm outside Paris
(Ed Feingersh / Michael Ochs Archives / Getty Images)

Hubert and Audrey at another fitting *(© Pierluigi Praturlon / Reporters Associati & Archivi—Roma)*

Our peaceful Swiss haven—La Paisible *(Hepburn family archive)*

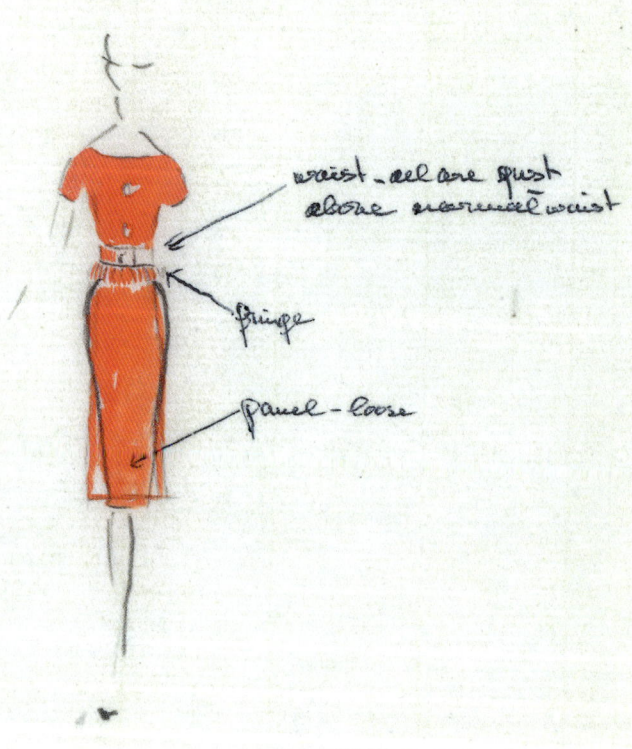

"There is a shade of red for every woman."—Audrey Hepburn *(Hepburn family archive)*

Still in love with Mel Ferrer *(© Philippe Halsman / Magnum Photos)*

Filming *The Nun's Story* in the Congo *(Leo Fuchs / Leo Fuchs Photography Archive / Courtesy of Paramount Pictures)*

With the monkey that bit her *(Leo Fuchs / Getty Images)*

Glowing with happiness—and me *(Mel Ferrer / Hepburn family archive)*

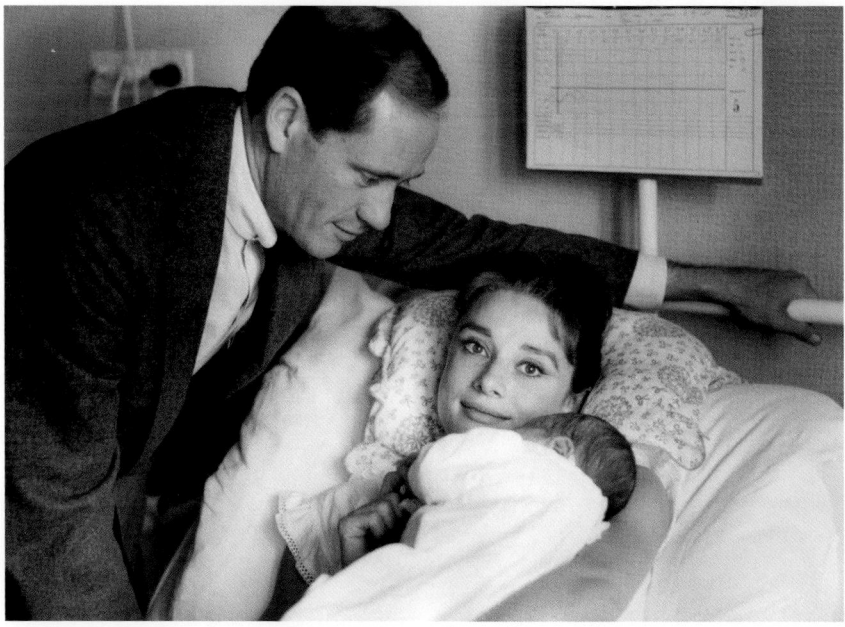

Proud parents with nine-pound me *(© Pierluigi Praturlon / Reporters Associati & Archivi—Roma)*

Her longed-for baby *(Mel Ferrer / Hepburn family archive)*

Dressed in her favorite matching white *(© Bud Fraker / mptvimages.com)*

Pool time with Mama *(© Bud Fraker / mptvimages.com)*

With my father, Mel Ferrer *(© John Swope / Courtesy Margaret Herrick Library, Academy of Motion Picture Arts and Sciences)*

Mr. Famous and me, Switzerland *(© John Swope / Courtesy Margaret Herrick Library, Academy of Motion Picture Arts and Sciences)*

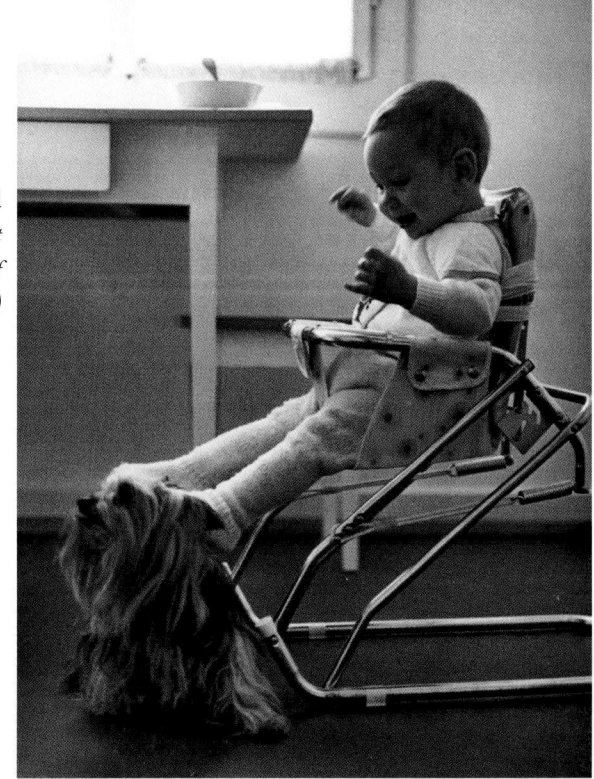

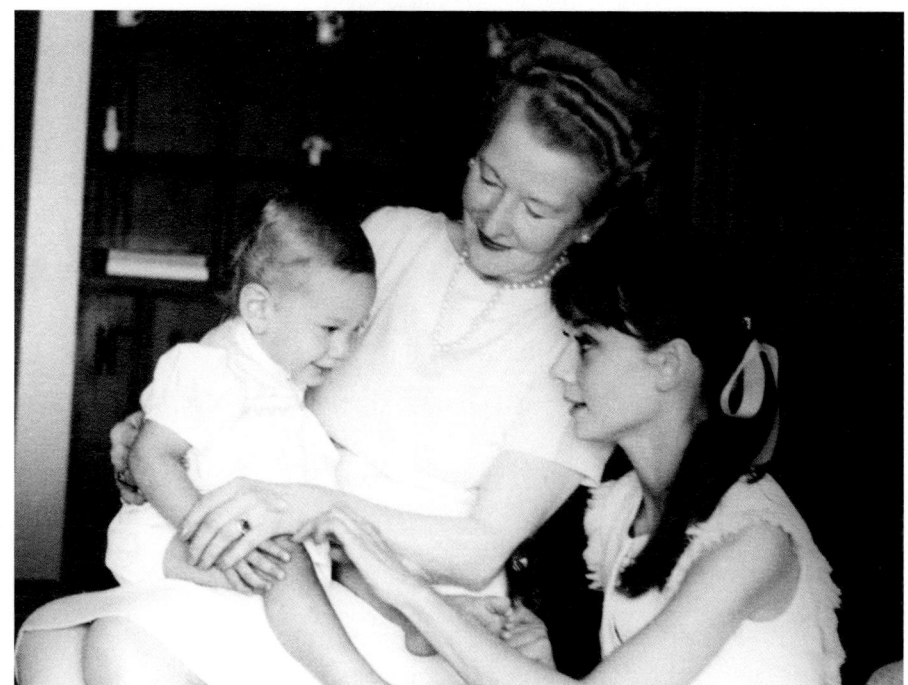

My grandmother and protective mum *(© Bud Fraker / mptvimages.com)*

A new mum missing me in New York on the set of *Breakfast at Tiffany's (Courtesy of Paramount Pictures)*

Before hair and makeup for *Breakfast at Tiffany's (Courtesy of Paramount Pictures)*

Publicity shot for *Breakfast at Tiffany's (Courtesy of Paramount Pictures)*

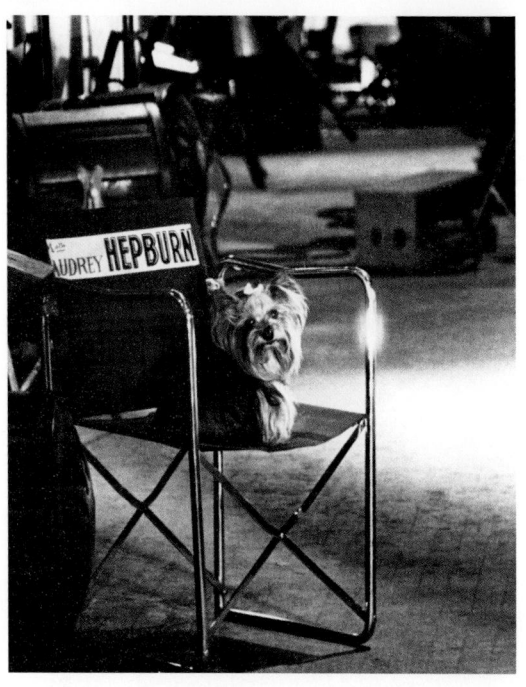

Mr. Famous, her surrogate son, on the set of *Breakfast at Tiffany's (Courtesy of Paramount Pictures)*

Reunited, best friends from the start
(Mel Ferrer / Hepburn family archive)

Waiting for her cue on the set of *The Children's Hour (© Pierluigi Praturlon / Reporters Associati & Archivi—Roma)*

Rex Harrison, Audrey Hepburn, Jack Warner, and George Cukor pose with the Oscars they won for *My Fair Lady* (B.D.M. / mptvimages.com)

Sweet note from designer Cecil Beaton *(Cecil Beaton Archive © Condé Nast)*

Winter in Bürgenstock was always fun *(Mel Ferrer / Hepburn family archive)*

Playing with a lion cub at the circus in Paris *(© Pierluigi Praturlon / Reporters Associati & Archivi—Roma)*

With her beloved makeup man Alberto de Rossi and his wife, Grazia *(Hepburn family archive)*

Hugs galore with the most beautiful mother in the world *(© Pierluigi Praturlon / Reporters Associati & Archivi— Roma)*

now beginning to feel much better...her spirits and physical being are much improved."

What he didn't say was that he was booked for minor surgery for hemorrhoids and, having been told there was a chance they might turn cancerous, he went ahead with the operation even though my mother felt somewhat abandoned by him in her grief. The "oodles of children" she'd longed for since childhood still felt like an impossible dream, and her spirits sank. She penned her father her own note, writing, "There is much to go through still, I pray...for strength and gentleness."

Throwing herself back into work, she agreed to appear in *Two for the Road* with Albert Finney, a friend of Peter O'Toole, who had sung Finney's praises. As she wrote to her father: "Am well again and not so sad anymore....I start work on the 1st May first in St. Tropez then Paris...a wonderful script....xxxx M.P."

It was while she spent four months working with "Albie" in the South of France that my mother began a fling with her younger costar, which they managed to keep from my father—and the press. The irony was that in playing a woman whose marriage is on the rocks, she was the happiest she'd been in years. Her friend and hairstylist Grazia de Rossi was by my mother's side throughout, as the movie used different hairstyles and clothing as a guide to the decades portrayed. I joined her with my nanny on set and was never happier than when playing in the props truck and all its magical drawers. I remember golden days with the happy gang in the South of France.

When asked by a reporter how she was getting along with Finney, my mother replied, "I love Albie. I really do. He's so terribly, terribly funny. He makes me laugh like no one else can. And you can talk to him. Really talk. He's serious, too, completely so about acting, and that's wonderful. It was just plain wonderful, that's all there is to it." Those who knew her said the pair behaved like teenagers in love, and there was a light in her eyes that had been missing for a while.

Stanley Donen, who'd previously directed Mum in *Funny Face* and

Charade, had worked hard to persuade her to make *Two for the Road* even though it featured a love sequence where she'd appear half naked in bed, and there were other scenes in which her character would commit adultery and swear. This was a major departure from her other roles, and although anxious at first, she accepted Donen's directorial challenge, describing the script as "refreshing," adding tellingly that there was "no awful penance" for the plot's adulterers.

WHEN I LOOK BACK AT my mother's schedule, I can hardly believe she had the time to do all that she did with the sadness she was carrying. I never felt neglected or abandoned to the care of my nanny. Mum was constantly juggling her commitments to make sure that my needs and those of my father were met. She never stopped trying on every level to please, to be happy, and to be loved.

Some of my fondest memories are of the sleepovers we had when she came home from that shoot and from her many other commitments on weekends. We would lie in bed with the lights out, chatting about what we'd each been up to and how we were feeling. We talked for hours about life, relationships, and friendships and what I'd be like as a grown man. "To be a gentleman, you must first be a 'gentle man,'" she advised. They were some of the most meaningful conversations of my life as we lay together, two souls suspended in the dark.

I was enrolled in the local village school, where she wanted me to enjoy being like every other kid. I spoke French in class, but my parents had always spoken English to me, and Spanish when we were in Marbella, plus my nanny, Gina, spoke only Italian, so I grew up multilingual. Each night when I came home from school, Mum would help me with my homework, and on holidays and weekends she'd invite children from the local orphanage to come play with me in the garden.

We also went on fun excursions together, such as taking everyone to the cinema in a rented minibus to see *The Jungle Book*. And we took long walks every day—always briskly—before coming home, where she'd cook us pasta for supper, eating hers swimming in sauce. It was a happy time, and although I knew my father was away a great deal and difficult to live with, it never occurred to me that everything was about to change forever.

Not long afterward, in the fall of 1966, my parents announced that they were getting a divorce, although they didn't make the announcement public until a year later. My mother confided in friends that she had spent "two years in hell...the worst of my life," but told reporters, "In thirteen years of living together some dissension is inevitable, but I will not destroy what was between us with bitter words or memories."

Even though I knew my mother couldn't breathe in the latter years of her marriage, I will never forget the day she broke the news. I was six years old, the same age she'd been when her father walked out. She sat me down and started to talk to me about how people sometimes can't live together anymore even if they still have feelings for each other.

It was that meaningless conversation where the parents assure the child that even though they're getting divorced, nothing will change in their lives. But of course things did change, because I lived with her from then on and saw him only on holidays. When she'd finished telling me what was happening, she asked if I had any questions. I couldn't think what to ask, so she took me to Lausanne to watch a Disney cartoon followed by a stop at Manuel, our favorite patisserie.

Once divorce proceedings began, she was terrified of losing custody of me or having to give up the house that was her haven. By the time the paperwork was all finalized in December 1968, my mother had not only given up work to look after me full-time but managed to keep her beloved home. Dad kept the Spanish property, to which he decamped to lick his wounds. Although he didn't always know how to show it, my father loved my mother to death and regretted losing her for the rest of his life. He had been the second person to really shape her, after my grandmother, and he believed in her both as a person and for what she represented.

Mum was equally destroyed by the divorce, which she saw as a failure on her part as much as his. It didn't help that from then on, whenever I spent time with him in Spain, his bitterness over the split led him to tell me things that he knew I'd go home and tell her, making her break down in tears. Her heart in pieces, she refused to blame my dad, however, and only wished he could have overcome the darker side to his personality and remained in the family home. We both did.

IN THE SUMMER OF 1968 my mother met a thirty-year-old Italian psychiatrist named Andrea Dotti on an Aegean cruise with friends. With her hair newly shorn in defiance of my father's desire for her to keep it long, she swam and drank, ate well, and flirted with the handsome young bachelor who made her laugh.

"We fell in love somewhere between Ephesus and Athens," she later said. "Do you know what it's like when a brick falls on your head? That's how my feelings for Andrea first hit me. It just happened out of the blue."

Andrea swore he'd met her once before, in 1952, when she was filming *Roman Holiday*, although my mother had no recollection of that. The story went that he was fourteen and standing with all the people watching the filming when he broke away and ran up and shook her hand. He claimed he then ran home and told his mother he was going to marry Audrey Hepburn. It took him sixteen years, but the couple got engaged on Christmas Day 1968. He might have been fulfilling a boyhood dream, but saying yes to his proposal was a knee-jerk reaction by my mother, who was a self-proclaimed "incorrigible romantic."

Everything happened so fast that I didn't have time to form an opinion, other than that I was relieved to see her so happy again. My grandmother was far from happy, however. The baroness was opposed to the relationship from the outset, although her reaction surprised no one.

For years my father and I had witnessed the tension between the two women. You could almost feel the chill in the room. Both strong individuals, they held each other at arm's length emotionally, and they fought—if always politely, as my mother wasn't a fighter at heart. Ella was no longer physically formidable, although she retained her baroness title until her dying day, even when bedridden. She lived with us for the last twelve years of her life, after a decade in San Francisco, where she'd helped soldiers returning from Vietnam.

Despite her frailty, she and my mother were like two champions circling each other. In Granny's company, Mummy lost her sense of humor. Whenever I saw them together, she reminded me of a tennis player—hunched over slightly, tense, and ready for the criticism that would come at her sooner or later. She never returned it.

The barbs would usually be petty and always about something from the past that couldn't be changed. Granny would say things like, "Well, if only you hadn't done this (or that)—relationships, friendships, career—we would have/could have..." Whatever. She was never sympathetic. Even when my mother had her miscarriages, she wasn't the type to hurry to her grieving daughter's side.

By the time Granny moved to Switzerland in the early 1970s, however, Mum was fully independent of her, both financially and emotionally. All that was left between them was vestiges of their old stresses with nothing new to build upon. Their relationship had always been complicated and, toward the end, was based largely on a sense of duty and responsibility on my mother's part to take care of the woman who'd looked after her in the war and when she was a young woman pursuing her dream.

It wasn't that she was ungrateful for the sacrifices made, but she expressed her gratitude through her actions, not words of affection, which had never felt appropriate between them. She also expressed it through food, cooking my grandmother's favorite chicken curry, which she had first come to love during her years in the Dutch East Indies.

Mum had undoubtedly valued the baroness's moral and physical support during her early years, and she fretted about her mother's health in her declining decade, but she chiefly showed her appreciation through acts of generosity. When Granny canceled her insurance to save money but then became seriously unwell, it cost Mum around 250,000 Swiss francs in medical bills. That was a figurative thank-you.

My grandmother eventually managed to swallow her distaste for Andrea Dotti, the aristocratic young Italian doctor nine years my mother's junior who became her son-in-law in January 1969, just a few weeks after my parents' divorce was finalized. I, on the other hand, liked him immediately. Andrea had always wanted a son and was kind, spending time with me and telling me to call him by a nickname of my choice, Coco, rather than Daddy, so as to relieve any tensions.

The wedding was a simple civil ceremony at the town hall down the hill from my mother's Swiss hideaway. I was just eight years old, and in the photos of me at my mother's side, I look as dazed as I felt from the latest shift in my life. Hubert de Givenchy had made her a pale-pink minidress in cashmere jersey with long sleeves, a funnel neck, and a matching headscarf to protect her hair from the winter rain. She wore the unadorned sheath dress with white ballet pumps, white tights, white gloves, and a delicate bouquet of white freesias as she gripped my hand and negotiated a path through the waiting crowds.

Around ninety of their friends and family were invited to the wedding, although my mother didn't ask her father or stepmother but wrote to them a few days later, saying, "I was married on Saturday—quietly, quickly and somehow beautifully." She added, "I have found such peace and happiness and just wanted to tell you how full my heart is."

As she packed up her most precious possessions and prepared to move to Rome, it must have felt to my mother like the start of something new and good. Little did she know that she was heading into an inferno of pain. A "Roman hell."

10.

When I fell in love and got married, I lived in constant fear of being left.
Whatever you love most, you fear you might lose.—AH

INT. VIA DI SAN VALENTINO, PARIOLI, ROME, 1975

AUDREY sits on the edge of her bed sorting freshly washed laundry. **GIOVANNA** walks in, her face ashen.

            AUDREY
      (glances up and smiles)
  Sì, Giovanna. What is it?

GIOVANNA remains silent, her eyes full of tears as she stands a few feet from her mistress.

            AUDREY
    (suddenly concerned)
  Sean? Luca? What is it? Is everything OK?

                    GIOVANNA
               Sì, sì, stanno bene, signora.

                     AUDREY
             Then what on earth is the matter?
               (she pauses, then pats the bed)
                 Here, come sit next to me.

GIOVANNA stares at the bed as if it's the last place on earth she wants to sit.

                    GIOVANNA
              I can't, I can't live with this
                        anymore...

                     AUDREY
                  (softly but gravely)
                       Tell me...

                    GIOVANNA
            He brings them—he brings them here...

The color leaches from **AUDREY**'s face, and she stares up at the woman who has been by her side for years, as if willing her not to say another word.

                     AUDREY
                       (softly)
                        Go on.

> GIOVANNA
>
> He—he—brings them here—when you are away, signora. He—he—brings them to this bed... for the night, signora. He—he has us serve them breakfast—in bed... in this bed...

GIOVANNA clenches her fists and brings them to her forehead before pounding it as if to beat away the memories.

AUDREY sits very still.

> AUDREY
>
> When?

> GIOVANNA
>
> Always...signora. Every time you go!

GIOVANNA starts to sob, covering her face with her apron.

> GIOVANNA
>
> I can't do it anymore. I can't lie to you! He tells me to say nothing. *Niente!* But I can't. Please, signora, please forgive me!

GIOVANNA falls back against the wall.

AUDREY remains dry-eyed. Quietly she stands up and turns to the window to look out onto the Eternal City. Reaching into her pocket, she retrieves a

pack of Kent cigarettes and lights one, her hand
shaking.

                      AUDREY
     Grazie, Giovanna. You did the right thing.

GIOVANNA, looking distraught, takes a step toward
her as if to comfort her, but **AUDREY** raises a
hand.

                      AUDREY
         I need a moment.

GIOVANNA pauses, staring at her mistress's back,
before leaving the room with her head bowed.

WHAT HAD STARTED SO PROMISINGLY as a whirlwind romance on a yacht bobbing on the Aegean Sea quickly turned into a nightmare from which my mother felt she couldn't escape. Most people, and women especially, imagine Audrey Hepburn as a woman in control of her own life, a star who stood apart from the rest, but when it came to romance, she was as vulnerable as she often appeared on-screen.

From the day she married Andrea, she was determined to distance herself from the industry that had made her famous and focus on becoming the best psychiatrist's wife. As plain Signora Dotti, she quickly settled into domestic life and got acquainted with her new husband's large, exuberant Italian family. In those early days of her marriage, Mum seemed very comfortable back in the city where she had made three films, surrounded by her new relatives who loved to laugh and eat. Once again, she was part of something she'd always longed for.

She even got on well with Andrea's formidable mother, the countess Paola Roberti Bandini, one of the heirs to the Cirio food empire. It was this matriarch who presided over every noisy dinner as my mother played the dutiful daughter-in-law.

Mum refused to call herself a baroness, though she was one (as her mother had been), having decided long before that all family pretension would end with her. All she wanted was to be a nondescript Roman *casalinga*, or housewife. Being European and speaking five languages elevated my mother from being just another American starlet who spoke only English. Switching effortlessly from language to language, she conversed in whichever felt appropriate at the time, although English and French tended to dominate when she was with my father and me. She spoke Dutch with her mother, then Italian with Andrea and his family, and French and English to me later.

Mum's staff consisted of Giovanna, who moved with her to Rome, Giovanna's sister Tina—the cook—and Engracia, a happy soul from Talavera, Spain. Despite being surrounded by Italians, my mother sometimes muddled her feminine and masculine. Famously, at one dinner party a friend of Andrea's asked her what she most liked about living in "Roma." Her reply—"Mi piace aprire le finestre e vedere le tette di Roma"—made everyone laugh. She was trying to say, "I love to look out and see all the roofs." But instead of *tetti* for "roofs" she used the word *tette*, which means "breasts."

Linguistic mistakes aside, she glowed with contentment and told the reporters who started hanging around outside our home, "My life is filled with affection. Andrea is a terribly sweet-tempered, kind man. Full of fun. Very bright." They were especially fascinated by her decision to walk away from the industry, as film scripts sent to her were politely returned, but she had no intention of jeopardizing her new relationship with long absences—a factor of her acting career that she partly blamed for the collapse of her marriage to my father, who had wanted her to work only alongside him, ideally. "Movies have no bearing on my private life," she announced. "The fact I've made movies doesn't mean breakfast gets made, or that my child does better in his homework. I still have to function as a woman in a household."

Andrea was the total opposite of my father in every sense of the word, and my mother felt enormous freedom in that at first, but in truth their marriage was good only for the first few years. The rest of the time they were patching things up and trying to find a way to stay together, mostly because she didn't want to hurt my younger brother, Luca.

I was enrolled at Rome's French-language school Lycée Chateaubriand as my mother and stepfather searched for a new home nearby. They found it in a beautiful penthouse overlooking the Tiber River. It had twelve rooms and an enormous wraparound terrace, and, at ten thousand square feet, was like a house within a building. Enormous and already elegant, it only became more so with my mother's special touch as she spurned the heavy curtains and gilded ancestral paintings of many Roman homes and filled it with airy yellows and white.

With my stepfather busy as a professor at Rome's Sapienza University as well as with a private practice in the afternoons in which he treated patients with everything from eating disorders to schizophrenia, my mother got into a daily routine that seemed to satisfy her urgent need to make this marriage work after the failure of her first. Rising at dawn to make Andrea's morning coffee and get him off to work, she'd then take care of me before exercising our two dogs—a Jack Russell terrier named Jacky and another JRT crossed with an Italian whippet foundling called Picciri, which means "little one."

She still walked everywhere and loved to wander incognito to the market and little shops to select ingredients for supper before collecting me from school each day for lunch. She devoted her evenings to her new husband once I'd been fed and put to bed.

Relatively young for a professor, Andrea was doing research into the use of lithium for the depression and bipolar disorders he specialized in, and my mother offered to help him with his laboratory work. I helped too sometimes, caring for his aquariums full of *Betta splendens*, the Siamese fighting fish he tested microdoses on. Mum also attended lectures and medical conferences with him so she could learn more and immerse herself in his work.

So as not to detract from his professional life, she tried not to be noticed, donning oversize sunglasses and one of the many headscarves she'd collected since that first Dior square in Arnhem. She knew that her fame might also have been an issue between her and my father, who had felt somehow diminished by her success, and she was determined not to let history repeat itself.

Throwing herself into decorating the house and cooking, she'd sometimes prepare food to take to Andrea in his office before the pair went out to nightclubs with his eclectic mix of friends. After years as an aristocratic playboy, my stepfather wasn't prepared to relinquish his relentless socializing after marriage. Nor did he expect my mother to accompany him but rather preferred her to stay home.

Although she'd made *War and Peace* in the city after *Roman Holiday*, she had few friends there and soon began to feel lonely. Being Roman by adoption because of her Oscar-winning role wasn't enough to keep her occupied. Salvation came in the form of the titled sisters Afdera and Lorian Franchetti, the wife and sister-in-law of Henry Fonda, with whom my mother had starred in *War and Peace*. The sisters introduced her to new people and reconnected her with Olimpia Torlonia, the granddaughter of the former king of Spain, on whose yacht she'd first holidayed with Andrea after meeting him at Lorian's home on Giglio Island.

Being spotted out and about with Andrea and friends in Rome, my mother began to attract a fresh wave of interest from the media, most of which was unwelcome for someone who cherished her privacy. When the paparazzi began to intrude in a way they never had in rural Switzerland, she did her best to disguise her growing discomfort. Smiling into the cameras with outward composure, she told them cordially,

"I'm in love and happy again. I never believed it could happen to me." She was at pains to add that her new husband was not only cheerful and enthusiastic but also romantic and loving. What she didn't say was that he drank too much, and when he did, he lost all resistance to other women.

My stepfather had none of my father's neuroses or mood swings and was good with me, which Mum loved. He and I played games like Battleship, while she cooked for us or filled the apartment with flowers, modern art, and music. During her Rome years, she listened to everything from the Beatles to the Carpenters to Johann Sebastian Bach. I can't remember having a meal without music.

When she fell pregnant four months into her marriage, Andrea was delighted, as he had long wanted a son and heir. Mum was happy, too, but her old anxieties about losing the baby soon resurfaced. Knowing she needed to rest, she took the advice of friends, including the actress Sophia Loren, and first took to her bed in Rome before moving back to La Paisible for the last few months of her pregnancy. Andrea remained in Rome, visiting when he could.

Sophia was another of my mother's friends whose life had uncanny parallels to her own. The pair first met during the filming of *War and Peace*, produced by Sophia's husband, Carlo Ponti. Five years younger than my mother, Sophia was also of noble descent and had been abandoned by her father. During the bombing of Naples, she was so undernourished that people called her "the toothpick." She was hit in the head by shrapnel like Mum. She was eleven when war ended and survived only because American soldiers gave her all their rations. She was signed up by Paramount in her early twenties. After suffering two miscarriages she was told that she'd never have a baby but went on to have two sons.

Heeding her advice about resting completely, my mother took to her bed. Despite all her fears, the birth of my brother, Luca, by cesarean section in the Lausanne hospital on February 8, 1970, just over a year after Mum married Andrea, was uneventful. Givenchy created Luca's christening gown, just as he had mine. My mother wrote a happy letter to her father saying Luca had "long legs, hands and feet and the most perfectly shaped head I've ever seen—what a joy for us all." She added, "My life is just the fullest and happiest ever."

Her decision to give up her acting career altogether and stay home to raise us both was an easy one. At the age of forty, she couldn't bear the thought she might fail as a mother. Motherhood was too important to a woman who had longed for babies since childhood and now felt complete. She described her semi-retirement as no sacrifice and an almost selfish decision that brought her great personal joy. Her time and attention were the greatest gifts a parent could give a child, but she refused to be called virtuous, reminding people that—aside from her love for us—she deserved a break after working nonstop since her teens.

Delighted to have given me a little brother, she devoted her days to our needs and to appreciating the simple pleasures of motherhood. "My children are my joy," she said. "Sean is a big, healthy, sweet boy who is enormously tall... and I've made this other boy who is so very alert and very sweet and a beautiful baby. He looks very much like Andrea."

All seemed rosy, until the betrayals that would shatter her heart anew surfaced.

WHETHER SHE WAS HOME OR in Switzerland, Andrea continued to go out every night and was frequently photographed in the company of beautiful women, with the pictures sold around the world. The paparazzi lapped up his brazen indiscretions, and no matter how hard my mother tried to believe his protestations that his companions were just friends or even patients, she had her doubts. She'd never signed up for an open marriage and blamed herself for being too old for him.

She had carried the sorrows of her childhood throughout her life, and then the sadness of her failed marriage to my father. In Rome she was carrying the weight of disappointment in Andrea too. Even though I was still young during this time, I could tell how much his infidelity devoured her. Our lives had so often felt like Mum and me against the world, and in the previous few years I'd become her best friend—the one person she told everything to. I was the one who saw what she was really like behind closed doors, wringing her emotional hands.

Homesick for the garden, trees, and privacy of La Paisible, especially in the sweltering Roman summers when water supplies became patchy even in the smartest districts, my mother was desperately unhappy. "There is the thing about society and life in the city that oppresses me," she said at the time. "The air is polluted, the backfire of cars is reminiscent of guns, and the noise is so bad you can't hear properly." And then there was the oppression of her relationship.

Sensing her need to get out of the city, Andrea rented a summer house on the beach and joined us there on weekends when he wasn't working. They were happier days, but he still had a destructive side to his character and continued to have flings whenever he was alone. Within a few years of their wedding, he'd been photographed with some two hundred women, and these pictures were splashed across the front pages of magazines and newspapers the world over. My mother was desperate, and even though she confronted him about his indiscretions, he never took full responsibility for them and protested that this was just how life was in Rome.

After Giovanna finally broke down and confessed that Andrea had brought some of his women home to their marital bed, part of her didn't even want to hear it. Instead of being a fresh start, her marriage was proving to be a cliché and a rotten dead end.

Wandering around the huge apartment filled with all the things she'd bought to make it cozy, she longed to run away from the world that had made her famous and missed her roses, the mountains, and the lake. She longed to dabble again in her watercolors, pick flowers, and enjoy the solitude of Switzerland. She berated herself for her failures and agonized over what another divorce might do to me and how it might affect young Luca. One friend who visited was surprised to see her pour herself a small whisky in the middle of the afternoon. "It must be six o'clock somewhere," she said with a wry smile.

Realizing how sad she was, I did my best to cheer her up. Relying on the humorous genes that run in the family, I became a comedian and imitated her friends in various accents to make her laugh from her belly, doubled up, the way she loved to. Her favorite was my imitation of a butler named Alfonso who worked for one of her friends. Without any dialogue, it was all about the facial expressions and the way he approached people so obsequiously, and it would almost always have her in hysterics. That worked for a while, until it didn't.

One day, my mother came to me with red-rimmed eyes and confessed what Giovanna had told her about my stepfather and his lovers. I was painfully aware that there were problems, but when she asked me what I thought, I didn't know how to help her. "Seanie, do you think people can change?" she eventually asked. Floundering for a moment, I thought about it and then told her that no, I didn't.

From then on, for the next four years, I believe she remained with Andrea only for Luca's sake and because of what she called her deep respect for marriage. Once I'd been made aware of the situation, my relationship with my stepfather cooled and I kept my distance, burying my anger over how much he was hurting her. My mother, of course, pretended that everything was fine if anyone asked, telling one reporter, "I'm a Roman housewife, just what I want to be. Despite what you sometimes read, my marriage is working out beautifully, and watching my sons grow is a marvel.... I was never part of Hollywood or anywhere else, and I've finally found a place that I can call home."

I have no idea how long she could have hung on in her fragile emotional state, but a combination of factors eventually forced her hand. When we'd first arrived in Rome, we were able to move about freely, take the dogs to the park or go to the cinema without being bothered by anyone, but all that changed once my stepfather's personal life became hot international news. Paparazzi hoping to sell their photos for thousands would lie in wait in bushes, climb trees, and jump out at us, startling my mother and especially Luca, who'd howl in fear. Unfailingly gracious with them all, she'd smile and pose for a moment but was inwardly seething at their intrusion and full of guilt for bringing them into our lives.

Unable to walk the streets without interruption, she ended up having to take Luca to a friend's private garden for some fresh air and exercise, and when we went to Sunday lunch at Andrea's mother's he would drive like a madman through the streets of Rome, trying to lose the photographers following close behind on Vespas. Not realizing the dangers, I would watch the paparazzi pursuing us with delight from the rear window, imagining we were in a movie chase.

It was the attention of the media that first made me think about who my mother was and what she did for a living. Prior to that, what Mum did had come to me only in small pieces. It was never something she spoke about much, and her Oscar propped up books on our shelf like any other ornament.

As far as I was concerned, I was growing up with a regular mom who had become the best friend one could hope for. She granted me the gift of a normal childhood as she walked me to school, helped me with my homework, and took me to buy books and socks. She was there to run her fingers through my hair whenever I woke up scared, and she made cakes for boisterous birthday parties with my pals. She was the person most dear to me, and for a long time I thought the photographers waiting for her to pick me up from school every day were there only because she was so beautiful.

There was no screening room in our home, and Mum never sat me down to show me her films or tell me about her life in front of the camera. When I was fourteen, however, my curiosity got the better of me, so I strung up a sheet in the attic of our Swiss house that summer, found some of her sixteen-millimeter films, and fed them through an old Bell & Howell projector to watch one after the other. That is how I discovered the magic of this person called Audrey Hepburn—lying on the floor on pillows watching her flickering image on a sheet with the unmistakable tick-ticking sound of the sprockets. I have to say, discovering those movies that way was pretty wonderful.

During my personal Audrey Hepburn film festival my mother climbed the attic stairs a few times to check on me, but she never made a fuss. She hated to see herself on the screen, as she was always so critical of her work. She'd ask, "Did you like that one?" and I'd share my thoughts. If I said it was a good film, she'd attribute its success to the vision and talent of the director or the rest of the cast, never herself, dismissing her own role as far less significant.

We'd discuss any aspects of a plot I didn't fully understand, or I might inquire about the location or the cars, but that was about it. She didn't boast about whom she'd met or how she'd won any awards. Having never grown up in that Hollywood culture of being famous or part of some anointed group, I sometimes found it hard to reconcile the woman projected onto a sheet with the one I knew as Mum. It was only later that I realized just how much depth she had to have to be so utterly convincing in every role.

The film she felt the strongest personal attachment to was *Roman Holiday* because it was her first major role and the movie that had won her an Oscar. The storyline also mirrored her life once she was famous. My mother became a princess of Hollywood because, as Bernardo Bertolucci once said, "Hollywood actors are the royalty of the twentieth century." Her character in *Roman Holiday* wants nothing more than to put on casual clothes and go out incognito. All my mother yearned for was to go to the cheese shop or the market as a normal person, without the paparazzi shoving cameras in her face. She felt guilty that they had become part of our lives because of her when she was happiest staying in, curled up on a sofa with us, her dogs, and a good book, after a simple plate of homemade spaghetti al pomodoro.

My favorite of her films is *Funny Face* because of how much she'd loved doing it, which was so plain to see. The movie made three years before I was born still fills me with happiness every time I watch her soar and dance away all those dark years of war. And for the girl who'd longed to be a ballerina, to dance with Fred Astaire—a man she'd long admired—was a dream come true. To see her fly across the set, free from her past, with a huge grin on her face is still such a joy.

GETTING TO KNOW WHO SHE was and how much she was admired around the world was a revelation that only made me love her more. But our carefree days in Rome together were very short-lived because of the spate of high-profile kidnappings happening across Europe and elsewhere in an era of political turbulence and high unemployment.

In the summer of 1973, John Paul Getty III, the sixteen-year-old grandson of the oil tycoon, was grabbed off the street in central Rome. His kidnappers demanded a $17 million ransom, which his grandfather initially refused to pay. Kept for five months in a cave in Calabria, the teenager was physically and psychologically abused by his captors, who cut off one of his ears and sent it to a national newspaper. He almost died of the subsequent infection and was released only when a much smaller ransom was paid. Badly affected by his experience, Getty died at the age of fifty-four.

The kidnapping was all anyone could talk about in Rome, and my mother became paranoid about our safety. I was thirteen and Luca three, and we couldn't leave the apartment unsupervised. Our driver, Franco, would take us everywhere, and although he wasn't a trained bodyguard, Mum was comforted by the fact that because of his sheer bulk it would have been hard to get past him.

Then in 1974 she fell pregnant again, at the age of forty-five. It was, I think, a desperate and slightly insane final attempt to create the family she'd always hoped for, even though she was married to a philanderer. Sadly, she lost the baby early on. Her distress at not being able to have another child chipped another little corner from her heart and only added to her longing to be back in Switzerland to recuperate in her beautiful garden.

The following year, I was home with Mum one lunchtime when Andrea came bursting in with a gash to his head and blood on his shirt. He was very shaken and told us that four masked men had jumped on him as he was leaving his practice and tried to drag him into a waiting Mercedes. When he fought back, they pistol-whipped him, but he escaped from their grip and crawled under a parked car, where he created such a disturbance that nearby security guards came to his rescue.

My mother was aghast and began trembling with fear. She accompanied him to the hospital to have his head wound stitched, but she was so upset by what had happened that long after I went to bed, I could hear them discussing the situation loudly through the bedroom wall. It isn't too dramatic to say she was traumatized. Writing to her father with the news, she said, "They tried to kidnap Andrea in Rome, nearly killing him in the attempt, his head was split open with a revolver butt." As usual, her father did not reply, but his wife, Fidelma, did so sympathetically.

The day after the attack, she came to my room and sat on the edge of my bed. She told me how terrified she was of anything happening to me and explained that I had two choices—I could stay in Rome with bodyguards flanking me day and night, or I could go to a boarding school in Switzerland, where I'd be in a secure environment. If I chose the latter, she'd take Luca to La Paisible and enroll him in the local school, seeing me on weekends and holidays. I could see how scared she was, so I asked her, "Which would you be most comfortable with?"

"Well, I know we wouldn't see each other as often," she said, biting her lip and fighting back the tears, "but I'd prefer it if you went to Switzerland to ensure your safety. There haven't been any kidnappings there, and the school is very secure." So I agreed. She and I had always been inseparable, and I was heartbroken at the thought of leaving her, but I also couldn't bear to see her so worried, so I did as she asked and gave up my entire life, school friends, soccer, and the Roman dolce vita.

Within three days, I'd been shipped out. I never went back to the school I'd grown to love or to the friends I'd made there, including a Vietnamese boy named Bang, my closest pal. Instead, I was enrolled at the Institut Le Rosey private boarding school in Rolle and Gstaad, which was attended by everyone from the princes and princesses of the world to the children of stars like Elizabeth Taylor and David Niven. It wasn't until years later that I found out Mum was so worried I'd be too isolated there that she'd called up the mother of one of my friends in Rome and offered to pay his tuition if he could accompany me. The woman understood her concerns but wanted to keep her son with her, so I had to go it alone.

I missed my mother and friends terribly, and she missed me but couldn't dare risk me being snatched. Although she returned to Rome frequently to spend time with Andrea, she was right to be concerned, as kidnapping and hijacking only increased. A year after the Getty kidnap, the nineteen-year-old heiress Patty Hearst was kidnapped in California by members of a "liberation army" who demanded millions. After two months in captivity, she was indoctrinated into the group and persuaded to take part in a bank robbery and hijack that resulted in her arrest.

Two years later, in the same US state, an entire school bus was hijacked and the twenty-six elementary school children on board were forced into an underground bunker with their driver. They managed to escape before any ransom demands could be made. And in 1978 a Franco-Belgian tycoon was kidnapped in Paris by a guerrilla group demanding 80 million francs. They cut off one of his fingers and held him for sixty-three days. All these incidents happened in the years before the kidnapping of my mother's friend Freddy Heineken, the Dutch brewing heir who was chained to a wall for three weeks until his family paid a ransom of $18 million and he was released.

Interviewed in Rome in the mid-seventies, my mother spoke openly of her fears. "It is a very anguishing period," she said. "They're even kidnapping tourists for fifty dollars apiece, ransacking apartments and breaking into cars... the joy of Rome was to walk around the streets at night. Not anymore. The whole world has changed."

For my mother and me there was an ironic and unexpected twist to the attempted kidnapping of Andrea that shook us both to the core. Years later we discovered that it hadn't been a kidnap attempt at all. An unhappy husband had found out Andrea was having a fling with his wife and sent the masked men to beat him up. So it was a direct consequence of my stepfather's infidelity that I was sent away from my mother and lost four years of family life. That was something I found terribly difficult to forgive.

DESPITE BEING SO DEEPLY UNHAPPY, my mother still held off on filing for divorce. Desperate to maintain the emotional equilibrium she'd never known as a child, she was anxious that five-year-old Luca remain close to his beloved Papà and feared his response to being separated. She was also aware of the Italian law that required a five-year legal separation period before a divorce could be granted.

The tragic irony of her second failed marriage is that Mum had never expected Andrea to sit in with her every night watching TV or reading a book. That would have been too risky, as she knew someone like him would soon grow bored. She also knew from the start that nightclubbing was his way of relaxing and was something he'd done since his late teens. But he was acting as if he weren't married at all and didn't seem to appreciate how humiliating it was for her to have his affairs so publicly flaunted in the gossip columns.

Even though I'd been fond of my stepfather to begin with, when I discovered that as well as cheating on her he had a much colder side to him, I struggled. He even started trying to excuse his affairs by turning them back on my mother, blaming her in some way and still insisting that seeing other women wasn't such a big deal for an Italian. He was alternately affectionate and apologetic and then hard-hearted and mean. His behavior would be called gaslighting today, and it was despicable.

As a person who was naturally kind and empathetic, my mother was tormented by his inability to understand how much he was hurting her. He, in turn, played psychiatrist, accusing her of being difficult to live with and overemotional, especially when her makeup man Alberto de Rossi died. In one TV interview she said, tellingly, "Doctors are great with their patients, but they never take care of their families." I'm sure people picked up on the not-so-hidden message in what she said and came to their own conclusions.

Completely deflated by the unhappy situation she found herself in, my mother didn't feel strong enough to go back to work and instead spent the days limply hanging around the house. In an attempt to distract her and enlisting the help of her friend Arabella, who'd been her public relations manager for many years, we persuaded her to return to the movie industry after an eight-year gap. With our coercion and the suggestion that she could introduce Luca to one of his heroes—James Bond—she agreed to play Maid Marian in *Robin and Marian* with Sean Connery. Their costars would be Richard Harris, Robert Shaw, and an entire cast of illustrious actors.

The cast and the parallels between the film's plot and that of *The Nun's Story* were too tempting for her, and the writer, James Goldman, had won an Oscar for a Peter O'Toole/Katharine Hepburn film she loved called *The Lion in Winter*. Like *The Nun's Story*, *Robin and Marian* features a woman who seeks spiritual comfort in religion but ultimately relinquishes her vows to do something she never imagined she'd do. And, like Lou Habets and Maid Marian, my mother was—in her own way—returning to the world from a cloistered life. She thought the idea "poetic" and was glad to have at last been offered a mature role, one suitable to her age—forty-six.

Filming took place in Navarre, Spain, and Mum took Luca with her for part of it so he could meet Sean Connery and play with the horses. The period piece didn't call for Givenchy clothes or much styling, as she was in a habit for much of it, so—with her favorite cinematographers unavailable or dead—she found herself largely surrounded by people she didn't know.

I think it's fair to say that, although my mother loved her fellow actors, her return to the screen wasn't an entirely happy one. The script she'd originally agreed to had been altered; for the first time she didn't bond with her director, Richard Lester; and everything had changed since she was last on a set. Under the new regime, she wasn't offered the chance of a camera test, a preproduction evaluation to check lighting and lens settings first, or given the opportunity to see the raw, unedited footage from each day—known as rushes—which she liked to view to see what she could correct. The movie was shot at breakneck speed, and it was all a far cry from the old studio system she'd known. Completely out of her comfort zone, she admitted at the time to being "petrified" throughout much of the filming, shaking with every take. In one scene, she feared she might drown when the horse-drawn wagon she was in accidentally overturned in a muddy river.

Acting "gets harder and harder," she said later. "I really die a million deaths every time. My stomach turns over, my hands get clammy, I do suffer. I really do."

When the film was released to critical acclaim, however, she was relieved, but she quickly tired of the constant press inquiries about her so-called comeback. "I'm not Garbo," she protested. "I always hoped to make another film...I'm not making a 'comeback' because I never consciously went away. And now that I've come back...I may not stay back." When further pressed, she admitted that she fell into acting as an unknown and inexperienced teenager. She stressed once more that being a mother and a wife meant much more to her. "Home is the last stand," she said, with feeling. "It's the last thing we've got." It was a far cry from the days when she'd called off her engagement to James Hanson so she could concentrate on her career.

In an article for *McCall's* magazine titled "The Return of Audrey Hepburn" in which, unusually, her husband was interviewed, too, Andrea was asked for his professional opinion about the impact my mother's childhood had had on her. "She's a perfectionist with a strong need for security," he replied, adding that surprises unsettled her and she needed to have her life under control. "She's composed of categories, like boxes. It's either good or bad. It can be done, or it can't. In between, we don't discuss." It was a brutal assessment of a woman whose chief idea of security was a husband who didn't bring strangers home to their bed.

As my mother continued to plead and negotiate with Andrea and pray that she could turn her marriage around despite him still blowing hot and cold, film scripts began dropping into her mailbox again, most of which she turned down for being too full of sex or violence. Then she was offered *A Bridge Too Far*, about Operation Market Garden's disastrous assault on Arnhem, starring Sean Connery, Laurence Olivier, Gene Hackman, and Robert Redford. Director Richard Attenborough thought Mum perfect to play a Dutch woman who worked for the Resistance, but he didn't count on her own deep resistance to revisiting a part of her past that she knew would bring unpleasant memories bubbling up. She also turned down the lead roles in *Out of Africa* and

The Turning Point, which went on to be huge successes for the actresses Meryl Streep and Anne Bancroft, respectively.

Terence Young, a family friend known to us all as T.Y. and her former director on *Wait Until Dark*, tried several times to get her to be in one of his projects, without success. He told one interviewer that it could take her a year or more to even accept an idea, and she would then have to be persuaded that she wouldn't be "totally destroying" Luca's life by spending weeks away from him. Even if T.Y. was able to get her past that hurdle, he said she'd often thank him profusely for thinking of her before declaring that she had to end their call and cook the evening meal.

My mother adored T.Y., not least because they'd discovered an uncanny wartime link between them. As a tank commander in the British Army, he had been one of those who'd aimed guns at the very area of Arnhem in which she was sheltering with her family. His quip about that—"If I had aimed slightly to the left, I'd be out of a job right now"—became their private joke. My mother, of course, convinced him that they'd welcomed the shelling, as it had let them know how close the Allies were.

Close as she was to T.Y. and others, few knew how hard she tried to cling to what was left of her marriage despite Andrea's continued indiscretions. All she really wanted at that point in her life was someone to cherish her. No one knew that she was absolutely at the end, and the pain was eating her up.

In the spring of 1978, I was allowed home to La Paisible to study for my baccalaureate examinations. I arrived back at the "house of peace" to find it far from peaceful. The staff were in a panic. A doctor had been called because when the maid took in my mother's breakfast tray, she'd found her lying in bed, staring into nothing, an empty bottle of sleeping pills by her side. The doctor arrived and went in to see her while we all waited outside. When he found out which pills she'd taken, he arranged for her to be taken to the hospital immediately to have her stomach pumped. At age seventeen, I watched in shock as she was carried out.

When she returned home from the hospital the following day, she was pale and exhausted, but I was the first person she sought. Sitting me down quietly, she said, "I know what this looks like, Sean, but please try to understand. I was in so much pain that I desperately wanted to knock myself out. I overdid it with the Mogadon, that's all. I've been hurting too much and needed it to stop. I'm so dreadfully sorry. I never meant to take my life." The way she said it, I believed her. She clearly felt terrible, and with hindsight I think she was the kind of person who would have done the deed if she'd really wanted to.

The fact that she'd been so low that she'd risked leaving me and Luca motherless was enough to convince her that her marriage was truly over. It took years for the divorce to be finally granted, in 1982, but that was merely a legal formality. Resisting her overwhelming desire to remain at her Swiss sanctuary, she moved back to Rome and for two years lived in the building opposite Andrea's so Luca could continue his Roman education and see his father every day. It was only when my brother was enrolled at the Beau Soleil boarding school in 1984 that she finally returned home—just in time to spend my grandmother's final days with her.

I was abroad when Granny Ella called to tell me she loved me. She died not long afterward at the age of eighty-four. There was some sadness but mostly a sense of relief, not only because she hadn't been well but also because the tension in my mother melted away. Her funeral drew a line under a long and difficult relationship that was never fully resolved. Yet my grandmother was more than partially responsible for so much about my mother that was unique, especially her self-discipline, her determination to put others before herself, and her need to be loved.

Mum was a one-off, but so was my grandmother in a different way, and I guess that apple didn't fall very far from the tree. Both women suffered tremendous loss in their lives and found themselves cast adrift. Each had to find her own way to survive. Ella did it through endless charity work, making up for her prewar Nazi sympathies by volunteering to help returning Vietnam veterans until illness forced her to retire. My mother drew on her own pain, first to bring real emotion to her acting and then to marvelous effect with her family and with all those she met through UNICEF.

It was the loss of her babies and the failure of her marriages that almost broke her. She spoke of how desperately she'd tried to avoid divorce. "I hung on in both marriages very hard, as long as I could, for the children's sake.... You always hope that if you love somebody enough, everything will be all right, but it isn't always true." She described the lengthy legal proceedings to separate us from Andrea as "one of the worst experiences a human being can go through." The provision under Italian law that a couple had to be separated for five years before seeking a divorce only prolonged an already agonizing process.

When their divorce was eventually finalized, she slumped. She thought she'd let her husband down as a wife and let us down as a mother and that she had been unable to protect us from the childhood pain she had endured from a broken marriage. It took her a long time, right up to her deathbed, to be convinced that she had raised us with more than enough love to compensate for everything that had happened and that it wasn't her fault. Even though she was the most wonderful mum and friend, she was still constantly seeking reassurance that she was loved and that she mattered.

Her confidence shattered, she was approaching her fifties and reluctant to go back in front of the camera because of her insecurities about her looks. She was twice divorced and single. I think she also felt somewhat abandoned, as she'd recently helped me fulfill my burning desire to work in the film industry that I'd grown to love ever since I'd seen her on set in the South of France. When she put me on a plane to South Korea to work on a war movie for T.Y., her parting words of wisdom were, "Everybody is expendable and replaceable, Sean. Don't ever believe otherwise. Treat this job as if it's your last and the most important one." I could almost hear my grandmother's voice in hers.

Alone in Switzerland to stay close to Luca, who was at school and struggling from the marital fallout, she found herself more isolated than she had ever been. It was her dearest friend, Connie Wald, who came to the rescue, suggesting in 1980 that she accept an invitation to an event in California and stay with her. Flying to Los Angeles soon after hearing that her dear friend Felix Aylmer had died at age ninety, my mother must have wondered what cards the twisting, turning hand of Fate was going to deal to her next. All the men in her life had disappointed her so far, and it upset her terribly that, just like her own mother, she'd ended up a lone parent after two broken marriages.

Channeling thoughts of Anne Frank, she told herself to think of all the beauty still around her and try to find happiness again. In Connie's comfortable living room that first night, she started to relax as her friend told her of a Dutchman she wanted Mum to meet. His name was Robert Wolders, and he had recently lost his wife, the sixty-eight-year-old actress Merle Oberon, to a stroke. At forty-three, he was seven years younger than my mother and had starred in the television Western *Laredo* until he'd given it up to marry Merle five years earlier.

The next night, at one of her supper parties, Connie led my mother toward the handsome bearded man with dark hair and kind eyes. "Audrey, this is Robert," Connie announced. "He was extraordinarily good to Merle in her final months. Robby, Audrey's marriage has just come to an end too. You both grew up in Holland during the war, so I'm certain you'll have lots to talk about, and I just know you'll get along." She was right, and within a very short time, the unfailingly courteous and polite Rob Wolders became my mother's latest love.

After a faltering start to their romance, Mum invited him to visit her at La Paisible, where he surprised everyone by slipping into her world as if he'd been born to it. He even won over my dying grandmother, the pair chattering away in Dutch. For the first time since James Hanson, the baroness approved of her daughter's romantic choice. Not that she ever admitted it.

Lighter in her step and in her heart, my mother told friends that she'd finally found someone kind whom she could trust. Referring to him as "my Robby," she said they'd discovered each other "at a time in our lives when we were both very unhappy, and we're terribly happy together." When journalists got wind of the relationship and asked my mother if she'd consider getting married again, she ignored them, but Rob spoke more openly. "Everyone knows how unhappy her marriage to Mel was, and the second to Andrea was even worse," he said. "It would be like asking someone who has just got out of an electric chair to sit back on it again."

That kind of comment didn't endear him to my father, a genius at acid commentary who described Rob as "the door opener." Of all her romantic relationships, the one with my father had been the most valuable, but also the most difficult. To my mind, Andrea was her most pleasant partner, though completely unreliable, and Rob was adorable but a doormat. Nobody could deny, however, that he made Mum laugh for the first time in years as they shared their passions for everything from dogs to the countryside, books to gardens. She often referred to him as her spiritual twin, and he helped her through her difficult divorce negotiations.

The fact that Rob was Dutch and had been in Holland during the war was another link in the chain that bound them, along with his large and loving family, who embraced her wholeheartedly. Born in Rotterdam, he'd lived in a suburb of Arnhem during hostilities, enduring much of what my mother and her family suffered—bombings, atrocities against Jews and others, and ultimately near starvation. He was just nine years old when the Allies liberated the country. In his mid-twenties he went to America to pursue an acting career and appeared in several television shows. He met Merle Oberon on a film set, and despite the twenty-five-year age difference, the pair married after her divorce but had just four years together before she died.

My father's disparaging description of Rob did have an element of truth to it, as the new man in my mother's life appeared to have no aspirations other than to play the devoted escort. This meant that, for the first time, she was allowed the space to truly be herself without anyone else forcing an agenda on her or behaving toward her in cruel or hurtful ways. Although they had their occasional differences, Rob was loyal and loving, a welcome change after the misery of the Andrea years, although—ironically—she and her second husband remained civil long after their divorce, chiefly for Luca's sake.

With Rob's constant encouragement and unfailing affection, my mother finally began to accept herself and strengthen her own sense of identity. Viewing her life through the eyes of someone else, she learned to appreciate what a singular life it had been and how her experiences had helped shape her. She also began to realize that it was time to put her bottomless pit of love for children to some practical use, which was when she agreed to work for UNICEF.

This was the second time she'd decided to do something other than what she was most famous for. The first was when she gave it all up to look after us. I think it was her way of refusing to let her painful memories destroy her. As my daughter, Emma, pointed out, "Audrey represented the first on-screen union of the Hollywood world of glamour and the developing world—something we take for granted today."

The work she did proved to the world, if it needed convincing, that she wasn't a two-dimensional personality, though she was dismissed by many as a mere fashionista. In fact, she was a huge-hearted human being who was prepared to risk her life in places no one else would go. The world saw her humanity for the first time, and they rewarded and applauded it. Those of us who really knew her had been clapping from the wings for years.

11.

Nothing is impossible.
The word itself says, "I'm possible." —AH

INT. SEAN'S BUNGALOW IN LOS ANGELES, CALIFORNIA, 1988

Fifty-six-year-old **AUDREY** sits on a large white sofa with her legs folded neatly beneath her. Reaching into her handbag, she retrieves three crumpled handwritten letters on flimsy writing paper. After pressing them flat on her lap, she looks up at **SEAN**, twenty-eight, and gives him a smile.

AUDREY
These are the letters from Bang I told you about. He sent them via the UN, UNICEF, and the UNHCR. He must have worried that I'd never receive a single one, let alone all three.

SEAN reaches for a letter and reads aloud the first few lines.

SEAN
"Cher Madame Hepburn, Je ne sais pas si vous vous souvenez de moi, mais je m'appelle Hoang Chiem Bang et je suis allé à l'école à Rome avec votre fils Sean..."

SEAN looks up with a sad smile.

AUDREY
(nodding)
I know. He thought that I wouldn't remember him as your best friend in school during our years in Rome, even though he was the only one called Bang and the only Vietnamese child there. He even sent me what is probably his only photo of the two of you together.

SEAN reads on in silence, a frown deepening on his brow.

SEAN
He says his father was listening to Voice of America illegally on the radio and heard that you'd started working for UNICEF. Now he's asking if you can help get him and his family out...
(looking up)
All eight of them? How was he even able to send letters out of the country? The government would surely have punished him if he was caught.

AUDREY
(her jawline hardening)
Which makes my task all the more urgent.
He says he has papers to prove his father
was a diplomat for the South Vietnam
government in Rome and worked for the
French in Laos. There are relatives in
Europe with the means of support for
them all. I need to get those
documents to the right people...
get the ball rolling.

SEAN looks up and studies his mother's face. His expression reflects his worry that she looks tired, and not just from the jet lag of flying around the globe. Yet he also recognizes her determination to get it done.

SEAN
His family has endured terrible hardship
and famine since the takeover ten years
ago. Their relatives in France have
tried multiple times to get them out
with no success...you're their
last chance.

AUDREY
(sighing)
Which is why I must try my utmost. I remember
Bang so fondly, and his beautiful family.
I will do everything I can to help them.

SEAN

Thank you...
(dreamily)
I used to love going there for Sunday lunch. His mother made the most delicious nems with lettuce and mint.

AUDREY

And I remember Bang joining us for weekends in the Italian countryside. He was so kind when you started at the Lycée Chateaubriand midterm knowing no one. I was so glad you'd found a friend.

SEAN

I was a loner, too, and when I saw that none of the other children were playing with him, we made an instant connection. After his father was recalled to Saigon with his wife and youngest children, Bang was supposed to come back and live near us in Switzerland to carry on his education, but then the Vietnamese war ended... with his side's defeat. He sent me his new address, and I wrote but never had a reply. Do you remember how worried I was and asked you about trying to find out what had happened to him?

AUDREY

(picking up another of the letters)
I do, but there was no information available at the time. Bang says here that his father was punished for being a servant of the southern

government and the family were sent south to a
"new economic zone" where they were forced to
grow their own crops in an infertile forest.
They had no food or money and little shelter and
had to attend military camps where they were
brainwashed in Vietnamese into supporting the new
system. They only spoke French or Italian, so
that must have been a terrible shock after Rome.

SEAN
What can I do to help?

AUDREY
(smiling and touching his arm)
Nothing, darling. It's up to me now. This
is where being me might actually be of some
practical use. I'm hoping that my name might
be enough to help save that lovely family from
all that they've suffered these past ten years.
If so, then it will all have been worth it.

——◆——

The story of my mother's involvement in attempts to rescue Bang and his family has never been told, but it speaks powerfully of her humanitarian spirit. This was the "mother to all" who felt the need to answer every call for help and who was determined to use her name for good.

She'd long had a will of iron when it came to fulfilling what she saw as her responsibilities, especially once she became a Goodwill Ambassador for UNICEF after a chance invitation by a diplomat cousin to attend an event in the Far East in the mid-1980s. She would get a look on her face that made it very clear to everyone around her that she had something she wanted to say or do and she wasn't going to let anything stand in her way.

Christa Roth, my mother's right hand at UNICEF, who became a friend, agrees: "Audrey was an unusual mix. She looked delicate but wanted no entourage other than her partner, Rob Wolders, was diligent in her research, fearless about where she wanted to go, and made her choices based on her hope to provoke something by speaking to the press afterward. She was very determined that way and extremely concerned about what was happening in some of these developing countries."

Having taken over the ambassadorial role from the actor Danny Kaye, who'd died in 1987 after years of charitable service, Mum found herself in the middle of massive geopolitical upheaval in Africa. This meant traveling to many more extreme and difficult regions than any ambassador had ever been to before. The depressing scenarios she read about and saw on television kept driving her on.

"She was immediately extremely professional," said Christa, who would drive to La Paisible with piles of faxes and reports for my mother to go through. "There were certain things she wanted to do and others that she didn't, so we arranged everything together and worked it out between us. When I told her she'd been my idol as a teenager and that I even dressed like her when I was growing up in Germany, she was very bemused but quickly directed the conversation back to what needed to be done."

Staff in the New York office would write her speeches for her, but Christa said my mother would rewrite them. "They were too bureaucratic and formal for her. She'd change them so that they were much more from the heart." I witnessed her doing exactly that on several occasions. I can see her now. It was just like when she used to go through her film scripts. She'd sit at our dining table, which was covered in reams of books and reports, with her reading glasses and a lit cigarette, scribbling copious notes and crossing out all the things she didn't like.

Christa added that the suffering my mother witnessed touched her very deeply. "I could see the sadness in her, but she was adamant that she wanted to continue." Giving press conference after press conference to tell the world what she'd witnessed only made her relive her past all over again, so the trauma never really went away. She was also full of rage that thousands of children were dying every day of preventable causes and the world was letting it happen. After each trip she needed time to adjust as she recharged her batteries, but then she'd ask, "What next?"

Against the wishes of her family and her protective housekeeper, Giovanna, my mother not only said yes to most invitations but pushed for field trips that UNICEF hadn't even asked her to do. "There was a time when everyone worried that we were asking too much of her," Christa explained. "I told them, 'No, we are not. She wants to go to these places and asks us to propose something.' Each time, I'd say to her, 'Audrey, if you don't want to do this, just let me know. I will tell UNICEF you're not going. You have to be sure that you really want to do this.' She threw herself into the work and felt she had to keep going, and no matter how tired or sad she felt, she wouldn't give it up."

In the five years Christa worked for UNICEF, she said my mother went on so many field trips and attended so many events that she raised more money than any individual ever had before. This was crucial for an organization that, although part of the UN, has no budget of its own and survives solely on donations from governments, corporations, and private individuals. "She was phenomenal and unflinching. She was also angry that so little was being done to save millions. When she stood up for certain things, she could be extremely outspoken, pointing her finger on things she felt were wrong. That was something she had—a real strength about her. It was a resilience I hadn't expected."

———◆———

So when my twenty-seven-year-old former school friend Bang first sat at his father's small kitchen table in early 1988 to write three letters to "Madame Hepburn," little did he know whom he was dealing with.

He and his family were desperate and had all but given up hope of being rescued from Vietnam. Their home and property in the former Saigon, renamed Ho Chi Minh City by the Communists, had been requisitioned to become "collectively owned" by the new government. There was no free press, and no dissent was permitted. Education and religion were under official control, too, and food handouts were based on a person's status or productivity. Families like Bang's were forced into areas where indigenous people had been displaced, and millions suffered from malnutrition and malaria.

The weekend he wrote the letters, he was visiting his parents from the south, where he worked in an oil recycling plant. All the dreams he'd had as a schoolboy in Rome of studying hard, going to a European university, and becoming a doctor like one of his brothers or a diplomat like his father had been shattered. Back in his home country but unable to speak Vietnamese, he'd dropped out of school at fourteen after what he described as "a wasted chance at education" and was forced instead to work alongside his parents for two years as an agricultural laborer.

"There was a lot of misery and famine, with very little to eat. Like my parents and siblings, I was extremely thin and undernourished and couldn't keep up with the arduous work. After two years of chopping down trees, digging fields, and tilling the land, I went to work in the city at a plant nursery growing food for the regime. I was seventeen and lonely, separated from everyone I knew, so I moved to the oil plant to be with one of my sisters, who worked there."

Bang never stopped dreaming about going back to the kind of life they'd had in Italy, where he and his family lived in a large apartment with plenty of food and total freedom. "I was too young to appreciate the seriousness of our situation in Vietnam and wasn't overly scared when I wrote to Madame Hepburn, even though I knew the risks, as the authorities didn't recognize Western governments. I had no choice but to send the letters by regular mail, and—incredibly—they all arrived."

He had never forgotten me either—the quiet boy with a mop of mousy hair whom he'd first met in school in 1970 when we were both ten years old. I was shown into the classroom by the principal, accompanied by my mother, and introduced as the new boy who had recently arrived in Rome. Bang and his father, Hoang Huu Than, the consul at the South Vietnamese Embassy, had done the same when they'd settled in the city a year earlier.

"I had no clue who Sean's parents were. I just remember them coming in and his mother smiling warmly at us all," recalled Bang recently. "Sean and I became instant friends and spent almost every weekend together for the next four years." Best of all, Bang knew the woman he called *madame* only as my mum. He didn't know she was famous until he saw the paparazzi waiting for us at the school gates. Even then, it didn't mean much to him because she never behaved as people imagine a famous person would. We were a normal family.

Whenever I went to Bang's apartment, I would join the large family for delicious lunches, and when Mum came to collect me, she'd bring flowers or a plant for Bang's mother, Huyên Khánh, before thanking her for feeding me. She didn't stay for anything to eat, but she knew how much I enjoyed being there, and she reciprocated by inviting Bang for sleepovers and weekends.

Bang was in his late twenties when his father told him that the beautiful lady he'd last seen when he was a teenager was working for UNICEF. My childhood friend was still young and hopeful, newly married to his bride, Thiên My, so he wrote to the one person who might be able to save them. He never really expected to hear back from my mother. And he had a lot to lose by even trying. Even if by some miracle she did respond, Bang doubted she could do anything for them. His sister Xuân Mai—who'd remained in Europe and married a Frenchman—had written repeatedly to the French foreign ministry over several years, appealing for the family to be reunited there, but had received no response.

"Then, from nowhere, a letter came from Madame Hepburn," he recounted. "It began, 'Mon cher Bang, Bien sûr que je me souviens de toi!'—My dear Bang, Of course I remember you!" She asked him to send her the dossier of papers that proved his father's employment history, as well as anything else that might help persuade the French authorities to let the family migrate. Once my mother received them, she wrote again to confirm their safe receipt and promised to do all she could.

I was living in LA by then and hearing bits and pieces about my mother's correspondence with Bang, so I knew she was trying, and I was very glad. If anyone could get this done, it would be she. As far as I know, she didn't enlist the help of anyone else to begin with, she just wrote directly to the French authorities as herself in the hope that her name would be enough. She was shocked and upset when she received a negative response. The French government had turned down Audrey Hepburn...the star and globally renowned UNICEF ambassador.

The next package Bang received from my mum was the most disappointing of his life. She was returning his dossier and all the files, informing him that she'd exhausted all avenues and that she was sorry but there was nothing more she could do. "I lost all hope in that moment," he recalled. "I thought then that things would never change. We'd had this dream for all those years, and now it was broken. I would have to stay in Vietnam and raise a family there with no chance of a better life for them or me."

Bang underestimated her. What he didn't realize was that whenever someone told her she couldn't do something, that was when she really dug in her heels. For her, the fight was far from over, and her response was, "Well, let's see..." She wasn't done.

The life of my childhood friend changed forever a year later when my mother wrote again. The woman who had once said "I believe in being strong when everything seems to be going wrong" asked Bang to send his father's file back to her. With those few words, his hopes rose again, and he allowed himself to believe that there might be a chance to escape after all.

Neither he nor I know what my mother did with that well-traveled dossier or how many strings she must have pulled, but we learned later that she involved the UN's High Commissioner for Refugees, who intervened personally with the French authorities. In early 1989, two years after Bang first wrote to her and a few months after she asked for the files to be returned to her, Bang's sister was summoned to the French foreign ministry in Paris.

"This was the first time my sister had any contact from them at all, and she was called in to be interviewed and prove that she could support us if we came to France," Bang said. "There were eight people on the application form, including me, my wife, my parents, a brother, two sisters, and a brother-in-law." After Xuân Mai provided all the correct documentation, the family was put on a priority list and finally approved. But that wasn't the end of it. They then had to go through the complicated bureaucratic process of applying to leave Vietnam, which took almost a year.

"The dream to get back to Europe took fifteen years, but it was Madame Hepburn who turned it into a reality," Bang recalled later. "We were all so happy. It would never have happened without her intervention, as our relatives had already tried multiple times. Our chances seemed exhausted, but then she saved not just me but my entire family. It wasn't normal that somebody like her would remember me all that time later. I found that totally extraordinary, and such providence. If she hadn't saved us, we would all still be there."

In December 1989 Bang and his immediate family were finally allowed to board a plane west to be reunited with their relatives in France. After so many years apart, they had a lot of lost time to make up for. At first they were confined to quarantine, where they were vaccinated and given extensive health checks, and then they were locked into a fresh bureaucratic process that garnered them identity papers but no permits to work or permission to leave the country. Once settled, Bang was finally able to send my mother a telegram expressing their profound gratitude. The family also sent her gifts, including a large painting of the head of Buddha in lacquered mother-of-pearl, which they'd carried all the way from Ho Chi Minh City.

In her note back to him from her home in Switzerland, she wrote: "My dear Bang, How happy I am to know that you are safely in Paris with your family! Your letter and beautiful gifts arrived bringing so much joy.... How did you manage to bring those lovely but heavy gifts all the way from Vietnam?" She went on to explain that she and Rob had just returned from a UNICEF trip to the US and were soon off to Japan and so were home only briefly. "In October we are going to New Zealand and perhaps... Vietnam!! Take good care of yourselves, my love to you all and a million thanks for the gifts. Audrey."

In later notes and cards that Bang has kept, my mother spoke of how she thought of his "dear family" with great affection and thanked them for their "kind and faithful wishes." Because she was traveling so much and he wasn't allowed to leave France, they were sadly never reunited, so he was unable to thank her in person.

Without any qualifications and almost thirty years old, Bang found work in IT until he retired. He and his wife had a son, who joined the military, and a daughter, who works in marketing. "Our children would have led such different lives if we'd stayed in Vietnam. It would have been much more difficult for them," he said. "We owe Madame Hepburn everything. She is our Madame Providence!"

This remarkable story illustrates exactly the kind of person my mother was. It was one of many private acts of kindness. As soon as she was aware of my school friend's situation, she set about doing something about it without shouting it from the rooftops. It wasn't ever reported on, and only Bang's family and a handful of people in our immediate family knew what she'd managed to achieve. That was her way, to proceed with quiet commitment and dedication. She was never about the glory.

———◆———

TRUE TO HER WORD, MY mother did visit Vietnam with UNICEF after she'd helped Bang and his family, her interest in the country piqued by all that she had learned. Her sole mission was to raise awareness of the needs of the children in the country, although her trip to the place where almost sixty thousand US soldiers had been killed in combat was considered controversial.

Undaunted, in November 1990 she flew to Hanoi and met up with British photographer Peter Charlesworth, who was taking pictures for UNICEF. He remembered that she was easy company from the start, even when their flight to a mountainous region in the north on an ancient Russian helicopter was delayed for hours because of fog.

"Audrey wasn't fazed at all by the delay," he recalled recently. "She sat on one of the whitewashed stones demarking the edge of the helipad and lit a cigarette. When she spotted me with all my cameras, she waved me over. After saying hello, she said, 'I'm a little bit vain, and I know you won't always be able to, but, if at all possible, I look much better if photographed from the left side.' From then on, she was a delight to work with, art directing almost every shot, looking around to assess how to make the best picture and then helping to make it happen."

In an area not far from the Chinese border populated by impoverished villagers from the ethnic Dao hill tribe, my mother watched trained medical staff treating people with a variety of conditions caused by malnutrition and vitamin deficiency, including goiter, which swells the thyroid gland. She also spoke to nurses treating pregnant women and children with malaria, the chief killer in the region. As on all her visits, women and infants swarmed around her, and she delighted in them all as she scooped up babies, congratulated new mothers, primed a new water pump, and addressed the villagers on the benefits of vaccination.

After her arrival in another remote village, giggling women swathed her in colorful local dress before she sat with the elders in a large hut on stilts for the obligatory presentations. "When it looked like the speeches were coming to an end, Audrey looked across at me and nodded at the door," Peter recalled. "I slipped out and, looking around, quickly figured out the best place for photos with the mountains as a backdrop once she emerged from the hut. Sure enough, everyone started spilling out, but her minders and I got a great shot of the women and children following Audrey devotedly down the hill."

Back in Hanoi, she visited a school where a portrait of the country's former prime minister Ho Chi Minh hung on the wall. She handed out books to children and, with a beaming smile, wrote "I Love You" on a blackboard. Later, after visiting a children's clinic, she met the country's deputy prime minister, General Võ Nguyên Giáp, a former war hero who'd led the Communist forces against the American forces.

"I could tell she was apprehensive about that meeting," said Peter. "She looked nervous, but when he arrived, she jumped up with a huge smile, and he was immediately putty in her hands. Had the war still been going on at that point, I truly believe she could have stopped it." Towering over the diminutive general with a motherly smile, she reminded him that his next and most important battle was to conquer childhood diseases.

Later she told the handful of reporters accompanying her, "I would like to give a much more accessible, human picture of Vietnam than just the Vietnam War. It's a ghost that has to be laid to rest." When asked about US trade embargoes that denied the country vital supplies and other aid, she replied with a steely stare, "I'm not in the business of politics. I'm in the business of children."

AND IT WAS THAT BUSINESS that also took her to Ecuador in October 1988, where she was assigned a young American translator named Gary Stahl, who was living and working there. Even though she had a good command of Spanish, Gary was hired to assist. It was to him that she admitted being hit by shrapnel as a teenager in Velp.

For Gary, working with my mother was a dream come true. "I had long admired her as a gay icon, and it was a joy to be working alongside her for those few days after she flew in from a field trip to Venezuela," he later said. "She was an amazing woman...so humble. We traveled up into the highlands about two hours outside the capital, Quito, to look at the ways in which UNICEF were fighting preventable diseases. It was there that I witnessed something quite amazing."

Gary couldn't believe the way children responded to her. "She was like a magnet, so open and friendly and never caring if she got dirty. I'll never forget the faces of the upper-class Ecuadorians in her entourage, who were shocked by all the grungy indigenous children buzzing around her."

After tenderly trying to calm sickly infants about to be immunized, my mother watched UNICEF staff teaching mothers how to administer the miraculous oral rehydration therapy to children who might otherwise die of dysentery. She then returned to the city to visit an open house that fed and cared for the hundreds of homeless street children with no families to speak of. Rob said afterward that seeing so many children who had nothing, and no one, touched her especially. "Being fatherless was something she could relate to," he added.

Her indignation at those she referred to as "men in power who allow children to suffer so" knew no bounds, and she didn't hold back when she met them, even telling senators in Washington, DC, that they needed to fulfill their moral obligation to those in need. And it wasn't only heads of state she called out if they did something she didn't like. At a press conference to discuss what more could be done to help UNICEF's mission to ensure the survival and development of children, a reporter asked an audacious and inappropriate question. Having discovered that Rob was accompanying my mother, the Ecuadorian reporter "thought she was going to get the juicy story of the century," according to Gary Stahl. She put up her hand before asking if Mum was traveling with her lover, and were they secretly married? Would she care to enlighten the press?

There were gasps, but my mother remained perfectly calm. She'd heard it all before. A decade earlier, when she and I were photographed at the Spoleto festival in Italy, the picture appeared in a paper with the headline "Audrey with the new love of her life." I wore a beard at the time and clearly the press had not recognized me. She laughed hard and then crossed out the word "new," cut out the picture, and framed it.

After the intrusive question at the press conference in Ecuador, my mother simply took her glasses off, leaned into Gary, and said, "This one I want translated word for word. No embellishments. Don't take any liberties. Make this as precise as you can."

He recalled, "I thought, *Oh God, what is she going to say?* She then looked the woman straight in the eye and, with her glasses in her hand, said, 'As a matter of fact, yes, he is the love of my life. I wouldn't be who I am without him. He is traveling with me. I love him dearly. We are not married. But I came here to give a press conference about the poverty in your country and what UNICEF is doing to address that, and I would truly appreciate it if those were the kinds of questions you ask.'

"I have never seen a press corps so floored," Gary added. "No one dared to raise their hand. It felt like an eternity before someone did, and then it was back on point. She had told that woman off so elegantly and politely with such a pleasant tone. It was her absolute self-assuredness and candor that I was most impressed by."

It wasn't the only thing that impressed him. When my mother turned down an invitation to dinner at the presidential palace for the second night running soon after arriving back from another arduous day in the field, she asked Gary, "Didn't you say something about whisky? If so, is there a bar somewhere where I wouldn't be noticed?"

He knew just the place and took her to the dimly lit, wood-paneled Reina Victoria, where they sat in a corner. As they sipped from tumblers of scotch—Mum's go-to evening drink—she told him about her childhood during the war and how UNRRA had saved her life.

"We really clicked and had a conversation that night which changed my life. It was the way she explained everything so clearly and believed so deeply. I was already impressed by the work of UNICEF, but I was suddenly seeing it through her eyes as she opened up, telling me what she'd experienced in her youth and then what she'd witnessed in other countries. Each agency had its own national goals, but UNICEF was pushing for 80 percent global immunization and a UN Convention on the Rights of the Child. She truly believed that every child needed to be protected and that we should all do whatever we could to make the world a better place."

Having already decided he wanted to pursue a master's degree and do something meaningful with his life, Gary returned to America soon afterward and applied to eight schools, submitting an essay about his experiences in Ecuador and with my mother. Seven accepted him, but the Harvard Kennedy School offered him a scholarship and paid for everything. "I asked them why they'd been so generous, and they told me, 'When we read your essay, we felt your passion and drive to change the world and that you believe you can do it.' Audrey was a big part of that journey."

He felt personal pride when he saw that she had been invited to the UN to address an international task force on hunger after a trip to Sudan the following year. Then, almost a year to the day after her brief trip to Ecuador, she was back in New York on World Children's Day to celebrate the adoption of the UN Convention on the Rights of the Child, which she had been longing for. In the building where the

General Assembly had decreed that "mankind owes the child the best it has to give," my mother was asked to read out the preamble to the convention, something she did with passion after stating what "a very great privilege" that was.

Visibly emotional, but with a resolute stare into the TV cameras, she read out the ten principles of the convention. They included these lines: "The child shall, in all circumstances, be among the first to receive protection and relief in times of emergency and disaster. The child needs love and understanding and shall have the right to grow up in an atmosphere of affection and security. The child shall be entitled to grow and develop in health, and shall have the right to adequate nutrition, housing, recreation and medical services."

Inspired by her example, Gary Stahl went on to work for UNICEF for almost three decades, starting as a coordinator of the emergency operation in the aftermath of the Rwandan genocide and ending as head of mission in New York and senior adviser for strategic partnerships in Geneva. "I covered pretty much every big emergency on the planet, and it's true to say Audrey Hepburn was partly responsible for that. Sadly, I never saw her again or got a chance to thank her for influencing me so deeply. No one ever knew what she had done for me, but I knew, because she was passionate and committed and the most educated and well-informed Goodwill Ambassador I have ever met. She knew that UNICEF could change the world, and she was quite blunt with people who didn't get that."

I didn't know about my mother's effect on Gary's life until recently, but I'm not surprised. People fell under her spell because of her charm, her warmth, and her grit. They still do, to this day, more than thirty years after her death, and that's an extraordinary achievement, one she could never have imagined.

———◆———

12.

To plant a garden is to believe in tomorrow.—AH

EXT. A ROSE GARDEN SOMEWHERE IN FRANCE, 1990

AUDREY, in a tailored white Givenchy suit, wanders through a beautiful rose garden in full bloom, beaming with happiness and stopping every now and again to press her face into a flower and inhale.

A few feet away a four-person film crew trains its camera on her face and zooms in to catch the light in her eyes as she gazes upon the beautiful scene.

Wandering on cue to a waiting bench on which lies a single pale-yellow rose, **AUDREY** sits neatly, knees pressed together, and picks up the delicate flower.

AUDREY
(to camera)
Few things are lovelier to me than a full-blown rose when it opens its heart. This rose, with its pale-gold, pink, and ivory petals blending to a lightly ruffled edge, has been called "the rose of the century." Bred in France from a single untested seed, it was smuggled in a diplomatic pouch onto the last plane leaving France before the occupation. At the end of the war in 1945, it was christened Peace.

DIRECTOR
Cut! OK, thanks, Audrey, that was great. Let's have a short break, and on the next take you can feed straight into the T. S. Eliot quote before we move on to the climbing rose segment.

AUDREY
Fine. And oh, I do love that story about the rose. Did you know that the horticulturist who developed it also sent cuttings to friends around the world for fear the cultivar would be destroyed by the Nazis? And in 1945, at the inaugural meeting of the United Nations in San Francisco, each delegate was given a Peace rose with prayers for everlasting peace. Isn't that marvelous?

DIRECTOR
You really know your roses, don't you?

AUDREY

Well, I have a beautiful rose garden in Switzerland, which is one of the greatest joys of my life. I also adore the first tulips of spring, which start off looking like onions and somehow survive winter before bursting forth full of beauty, cheer, and hope.

DIRECTOR

Tulips are closely associated with your native Holland, aren't they?

AUDREY
(laughing)
Oh yes, we loved them so much we even ate the bulbs during the war! And, rather splendidly, I have a tulip named after me now. It is an elegant white specimen, tall, straight, and skinny—like me!

DIRECTOR

Are you familiar with all the Latin names?

AUDREY

Not at all. I know those I was taught in England as a child, but not many. My job is to do the weeding and prune things that are easy. I clip off the dead flowers in the cool of the evenings and gather fresh flowers in one of my many baskets. But I also waste a lot of time gazing at the sky to see what the weather is going to do. I'm half English, and gardening is a national pastime in England, which explains my obsession with the weather!

A **MAKEUP ARTIST** moves in to lightly brush Audrey's face with powder, but **AUDREY** waves her aside when she asks if she'd like anything more.

               MAKEUP ARTIST
           (packing away her lipsticks)
Do you grow vegetables too? My granddad has an allotment and spends hours there.

               AUDREY
Oh yes. To me, one of the greatest luxuries in life is to wander out into my garden and pick tomatoes still warm from the sun. Or maybe gather fresh peas, leeks, onions, salad, and herbs. I can prepare a meal in minutes from these precious gifts from the earth.

ROB steps forward from behind the crew and, sitting next to **AUDREY**, takes her hand.

               ROB
You paint the garden too.

               AUDREY
Well, yes, in my own terribly naive style, but it's true that one of my favorite pictures is one I did of the vegetable patch in its full summer glory.

MAKEUP ARTIST
My favorites are wildflowers.

AUDREY
Oh yes. We have a little place in Gstaad, and in spring and summer the meadows on the lower slopes are full of them. They smell divine, and I especially love the white asphodel, which look like a thousand starbursts.

The **MAKEUP ARTIST** wanders off, looking as if she is dreaming of floral starbursts.

ROB
(quietly)
Are you OK? Not too tired? Do you need some water?

AUDREY
(smiling and laying a hand on his)
How can I be tired in such a beautiful garden as this?

ROB
I just don't want you overdoing it. You know we have to leave for San Francisco early tomorrow.

AUDREY
I know. I've almost finished working on my speech. I just want you to look at the ending and tell me whether it feels like too

much to include that Dickens quote about
children feeling injustice so deeply.

ROB
(leaning in to kiss **AUDREY** on the cheek)
Nothing you say is ever too much.
I'm sure it will be just right.

DIRECTOR
(clapping his hands)
OK, everyone, back to your positions.
Audrey, ready to go again?

AUDREY
(jumping up with a grin)
Of course!

THE TIMING OF THE TELEVISION series *Gardens of the World with Audrey Hepburn* couldn't have been better for my mother. After two years of harrowing trips for UNICEF to witness unspeakable devastation and misery, the self-confessed "garden nut" was flown to the serenity of some of the world's most beautiful gardens, as far afield as England and Japan, Holland, Italy, the Dominican Republic, France, and America.

Rather poetically, this—her first and last television series—was not only her final appearance in front of a camera but was aired four days after her death. A beautiful swan song for an exquisite swan. Mum was posthumously awarded a Primetime Emmy for the program, which was accompanied by a book she'd contributed to and from which some of the profits went to UNICEF.

For my mother, being asked to tour these heavenly places was—as she would say—"simply divine." And it came not long after she'd been approached in 1989 to play her final role—an angel called Hap in Steven Spielberg's film *Always*. In an early casting meeting hosted by the director, everyone was asked who should play the godly character named "God," or "Hap" if it was a woman, and the answer was unanimous: "Audrey Hepburn."

The director called UNICEF's Swiss office to ask if it could connect him to my mother, and it was Christa Roth, her right-hand woman there, who took the call. "When he told me who he was, I asked if I could help. He wanted to fax her a script, but she didn't have any such devices at La Paisible, so I told him to send it to me, and I would see that she'd get it." UNICEF's already overworked fax machine whirred away for about an hour, and when it finally stopped, Christa drove to Tolochenaz.

"I walked in and announced, 'Your film career is starting again. I have a wonderful script for you!' Audrey looked shocked and asked what I meant, so I explained, and her reply was, 'Oh God. Me? Well, I suppose if it's not too much time away from home, I might consider it, but let me read it first.' She did, and then she spoke to Steven Spielberg on the telephone, and they got along so well she decided to say yes. That film proved to be her last beautiful role."

My mother was secretly delighted to have been asked, and she called me in Los Angeles to tell me the exciting news that she would be starring alongside Richard Dreyfuss, with Holly Hunter and John Goodman in support. Although nervous, she found the experience thrilling.

Dreyfuss was equally delighted, but for different reasons. In a letter to my mother afterward, he wrote, "Now it can be told. In *Always*, the real reason I died was so that I could go to heaven and be with you.... Audrey, I have fallen in love with you again and again and again, and then I worked with you, and I fell again. Hopelessly. I have extraordinary taste, and I only fall in love with women who are graceful and thoughtful and earthy and talented and beautiful and elegant. So, it's all your fault. Richard."

Mum kept that letter as a reminder that life is full of surprises. Even though she was in her sixth decade, and after decades of praise, she still wasn't accustomed to such compliments and would admit only to working hard. "That I'll take credit for," she said, "but I don't understand any of it."

Then when the offer to host *Gardens of the World* came in, it was far too tempting to refuse. As she says in the program, ever since Eden, a garden has been a form of heaven on earth. And for her, gardens had always had such special meaning. Janis Blackschleger, the series producer, explained how the creators came to choose Mum as presenter. "We'd seen her interviewed by Barbara Walters and thought she'd be ideal, although we had no idea if a star of her magnitude would accept our invitation. Luckily, she agreed right away—donating her fee to UNICEF—but her first question was to ask which gardens she'd be going to."

As with her field trips for UNICEF, Rob traveled everywhere with her for the series and was grateful for the opportunity to see her at the work for which she was best known. I remember feeling the same a decade earlier when I joined the cast of the movie *They All Laughed*. Some actors need the first couple of takes to warm up, but my mother was already a "print" on take one: The next few takes would simply be more nuanced. Director Peter Bogdanovich, for whom I also worked as an assistant, could have filmed her all day but was at his wit's end because my mother's costar Ben Gazzara would get good only around the fourth or fifth take. Unable to wait that long, the director ended up using first or second takes, in which Mum, at least, gave an outstanding performance. Gazzara's slowness to warm up may have been one of the reasons that film was never really understood, although it has since become something of a cult movie.

Watching my mother film *Gardens of the World*, Rob was similarly astonished. He'd seen how professional she was with her UNICEF trips, doing extensive research and writing her own speeches, but this really opened his eyes to how smart she was too. "It became an intensely personal and creative process for her," he admitted. "She immersed herself in not only the beauty of the gardens, but also in their origins and evolution."

In an interview about the program in *House & Garden* magazine, my mother spoke of the parallels between her charity work and her determination to do right by the planet. "Everyone's concerned with the environment, but, of course, the environment includes flowers and trees as well as children," she stressed. "One cannot survive without the others. Today more than ever, gardens remind us of the beauty we are in danger of losing."

She was thrilled by the prospect of being flown around the world to see beautiful places instead of so much death and disease, but her dearest hope was that the series would be a similarly poetic experience for audiences. She wanted people to enjoy their virtual visit to the kinds of places they might never otherwise be able to see, while appreciating the beauty and fragility of our planet.

Janis Blackschleger discovered "no artifice" about her and was surprised to note that she not only did her own makeup but was "unassuming, modest, and refreshingly conscientious about her responsibilities." She worked closely with the writers, editing the script to make it sound more authentic to her voice and suggesting ideas to blend the historic and aesthetic elements of each garden.

"I found her to be serious, but not sad," Janis added. "When we first met at her home in Switzerland, she had only just flown in from one of her UNICEF field trips, and, as a former flight attendant familiar with jet lag and refugee flights, I had such empathy with how she must have been feeling."

During her five months working on the series, my mother was never afraid to do anything asked of her, whether it be traipsing through forests, wading through bogs, or working outside in all weathers. She loved aspects of all the gardens they visited, but her favorite was the Garden of Ninfa, a "mysterious, romantic" place created in the ruins of a medieval Italian town abandoned in the fourteenth century. Over one hundred hectares of land was cleared of centuries of undergrowth in the 1920s by a war hero who became the Italian ambassador to the United States, and he planted it with everything from roses to wisterias, magnolias to hydrangeas.

My mother also fell in love with the enchantment of the lush moss garden of the Kokedera, or "Moss Temple," in Kyoto, Japan, with all its softness and delicacy. She adored the blowsy English vegetable garden at Tintinhull, in Somerset, England, with its flowers and herbs. "I loved the soft colors of poppies, roses, and daisies, not hunks of color wedged against each other but in lacy, delicate, transparent arrangements," she said, her expression dreamy. These beautiful places provided a welcome antidote to the sights, sounds, and smells of Ethiopia, Sudan, and Bangladesh. The program and its accompanying book also gave my mother the chance to share her love of culture and art. For the pictures, she requested paintings full of light and color by two of her favorite artists, Camille Pissarro and Pierre Bonnard.

The timelessness and generosity of public gardens moved her, especially in Paris's Jardin du Luxembourg, which was built to improve the health and welfare of the city's inhabitants. There my mother wandered happily through the familiar avenues of trees she'd known ever since she first visited the City of Light to meet the author Colette.

The crew took one shot of my mother standing there in a traditional pose, hands clasped behind her back. She is staring into the middle distance, as if imagining that the children playing there would one day return with their own children, an idea that gave her great comfort. "It was the continuum of humanity she loved," said Janis. "Audrey showed us life-affirming ways of living and being in the world."

ALWAYS A TRAILBLAZER, MY MOTHER had campaigned to save the environment long before that became a crusade for modern-day activists. And she knew instinctively that the love of nature she shared with millions was something else that could be harnessed for the greater good. Or, as she put it in the foreword to the companion book, "By looking at our world through its gardens today, we reaffirm the simple human capacity to create beauty on this earth....Perhaps if we now take a closer look at our gardens, we will better understand how to find a way to save our lovely Earth."

Ever since her childhood in Kent, where she'd helped to tend the vegetable garden of her kind hosts, my mother had appreciated the determination of plants to survive winter and bring hope, renewal, and sustenance each spring. She once declared that all of us search for what made us happy when we were children, and that was true of her and her bucolic years there. "One should go back and search for what was lost and found to be real," she said, adding that she would rather we, her children, went back to the country to "search for blades of grass than for more sophisticated things, which are terribly unreal and disappointing."

She never stopped growing her own food, and wandering out into her garden to pick fresh fruit and flowers was one of her greatest pleasures. It was also comforting for her to know that if there was another war, she could keep us all alive with the produce she grew, pickled, and preserved. She was delighted to discover that during the height of the Cold War in the 1950s, the ornamental gardens of La Paisible were transformed into vegetable plots as it was one of thousands of properties earmarked by the Swiss government as places to grow food for the populace, much as in the "Dig for Victory" campaigns in England.

When the world's economy looked set to crash in the 1980s, my mother assured us all repeatedly that even if we lost everything, we could become self-sufficient as a family, living on homegrown potatoes, tomatoes, pumpkins, corn, soft fruit, and eggs from the hens. Her haven would become our haven, too, she insisted, and the seedlings she nurtured so lovingly would be gifts from nature to provide us with the sustenance that the Nazis had denied her. The most telling part of her plan was that she still half expected another war.

As solace from the stresses of life and the pressure of her charity work, she loved the promise of tomorrow that a garden brings. She described tending her Swiss orchards as "a spiritual practice" and took inspiration from the indomitable spirit of plants that withstand all that nature throws at them. Afflicted by severe frosts, rainstorms, and gales that tore limbs from trees, her garden needed constant care. When winds collapsed a bed of corn or snapped the heads from plants, she'd be out first thing the following morning to prop them up with splints and beanpoles. "That's what's extraordinary about plants, their resilience," she mused. "With a little help, they revive."

She couldn't help but compare gardening to the work of UNICEF. "I think that's what life is all about, really—children and flowers.... It's not just a matter of a child surviving but giving it a future and allowing it to develop well and not handicapped; giving it the strength to have a future." She, of all people, knew what it was like to grow up without the support of nurturing caretakers.

Naturally stylish, she also found gardens appealing to her senses. She was in awe of the effortless elegance of an iris or the understated beauty of a freshly picked peach. The creative streak that informed the watercolor painting she took up in later life and her tastes in interior decor was allowed free rein in the design and layout of her little piece of heaven on earth. Inspired by the natural play of light and her instinctive desire for color and scent, she made her garden a nostalgic expression of who she really was, with an informal nod to her English roots. Apart from the traditional rose garden with its corner of sixty white roses gifted by Hubert de Givenchy, her garden was, as she put it, "a helter-skelter of flowers and vegetables with the Alps as a backdrop."

Wandering through it with one of her many baskets, listening to

Never happier than when in her garden *(Hepburn family archive)*

Fond memories of Spain *(© Henry Clarke, Musée Galliera / Artists Rights Society (ARS), New York / ADAGP, Paris 2025)*

Giovanna with Mr. Famous's replacement, Assam
(Hepburn family archive)

Mum and me on the set of *Two for the Road* (© *Pierluigi Praturlon / Reporters Associati & Archivi—Roma*)

Shopping with Mum and my stepfather, Andrea, in Rome, 1969 *(Hepburn family archive)*

With my Vietnamese friend Bang in Rome
(Hepburn family archive)

Mum with Luca
(Henry Clarke, Vogue © Condé Nast)

At home in Rome in her negligee *(© Photo Elisabetta Catalano)*

Mummy's boy
(© Henry Clarke, Musée Galliera / Artists Rights Society (ARS), New York / ADAGP, Paris 2025)

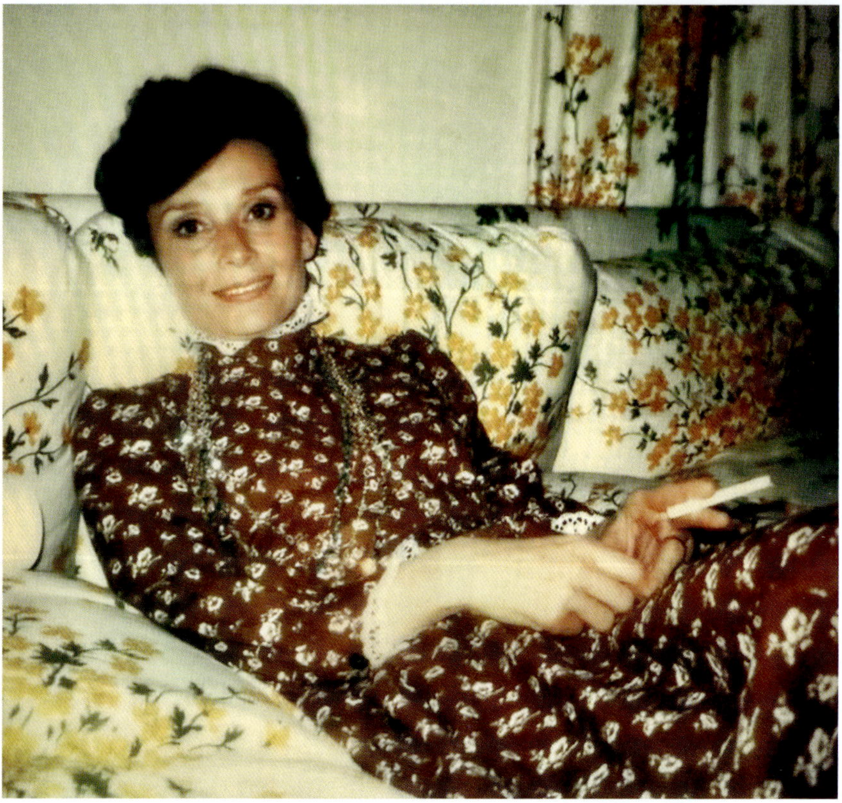

Home in Rome *(Hepburn family archive)*

Walking in the mountains with her beloved Connie *(Andrew Wald / Hepburn family archive)*

Healthy and happy at Connie's in Los Angeles *(Andrew Wald / Hepburn family archive)*

Mum with Luca *(Hepburn family archive)*

Mum at Connie's with two of the men in her life, me and Robert Wolders *(Andrew Wald / Hepburn family archive)*

"Ruby" and me helping out in Connie's kitchen in LA *(Andrew Wald / Hepburn family archive)*

"Say cheese!" at Connie's. Instamatic snapshots. *(Andrew Wald / Hepburn family archive)*

On holiday in France with Rob
(Robert Wolders / Hepburn family archive)

The ever-helpful Rob adjusting her hem *(Camilla McGrath, Earl McGrath / Hepburn family archive)*

My first Oscars with Mum
(Bridgeman Images)

Reunited with her childhood nanny Greta years later in Belgium *(Hepburn family archive)*

Stepping out with Mary Lazar, Billy and Audrey Wilder *(Hepburn family archive)*

With Hubert de Givenchy—the rock in her life *(Bridgeman Images)*

Sketch she did for a UNICEF Christmas card *(Hepburn family archive)*

Mum trying without success to connect with a blind girl in Baidoa, Somalia *(© UNICEF / UNI29045 / Press)*

"I've earned every wrinkle." Mum's (undoctored) favorite photo of herself, taken in an Ethiopian refugee camp. *(© UNICEF / UNI39753 / Isaac)*

Bring me the children. Always a magnet for those in need of a hug. Ethiopia.
(© UNICEF / UNI40120 / Hartley)

Just a little bit more. Spoon-feeding a seriously malnourished Ethiopian child.
(© UNICEF / UNI29047 / Press)

Dinner with Billy Wilder
(Andrew Wald / Hepburn family archive)

Filming *Gardens of the World*, her last TV appearance
(Perennial Productions)

Standing before her beloved willow tree at La Paisible *(Hepburn family archive)*

Basket of flowers handpicked and painted at home *(Hepburn family archive)*

Last photos: saying adieu to her LA friends *(Hepburn family archive)*

My family and my best friend Guy in Rome. From left to right, Gregorio and Santiago, my friend Guy, me with Karin, Athena and Adone, and Emma. *(Hepburn family archive)*

birdsong and the humming of bees, she reconnected with the simple things that meant so much to her. Even toward the end of her life, she wasn't a woman of faith in the traditional sense and favored no single religion. She thought the birth of a child or the miracle of a crocus pushing through the snow was the manifestation of whichever god we wished to believe in. And in those moments of solitude in her happy place, she was merely a mother and housewife planning to prepare something wonderful in the kitchen with whatever was available—the supreme curator supervising the tender charges in her care.

I am forever grateful that filming *Gardens of the World* gave her such welcome respite from her commitment to the voiceless. That period felt like a beacon of light in the midst of much darkness, and it beautifully mirrored her passion and her spirit. Whenever she was away from home, she longed to be back strolling through the vineyards with her dogs, picking roses, or making jars of compote from her apple harvest. Those were the things that brought her joy.

She was traveling abroad when she heard from her trusted gardener, Giovanni, the brother of her beloved Giovanna, who'd replaced Monsieur Nicole when he retired, that a favorite willow tree that she had nursed back to health appeared to have died. She was so upset she was almost tempted to fly straight home and see if she could save it. After she returned, in February 1992, there was a tremendous storm one night, and through the howling winds, she heard a thundering thump that shook the entire house. The next morning, when she went outside, she found that her beloved tree had fallen. She wept as if for a lost friend. With uncanny prescience she told Giovanni, "I'm next."

THE MORE SHE WITNESSED THE injustices of the world, the harder they were for her to stomach. In one interview around this time, she admitted that unless she stepped back from her charity commitments soon, she'd make herself unwell and might even "develop an ulcer," as she was "running out of gas."

Looking increasingly tired, she added, "It's a huge responsibility. Lots of work, lots of physical work, traveling, fundraising, but also lots of preparing. You can't just know where a country is on a map. You have to know its history, its problems, what can be done, what has been done. Because once you have been to those places, you have to face the press, and they ask lots of questions, and you have to make keynote speeches to whomever and raise awareness and funds."

Behind her outward stoicism, she privately admitted that she'd never expected her charitable role to be quite so demanding. Public speaking wasn't something she'd been trained to do, and it pushed her reluctantly back into the spotlight after decades away from it. "It scares the wits out of me," she said, explaining that being an actress didn't stop her from being shy. "Acting is something quite different from getting up in front of people over and over again in so many countries. Yet speaking out is something that is terribly important. And having to be responsible. You can't just get up and say, 'Oh, I'm happy to be here, and I love children.' No, it's not enough."

Even when she'd been one of the world's most bankable movie stars, her stage fright had never left her. Each time she had to appear at a press conference and report on what she'd witnessed, her stomach churned from fear. UNICEF field officer Ian McLeod was surprised at how nervous my mother was about having to speak publicly. "The first time I saw her step up to the microphone I wondered if she was ill, her hands were shaking so much. I asked if she was OK, and she told me it was just nerves. She said she had only one chance to speak on behalf of the unheard children of the world and that she was worried she might not get it right, for their sake."

Despite her anxiety, she refused offers of rest and insisted instead on giving as many as fifteen interviews per day, speaking several of the languages she was fluent in. She then took additional, often unscheduled flights to make personal, heartfelt appeals to heads of state, senior politicians, and the media at press conferences, world summits, and fundraising galas.

In one of her many addresses to the United Nations, the woman who came to be described by reporters as "the world's most powerful advocate for children" spoke with a glint of anger in her eyes as she summed up her frustration. "I speak for those children who cannot speak for themselves. Forty thousand still die every day from preventable causes.... No natural calamity, be it flood or earthquake, has ever claimed so many lives." When asked her reasons for visiting lawless Somalia against all security advice, she declared that there could never be enough witnesses to what was unfolding. "If I can speak up for one child, it will be worthwhile."

She told the House of Representatives, "I don't believe in collective blame, but I do believe in collective responsibility." Even though she raised millions—including an estimated $60 million for Ethiopia after just one high-level Washington breakfast of coffee and grapefruit—she worried constantly that she could be doing more. "We have ways to study war," she added. "We even teach it in universities. Wouldn't it be wonderful if there was a place where we could learn how to create and preserve peace? A university of peace." That was one of her most fervent hopes.

Although I was still enormously proud of my mother's dedication, I was deeply relieved when she recruited her fellow actor, friend, and neighbor Roger Moore to start stepping into her shoes—a role he performed brilliantly in her place until his death. More people were needed, though, and it's been gratifying to see that since then everyone from the English footballer David Beckham to actress Whoopi Goldberg has joined the cause. The human rights lawyer and activist Amal Clooney has been incredible in her support for women and children, and the actress Angelina Jolie stepped up, too, serving as a special envoy to the UN High Commissioner for Refugees for a decade. My daughter, Emma, became a young ambassador for the UNHCR and a spokeswoman for UNICEF. And so the compassion continues.

One cynical question sometimes put to her troubled her deeply: Was it morally right to prolong the life of a child who would only endure more poverty and suffering? Her answer was unequivocal: "Letting children die is not the remedy." She was, she said, a witness for the children and their needs. She was speaking for those who couldn't speak for themselves, "the first tiny victims of war." She pointed out that in our own homes a baby is the first to be protected because it is the most vulnerable. "Yet governments allocate first to arms and industries and last to children. What are we trying to do? We have already polluted our skies, destroyed our forests, and extinguished thousands of beautiful animals. Are our children next?"

It was in one of her programs on formal gardens that she summed up her ethos for life. "Every great garden has great bones, structural elements which hold it together. And every garden has its maker, an individual who shapes it with a personal vision." This was true of her, too, and her personal vision was for a place of wonderment and peace.

Just like Anne Frank, who gazed longingly at the sky and the chestnut tree from her attic window, my mother had glimpses of a tree from the family basement when she was hiding from shelling in the war. Hungry, frightened, and missing everything about normal life, she longed to run around the grounds of her grandfather's manor home or clamber into a tree with a cat and a good book.

How apt, then, that for a final scene in *Gardens of the World*, it was her suggestion that she sit beneath a huge oak tree in the garden at beautiful Mottisfont Abbey, England, to read an extract from Anne Frank's diary. It was a passage about how passionate the fourteen-year-old had become about nature after being cooped up inside for so long—a sentiment my mother knew only too well.

It was impossible to be sorrowful, Anne wrote, when there was still beauty to be seen. Like my mother, she recommended time outdoors as the perfect remedy for anyone who was feeling lonely or unhappy. It was a comfort Mum relied on time and again as the burden of her commitment to the dying and the dispossessed lay heavier and heavier on her slender shoulders.

EARLIER THAT SAME YEAR, MY mother had finally felt brave enough to resurrect her lifelong connection with Anne Frank, only because it would be in aid of the cause closest to her heart—children. In March 1990, she agreed to perform a series of readings from the famous diary on behalf of UNICEF on a tour of several cities. The words she was to read during Concerts for Life: An American Tour for the World's Children were to be accompanied by music composed for the occasion.

Although she was racked with nerves about appearing onstage for the first time in over thirty years, she was happy to accept the invitation. This time she wasn't being asked to "become" Anne Frank, she was merely repeating what the teenager had written. With her natural empathy, she was under no illusions that it would be easy.

"I think it's something very important," she told the press, pushing aside her fears. "[Anne's words] are very deep and they're pure because she was a child, and she wrote it from her heart. I think it's a lovely opportunity to relay her thoughts again. Her spirit." She believed that her collaboration with her departed soul sister to bring some solace to the starving children of the world would have made the young diarist happy. That thought gave her the strength to go on.

In advance of the performances, she carefully chose each sentence she would read aloud, learning entire passages by heart. The Californian composer, conductor, and pianist Michael Tilson Thomas, along with the New World Symphony from Miami Beach, Florida, loved what he called the "endearing" cadences in my mother's voice, which ultimately inspired the orchestral phrasing.

Her short but profound extracts were to be punctuated with sympathetic bursts of classical music inspired by the Jewish prayer of mourning, the kaddish. Descended from a long line of Jewish cantors and Yiddish performers and singers, Michael also felt an affinity with Anne Frank, and, to my mother's delight, he wrote what she considered the perfect soundtrack, one she described as "lovely and sensitive."

He, in turn, described Mum as "the dearest soul I ever met," adding, "She had that quality of recognizing you even when meeting you for the first time.... She made you feel there was some special secret you shared with her, some beautiful melody playing that perhaps the two of you could hear."

When UNICEF eventually persuaded their most visible ambassador to undertake the project, my mother reread the book, which was once again extremely hard. She said later, "It was like having the whole war played back to me." Bracing herself, she painstakingly listed her favorite passages and so did Michael. When they compared their selections, they were surprised at the similarities.

The tour's opening concert in Philadelphia raised several hundred thousand dollars. Three cities later, that figure had risen to several million. Wearing a simple but elegant black silk Givenchy dress and few adornments, my mother began with Anne's passage about having "melancholy days" and her declaration that she never intended to show the diary to anyone unless she found a true friend. Then she spoke of what happened when Anne's world went berserk, and how she'd felt standing on the edge of an abyss.

Before listing some of the Nazi edicts prohibiting Jews from everyday activities, Anne wrote of her panic at the thought of having to go into hiding—to effectively disappear, as my mother had done in her family's basement. Echoing scenes that she had witnessed herself at the railway station, my mother read Anne's words about seeing people dragged off the streets, returning home to find people had been taken, and how helpless she felt waiting for the misery to end.

The elegiac performance of Anne's precious words was far more musical than verbal, with the tension building musically to a dark climax. Mum's eyes glistened with memory as she held the script in both hands and gazed at her spellbound audience. It was mesmerizing. Recalling her longing for freedom and friends and her own feelings of restlessness, confusion, and frustration, she spoke of Anne being soothed by the sight of a bird in flight or the sun rising in the sky. When she came to what the teenager had written about courageously upholding her ideals until peace came, my mother's performance dripped with the emotion that Otto Frank—who'd died in 1980—knew that only she could have brought to the film role.

This uniquely compelling performance stemmed from my mother's ability to deliver her dialogue with a veil of vulnerability. She connected the words she was reading to the pain she hid away inside her but that was never very far from the surface.

Perhaps the most meaningful sections were those where the teenage Anne, who'd died forty-five years earlier, wrote of the pity and tragedy of war. My mother was fresh from her latest mission to yet another ravaged country where she'd witnessed children dying needlessly, and her voice wavered a little as she repeated sentences she could have written herself. The woman who'd once declared that war had "riddled her with apprehension about life and people" stared deep into the crowd as she read Anne's words asking why humankind couldn't live peacefully together and why so many were starving when the rest of the world had too much.

Change was needed, she wrote. It was no surprise that my mother had marked this section of Anne's diary with her own handwritten notes. Her personal and deeply held wishes for humanity were echoed in the words of a child.

At a similar event in Oslo, Norway, that summer, she began by quoting the Indian poet and Nobel Prize–winning social reformer Rabindranath Tagore: "Every child comes with the message that God is not yet discouraged of man." The quote was a favorite of hers. That night she shared the stage with her friend and former costar Gregory Peck, who read from the speeches of President Abraham Lincoln. She repeated segments from the diary, which were accompanied this time by the haunting new "Elegy for Anne Frank" by composer Lukas Foss, who'd fled Nazi Germany with his family before the war.

My mother's unique lilt with its hints of aristocratic European roots was raised only once during her measured performance before a huge audience. Speaking from the soul, she read of the teenager's deep empathy for the suffering of the world. Giving a final brave smile, she ended with a line about Anne's firm belief in the goodness of people at heart. It was a fitting final performance.

---✦---

13.

If my world were to cave in tomorrow, I would look back on all the pleasures, excitements, and worthwhilenesses I have been lucky enough to have had. Not the sadness, not my miscarriages or my father leaving home, but the joy of everything else. It will have been enough.—AH

INT. MASTER BEDROOM, LA PAISIBLE, January 1993

Near-complete darkness. Barely visible, **AUDREY** lies in her bed. **SEAN** sits beside her in a wicker armchair. At the foot of her bed, under the covers, lies Penny, her remaining Jack Russell terrier, keeping her feet warm.

SEAN
Mom?

AUDREY
Yes?

SEAN
Do you have any regrets?

AUDREY
(after a pause)
I guess...not meeting the Dalai Lama...
he has so much humanity...such a
wonderful sense of humor. And the
children...
(frowning)
So much suffering...the way we treat
them...we drag them into our conflicts...
we rob them of their childhood.

SEAN
I know.

AUDREY
But no, no regrets. I can't regret
what I cannot change.

SEAN
But you made a big dent...

AUDREY
Talking like this reminds me of
the nights we had sleepovers
when you were little.

SEAN
Oh, Mom...we still can.

AUDREY
Can what?

SEAN
Let our thoughts float in the dark.
Talk about everything and
nothing.

AUDREY
Don't worry, Sean. Everything
will turn out just right.

SEAN
How so?

AUDREY
It's nature...the taller tree
must fall to let the sun through...
for the sapling.
(pauses)
I'd have liked to have stayed
longer...to have seen...met your
children.

SEAN
Maybe a part of you will find its
way back.

AUDREY
Perhaps. I'm sorry I've been
such a terrible mother.

SEAN
Don't say that.

AUDREY
I was away too much...made some bad choices.

SEAN
That's not true. You did the best you could. Like we all do.

AUDREY
You'll understand better when you're a father. And you'll be a wonderful father, I know. Just love them and then get out of their way.
(pauses)
I feel closer now...to all those I've seen dying...

SEAN
How?

AUDREY
I know how they must have felt... towards the end. And I am strangely comforted that I won't survive them either.

SEAN
As dark as that sounds...I get it.

SEAN sits very still and stares at his mother's profile in the moonlight.

> **AUDREY**
> (softly)
> They are waiting for me...they are here...right there...at the bottom of the bed.
>
> **SEAN**
> How comforting.
>
> **AUDREY**
> You cannot understand. Maybe you will in time. I think I'll sleep a little now.
>
> **SEAN**
> I'll be right here.
>
> **AUDREY**
> Try to...
>
> **SEAN**
> Try to what, Mum?
>
> **AUDREY**
> Try to...smile in the dark...

ALL HER LIFE, MY MOTHER could hear my grandmother's voice in her head saying, "Don't draw attention to yourself," "Think of others first," "You're not that interesting." It was in her lifelong obedience to those instructions that she chose not to tell anyone how much pain she was in during her final trip for UNICEF.

Even Rob didn't know the full story as she struggled on with her mission to Somalia in 1992, the one she'd fought hard to be sent on and waited a year for—perhaps knowing it would be her last. Getting clearance to travel took the longest, even though Somalia was a lawless, visa-less country at its lowest ebb of humanity.

It was there that the full cataclysmic horror of war clenched her heart in its fist, never to let go. She watched helplessly as refugees staggered into the camps, having given up their animals and ancestral lands and trudged for miles without food or water, burying loved ones along the way. The pain etched into their noble faces reminded my mother of the Holocaust.

One incident in Somalia especially moved her. It was witnessed by Rob and photographer John Isaac, who'd accompanied her. A little girl was waiting in a long queue of children desperate for food. My mother walked over and began talking to UNICEF officials, who explained how many they had to feed.

As the girl moved up the queue, getting closer to the gruel that would go some way toward staving off her chronic hunger, she seemed mesmerized by the tall, thin white woman in their midst. She would never have heard the name Audrey Hepburn, seen her photograph, or watched any of her films, and yet she found something very compelling about her as she watched her stroke the cheeks of the malnourished and place a gentle hand on a baby's head.

John and Rob watched as the girl struggled visibly with her hunger and her burning desire to abandon her place in line to touch the strange woman. Peering hopefully at the front of the queue to see how far she had yet to go and then back at my mother, she hopped from foot to foot in an agony of indecision.

Just as she reached the head of the queue and was about to have food slopped onto her plate, my mother turned, and the girl caught her eye. With an impulse stronger even than starvation, the hungry child dropped her empty plate and ran to Mum's open arms, where she clung to her like a life raft, desperate for the sustenance she needed most of all—a mother's touch.

With similar incidents happening everywhere she went, it's no wonder that the profound emotional and physical consequences of what my mother witnessed in Somalia are plain to see in the photographs of that visit. The psychological pain she was in was only echoed by the pain in her belly that doubled her up on occasion. It was probably a side effect of the malaria pills, she told Rob and concerned colleagues, and then she blamed it on an amoebic or bacterial infection from the food or water. None of it was as bad as the pain in the eyes of the people she was trying to help, she insisted. Who was she to complain of a tummy bug when children were dying of dysentery? "Just get on with it," her mother would have told her, impatiently. So she did.

When Rob realized that her stomach problems were getting worse, he persuaded her to seek medical help as soon as she returned home. Forcing a smile, she promised she would and thanked him once again for his unfailing support. "I could never have done all of this work with UNICEF without Robby," she declared. "Apart from my personal feelings, there's just no way the job could have been done."

My mother extolled his virtues to me constantly, explaining how Rob helped with her speeches, made complicated travel arrangements, and checked the venues and sound systems before her engagements. He was also there to talk to and to cry with when things got too tough. But for her illness, I think their relationship would have been strong enough to last to the end of both their lives. I will always be grateful to him for taking such care of the woman most dear to me.

Back in Switzerland at last, she went to see the specialists Rob begged her to see, and they carried out numerous tests, including a colonoscopy, but in one of our many telephone calls she said the results had proved frustratingly inconclusive. "I'm sure it will resolve itself now that I'm home and eating normally, Seanie," she assured me.

When that didn't happen, it was decided in October 1992 that she'd fly to Los Angeles immediately after a UNICEF event in Washington, DC, and see the specialists recommended by Charlie Kivowitz, our longtime friend and family doctor. It was only much later that I learned she'd had to abandon her DC event early because she was in so much pain and that the Givenchy dress she'd planned to wear—and which she'd worn for years—no longer fit because her stomach was so swollen.

When I went to meet her at Los Angeles International Airport, I was shocked by how tired, thin, and tense she seemed. There it was again, that sadness that I had always known, only this time it was far more obvious and clearly wasn't just from the exhaustion of flying halfway around the world. I asked her about Somalia, and her jaw tightened. I could tell that the pain of memory was only adding to her physical discomfort, so I didn't persist.

The next battery of medical tests gave us no clear answers either, so in early November she went to Cedars-Sinai Medical Center for an investigative laparoscopy in which a narrow tube with a camera would be inserted into her colon via a small incision. Two hours later, the doctors had their answer, and it was what we had all feared: cancer.

They said it had started in her appendix as long as five years previously before metastasizing and spreading to her abdomen as a thin veil. Known as pseudomyxoma peritonei (PMP), it is a rare, slow-growing cancer that liquefies the intestine, earning it the peculiar nickname of "jelly belly." My mother's pain had been caused by repeated spasms in her small intestine, much of which had to be cut away.

The cancer had previously gone undetected because it had started in the appendix, that funny little inaccessible appendage that looks like a tail at the end of the colon. At the time, the appendix was considered by medical experts to be an organ without a function, but it has since been hailed as a tiny safe house for the good bacteria that keep our gut gardens healthy. Over the years I have often wondered if the appendix might also be a safe house for the soul, a place where all the pain and sorrows of a life are kept because they can never be fully digested. Perhaps my mother's soul simply overflowed.

When we went into the recovery room to wait for her to wake, it was all I could do to stop myself from feeling crushing despair. Her eyes flickered open, and she turned her head to give me a small smile but could see from my expression that something was wrong. After I'd gently explained the situation, she said quietly, "I knew it was more than a tummy bug." Later she joked about her abdominal cancer, referring to it as "abominable," as we all did our best to laugh.

I carried on talking, trying to keep her spirits up before the pack of doctors she jokingly dubbed "the Seven Dwarfs" arrived to say that they believed they'd cut away the malignancy and could offer her chemical treatments that could potentially give us more time. She listened and smiled, thanked them graciously, and said nothing more, but I sensed her skepticism.

"To allow time to heal, you have to be fed intravenously for a while, and then we can start the chemotherapy," they added. All I could think of was the starving children she'd so graphically described holding in her arms as they were placed on IV drips for dehydration. Now she was just like them.

As she recovered slowly from her major surgery, which had included a hysterectomy, we took turns sitting with her in the hospital, keeping the conversation breezy and helping her with anything she needed. She tried to make light of everything, and we all laughed in astonishment at the sheer number of bouquets being delivered to the hospital, each arrangement bigger than the last as friends vied for attention. Her friend Lenny Gershe, who had written *Funny Face*, sent her a book instead—Madonna's controversial new title, *Sex*. Later she rang him to thank her for making her the most popular patient in the hospital as doctors she'd never even met dropped by to casually flick through its pages.

Whenever someone took over from my morning shift, I would rush back to my office, where I had stacks of medical books and research studies, to read up on every possible cure for what turned out to be an extremely rare condition, quite literally one in a million. The more I read and the more experts I spoke to in hospitals around the world, the bleaker my mother's chances seemed.

Once she was released, we gently moved her to what she'd always referred to as her "second home" at Connie's. Our hostess took over Mum's care in the way that only Connie could and immediately started making homemade chicken soup for her beloved Ruby, her nickname from the scullery maid in *Upstairs, Downstairs*. Her efforts were largely wasted, as my mother had little appetite for anything and had to be coaxed to manage a spoonful or two. The parallels with what she'd seen in Africa were sometimes too great to bear.

On days when she felt up to it, we'd gather around Mum's bed or sit with her in Connie's living room and spend a few quiet hours together. When she was feeling a little stronger, we'd help her take a few steps in the garden or sit out by the pool for some fresh air and to hear the birds singing. It was amazing how just a few minutes outside seemed to revive her.

Missing her dogs terribly and realizing there was a chance she might never see them again, she asked that they be flown over from Switzerland, telling me, "I want them with me." Dear Giovanna, who was frantic with worry at La Paisible, jumped at the chance to come and flew to Los Angeles as soon as we could arrange it so that she could care for her beloved signora and bring the terriers that we knew would give her great comfort.

She enjoyed the dogs and Giovanna for a time, but then she had her first treatment of chemotherapy, via the same drug that had been offered to patients since the 1960s without any advancement. The first round went OK, but a few days later the pain returned, which meant that part of her intestine was being strangled again. Her doctors insisted she needed to return to the hospital for more surgery to remove further sections, and the prospect of that almost broke her. I was helping her get dressed to go when her defenses collapsed. She was more frightened than I have ever seen her, and that was the only time she allowed me to witness her tears.

Taking on the role of parent, I held her tight as she sobbed, "Oh, Seanie, I am so scared." Then she asked me where she would find the courage to go on. I could feel fragments of my heart falling away, but I tried my best to reassure her, telling her that she mustn't give up and promising her that I'd be there for her, no matter what. In truth, the research I'd done gave me very little hope. My mother and I were blessed with a bond for life, a spiritual umbilical cord, she called it, and I don't think we had ever been closer than in that moment. But we also each knew exactly what the other was thinking.

The tabloids had been running stories about Mum's cancer diagnosis for days, somehow getting access to private information from the hospital and predicting the worst. As ever, we kept them from her. When I drove her to the hospital for her surgery on the morning of December 1, she lay hidden on the back seat of my 1973 white Buick convertible, fooling the press photographers lurking under the palm trees outside Connie's house. They ignored us as we drove out, never imagining that Audrey Hepburn would ever be seen in such an old banger.

Once we were at the hospital and she was prepared for what was to come, we kissed her before she went into the theater and then took our seats as before. This time, however, the waiting was very brief—less than an hour—and the news was still briefer. There was nothing more the doctors could do, they told us. The cancer had spread exponentially. There was too much inflammation to operate, so they'd stitched her back up and said they would try to manage her pain. "The end will come quite quickly now," one told me. It took all my strength to stop my knees from buckling under me as a similarly winded Robby murmured, "Such a valuable human being."

When I had gathered myself, I went into the recovery room and sat on the edge of her bed. Taking her hand in mine, I told her what the doctors had said. She peered into my face for a glimmer of hope, but then her eyes softened, and she said simply, "How disappointing." She seemed remarkably at peace with the news. Calm. Accepting. No longer afraid of death. I, on the other hand, had never felt more helpless and was already beginning to ache all over with a burning sense of loss.

She and I then had a private conversation about managing her pain—which was her only fear—and I promised her that I would ensure it was always kept under control. Sitting in the silence of the soul for a while as her hand gently squeezed mine, we both let the importance of the moment sink in as I began to realize that, in many ways, this was the day that she died.

The doctors offered her more chemotherapy, but she refused, saying, "I just want to go home for Christmas." She knew she was on borrowed time, and true to the ethos of her life, she wanted to make the most of every moment for however long she had left.

Connie did a wonderful job over the next two weeks of helping my mother prepare to fly back to Switzerland.

We had been told it was risky for my mother to fly, as any dramatic change in cabin pressure could rupture her colon and give her peritonitis that could kill her in less than an hour. As she needed constant medical supervision, and no commercial airline would take the risk—not to mention that the eyes of the world were upon her—Hubert de Givenchy kindly called a wealthy friend who offered to lend us her private Gulfstream jet.

When I told Mum what he had done, she was completely overcome. Wanting to thank him personally for his "magic carpet ride," she asked me to call him for her, but when I placed the receiver in her hand, she could barely speak. "You have been everything to me in my life," he eventually told her through his tears, and—weeping—she sputtered, "Oh, Hubert—je suis si touchée." "I am so touched."

After speaking to medical experts, I contacted the pilot and passed on their instructions to make slow ascents and descents to avoid a sudden change in pressure and ensure her safe return home. The pilot promised to contact the relevant airports with this information and reminded me that our necessary refueling stop in Greenland would increase the risk. We were all set, but before we left California, there was something my mother needed to do.

"I'd like to see my friends," she said, and asked Connie to make some calls and apologized that she wasn't up to being Ruby in the kitchen anymore. On December 18, Billy and Audrey Wilder and Greg and Veronique Peck came and sat with my mother as she swallowed the pain I knew was eating away her insides. Sitting between Billy and Greg, who each held a hand, my white-as-a-ghost mother, who weighed less than ninety pounds, smiled at the camera as I took some photos on her Instamatic for posterity, at her request. Then, without a word, and so discreetly that few even noticed, she reached under her blouse and pressed the morphine pump that gave her a little relief.

Irving "Swifty" Lazar, the literary agent, came too with his wife, Mary, and Jimmy Stewart was the last to call, the morning before we flew to Geneva. They all knew it was the last time they were going to see her and were very lovely with her and with me, even though they were fighting back their tears.

Letting them spend their last precious moments together, I busied myself with the logistics and luggage, keeping an eye on the press waiting outside in the hope of snapping the last picture of Audrey Hepburn. They'd already printed leaked details of her surgery, and several tabloids claimed she had only weeks to live.

When it came to farewells with her dearest friends, they all behaved exactly as my mother wanted them to with gentle hugs and encouraging smiles. It was only when they got in their cars and started to drive away that they allowed their emotions to take over. Greg told me later, "I thought my heart would break then."

Connie was incredible, and when it was time to kiss my mother goodbye on the front lawn, she did it magnificently, both of them behaving as if it were just a regular departure and they'd see each other again soon. I thought it a performance worthy of an Oscar, and for a moment we all wanted to believe that they'd be reunited again one day. I was the last out of the house, and it was only after Mum had been settled in the limousine big enough to take her, the dogs, her nurse, and me that I saw Connie standing there with tears rolling down her face. Turning back, I folded her into my arms and thanked her for everything.

My mother declared that Christmas 1992 was the best of her life. With her family and close friends around her she was able to express her love for us, repeatedly, and we were able to tell her how much we loved her too. To the end of her days, she needed that reassurance.

We had arrived back at La Paisible just five days before with Betty, the excellent nurse who'd cared for her at the hospital and who gave up her own family holiday to remain at my mother's side. She and her husband described it as their Christmas gift.

Being back in Tolochenaz was the best possible tonic for us all. When she was feeling better, we'd sit together watching nature shows or comedies like *Fawlty Towers* on television as she dozed. "I'm so glad to be home," she'd say repeatedly, with an exhausted smile. As soon as she felt up to it, we wrapped her up against the cold and gingerly took her on walks around the garden, stopping at strategically placed chairs to allow her to tilt her face to the wintry sun and rest. Listening to the church bells or the birds, hearing cowbells in the distance or the wind rustling the leaves in her beloved trees lifted her spirits enormously.

Wandering slowly, we reminisced about the time I sneaked out of the house in the dead of night with a neighbor's son to watch a calf being born and about the fun trips we used to take with the children from the orphanage. There were all the fancy dress costumes she made for my birthday parties and the nights she fretted as I crammed for my exams, testing me last thing at night and first thing in the morning.

As we walked along the pathways she'd designed and past the vegetable garden she'd painted in watercolors, she'd point out which trees would need pruning in the spring, speaking of them as if they were her children. "He's over a hundred years old and has got far too tall," she'd say. Or "He really needs to be left to thrive, but trim him next year." I took careful note, promising to do as she asked, and I would obsessively fulfill her wishes to the letter in the coming years.

On a few of our strolls, she asked Giovanni to accompany us so she could remind him what plants would be coming up where and how to manage them. "But signora, you will come back to help me, when you get better," he told her, his eyes betraying his lie.

Smiling, she patted his arm. "Sì, Giovanni, I will help you...but not like before."

Several times, the paparazzi intruded on our lives in ways that infuriated me and saddened my mother. Some cut a hole in the hedge through which to stick long lenses and published photos of her looking extremely frail with one of us holding her infusion bottle. Others buzzed overhead in a helicopter, cutting short the precious twenty minutes or so that she enjoyed outside most days and forcing us back inside.

Then, before we knew it, Christmas Day was upon us. Only this one felt very different. Wherever we were in the world, we had always come home to La Paisible for Christmas, and this year was no exception. Often she'd invite lost souls like Cap—always Cap—who would otherwise be alone, or friends who'd been widowed or divorced or had had a difficult year. She called them her waifs and strays, and they could be anyone from Noël Coward or David Niven's Swedish widow, Hjördis, to a member of the UNICEF staff. Spending money on impractical

Christmas gifts was strictly forbidden, so we were encouraged to buy her toiletries or stationery, maybe a scented candle or a new scarf. She never did lose her love of scarves.

Christa Roth had been dropping by every other day from her office in Geneva, so for that last Christmas Mum asked her to join us too. Hubert de Givenchy had already been to say his tearful, private good-bye. He wrote later that she'd asked him to come and see her. "She welcomed me into the bedroom where she was lying in bed. 'I have a gift for you,' she said. 'Open this box.' Under the tissue paper was a coat, which she gave me, saying: 'If you ever feel sad, my dear Hubert, put it on your shoulders and tell yourself that I, Audrey, am hugging you to bring you comfort.'" Leaving them be, we had given the two of them some space to cry and talk together a little, as we knew that this would be one of the hardest of au revoirs for them both.

On Christmas Day we had a festive meal as usual, even though my mother—who was being fed through a stent—remained upstairs in bed while the rest of us ate. When the table had been cleared, we helped her downstairs for the giving of gifts. Unable to go shopping, she handed each of us something special from her own possessions, such as a sweater for Robby or a book. Luca and I received beautiful quilted winter coats, and Christa Roth was given a favorite monochrome Givenchy scarf. "Think of me when you wear them," she said, with a kiss. They were priceless items we would treasure for the rest of our lives.

After everyone opened their presents, she told me and my brother that we were the best things she had ever created, and then she read us something she oftentimes quoted in speeches to UNICEF. It was a favorite piece of lighthearted advice to make us smile. Written by humorist Sam Levenson for his newborn granddaughter, it began, "For attractive lips, speak words of kindness. For lovely eyes, seek out the good in people." It could have been written for my mother.

Exhausted by the effort and in a lot of pain, she asked me to help her back upstairs, and we settled into our usual positions with her lying in bed and me sitting next to her in the chair. I'd read several books on how to help someone face their own death and on the importance of spiritual healing, so we talked about that a little bit. I wondered how easy it would be for her to heal all the sorrows of her life that had begun when her father walked out and continued through the war when she watched Jews being loaded onto trains and young men murdered in the street.

"Oh, but I have had the most marvelous life, Seanie," she insisted. It was true. She had. But there had also been so much that was sad, evidence of which lay in the shadows behind her eyes. It was this, though, that made her so approachable and loved, I think. When we looked into those eyes, we saw our own pain reflected. We watched how she used that sadness to devastating effect on the screen, transferring it to her character and convincing us of each story's truth.

When I selfishly asked her to get better for all of us, she smiled. "That's easy," she told me. "I just don't know how to reconnect the top and the bottom." By that I think she meant she could no longer get her body to obey her mind. It made me wonder when the disconnect had happened. In Somalia, or before?

Rob came and went, and it was he who lay with her each night, but his grief was sometimes too much for her, as the man who had already buried one wife could barely face losing a second partner. "Think of the years we wasted doing all those difficult trips," he told her solemnly one night. "We could have been here with the dogs and your garden, just enjoying each other."

"But they were never wasted years, Robby," she chided. "Think what we have seen and what we were able to do...what we would have missed! That was such a blessing."

It seems incredible to me that even as she lay dying, my mother was still finding positives in the work she'd done and was doing her best to help Rob deal with the inevitable. After a lifetime of heartbreak, she had finally been free to find her place as a woman and be comfortable with it. In the final years of her life, she'd embraced the opportunity to play opposites. She could be a UNICEF ambassador one day, Hollywood royalty the next, or—twice a week—just a woman going to the market with her dog.

I think she always knew her fairy tale wouldn't end with her living happily ever after with the handsome prince. Her happy ending was accepting that and releasing herself from a lifetime of unattainable expectations. In her final years she'd been free to choose what kind of life and what kind of man suited her best. Now she was able to choose what kind of death she would have.

Using the last of her strength, she took time to speak to us all and to her closest friends in person and on the telephone, telling everyone what they meant to her. She was determined to leave everything in order and prepare us all. In showing no bitterness or anger at the cruel injustice of going too soon, she somehow defused ours. I had never seen her so mentally strong, even as her body withered.

As the bitter January days passed, so my mother began to gradually slip away from us, sleeping much of the time due to the combined effect of her illness and the morphine she'd been prescribed. When she woke, she always apologized for being a burden, ever gracious, ever wishing she could make our lives better. Sometimes the drugs confused her or gave her hallucinations of people around her, and other times she was fully lucid, but mostly she slept.

After one of his last visits to her bedside in LA, I'd asked our family doctor, Charlie Kivowitz, how much time we might have left. "Very little," he replied, which shook me, as I wasn't ready. Only a couple of days earlier she and I had walked in Connie's garden together, which had given me false hope that we still had a fighting chance of saving her. When our Swiss family doctor called in to see her at La Paisible, he saw my distress and patted my arm. "What you are seeing is a life well lived, Sean," he said, gently. "People who live well die well." As she'd lived, my mother was leaving this world so elegantly.

On January 20, worried about twenty-two-year-old Luca, his father, Andrea—who had flown in from Rome to support him—suggested they go to the cinema in Lausanne.

Sensing the end after another night of watching over her, I took her hand and told her how much I loved her. I was comforted by how peaceful she was in the bed I'd always known and by how she sensed that there were people waiting for her on the other side. I assured her we all knew how much she loved us and told her that if she was ready to leave us, that was OK. "Your little Seanie will go with you in spirit," I told her, not admitting that it would leave the broken shell of a thirty-two-year-old man behind.

Kissing her forehead tenderly, I went to call the pastor who had married my parents and who had christened me. A gentle humanitarian in his eighties, Pastor Eindiguer answered immediately and promised to come and read some prayers and give my mother the sacred rites. Needing some fresh air, I walked to the village cemetery with its distant view of the mountains. After finding the perfect spot, shaded by a little tree that I knew would burst forth with blossoms in the spring, I went to the town hall and made the necessary arrangements with the mayor, who'd been a family friend for years. To purchase the plot for eternity cost just 350 Swiss francs. The price of forever was as humble as her life had been.

My mother slipped away that evening at eight, while Luca was at the movies and Rob and I, along with a few close friends and family members, were downstairs comforting each other. It is often said that people choose to die alone, without an audience, and that was definitely true of my very private mother. When Giovanna found her and summoned us on the intercom, we raced upstairs to find that she had left us in her sleep, quietly and without any drama. There was a small, secret smile on her lips, as if she was pleased not to have caused any fuss.

The pastor read something beautiful as we all stood around her bed.

Giovanna's world had ended along with ours, and we held each other close. I called my father, who had flown to Switzerland to be near me, and he came to say goodbye. It had been a decade since they'd last seen each other, but he'd never stopped loving her. Kissing her forehead, he closed his eyes against the flood.

The morning of my mother's funeral, January 24, 1993, was just the type of morning she most loved, especially after a week of chill, gray days. Cold, crisp, and sparklingly clear, it was a day that made you feel painfully alive.

As I supervised the preparations for her service, I felt in a kind of trance, standing in her garden gazing at the mountains and thinking of all the times she had protected and saved me. Sad, so sad, that I had been unable to save her in return.

We had kept her home with us since her death, and then she was gently laid in a simple pine coffin, ready for us to carry her to the little church down the street. Luca and I were the pallbearers, along with Hubert, Giovanni, her half brother Ian, and her lawyer and friend Georges Müller. Rob and my seventy-five-year-old father walked slowly behind. At our request, Willy de Rham, a colonel in the Swiss army, had asked the authorities to declare a no-fly zone overhead so we wouldn't be disturbed by media helicopters and could hear only birdsong.

The 1,200 people living in our village lined the street in complete silence, their numbers swelled ten- or even twentyfold by the thousands more who had come to pay their respects. I thought back to the moment when Mum had told me about the chilling silence she'd encountered among 15,000 starving people at her first camp in Somalia. Smiling to myself, I remembered her wryly adding, "Can you imagine how deafeningly noisy fifteen thousand starving Italians would have been?" Her sense of humor, first molded in the basement in Velp, got her through many a dark day.

After a short but deeply touching service with hymns sung by a local children's choir, all of it broadcast by loudspeaker to the mourners outside, I recited the Sam Levenson poem she'd read to us on Christmas Day. Then I ended with, "Mummy believed in one thing above all: She believed in love. She believed love could heal, fix, mend, and make everything fine and good in the end."

We carried her to the cemetery, where we laid her to rest under the pretty little cherry tree. There would be no grand headstone carved with her name, just a simple pine cross. A few months later Hubert de Givenchy would return quietly on his own and plant some lily of the valley, one of her favorite flowers, a sprig of which she'd often worn pinned to her lapel when they first met.

Standing at her graveside on the day of her funeral, imagining the graveyard throughout the seasons, knowing how much she'd have loved the views, the butterflies, and the wildflowers, I felt strangely at peace. I don't think any of us had fully comprehended how much she had touched the world until she got sick. During her final weeks, we'd received so much mail that the village postmistress, who used to deliver on a moped, had to borrow a truck to cope with the bags and bags of cards and gifts sent from people around the world willing her to survive. Friends and strangers alike reached out to suggest cures and recommend doctors, all of them rooting for her to beat this and stay with us. To illuminate our path for even longer. She was very touched by their care and concern, as were we.

The effect she had on people really hit us when we carried her coffin from the church to her grave, gazing in wonder at all the people crowded at the roadside or standing like silent sentinels in the vineyards, weeping openly and bowing their heads in respect. That was an extraordinary sight. In the days and weeks following her funeral, I saw the same grief in the faces of people who discreetly walked up to me to share their condolences. I heard their loss in the timbre of their voices and noticed a new hollowness in their eyes.

It had been forty years since the world had first fallen in love with Audrey Hepburn in *Roman Holiday*, and it had been decades since she'd all but given up her movie career. Yet still she had endured in the hearts and minds of millions in a way that few others ever have.

Perhaps one of the reasons for that was my mother's fervent belief in the power of love, which she doled out in bucketfuls. Having been deprived of it as a child in a way that made her fearful that love would never stay, she overcompensated with almost everyone she met, showering them with kindness and compassion. In her own quiet way, living a life far from the spotlight and adhering to her own moral code, she crept into the public psyche as the epitome of goodness, courage, and decency. Then, when Luca and I flew the nest after she "got out of our way," she turned her loving eyes to other children, believing that her love could help them too.

"My life has been much more than a fairy tale," she told us. "There have been a lot of dark moments, but there was always light at the end of the tunnel." In the end, though, that innate optimism turned on her when she began to realize that no matter what she did or how much she loved, it wouldn't be enough. At one press conference she admitted bitterly, "I am becoming more raw, more hurt, more angry, feeling the pain more deeply."

The connection between emotions and the immune system is well documented, and I am of the firm belief that her body's response to her searing inner pain ultimately manifested itself in weakening her immune system. It seems no coincidence to me that Jim Grant, the children's advocate and tireless visionary of UNICEF who did so much for the organization, including signing my mother up in the first place, was diagnosed with cancer a few months after Mum passed and died two years, almost to the day, after she did.

The woman with the gentlest of hearts had never bargained for the toll her UNICEF work would take on her. She had transmuted her trauma of war and the Hongerwinter into love, but in the last five years of her life it transmuted back to trauma. Yet in some profound way she felt that dying before her time was a kind of symmetry. And as she had lived well, she died well. She was ready. The mere process of it made her feel closer to all the dead and dying children. Her final chapter brought her full circle, back to a different kind of hunger—the hunger of the soul for more humanity and greater kindness. Her legacy is timeless.

Almost three decades after she left us, the face of Audrey Hepburn is still ubiquitous, one of the most recognizable in the world. She has never really left us, and that is a great comfort. She is a myth. She is a legend. She is the proof that goodness exists. She is an example to us all, and—best of all—she is my mother. Seeing her everywhere reminds me that although she is no longer here, she lives on in our hearts and minds. She is the light at the end of our tunnel.

---- ◆ ----

Epilogue

INT. EMMA FERRER'S APARTMENT IN LUCCA, ITALY, 2025

EMMA FERRER sits on a sofa, her legs tucked up beneath her, like a fawn. It was the way her grandmother often used to sit. Opposite her is a woman with a notebook and a tape recorder.

INTERVIEWER
So tell me, when did you first become aware that your grandmother was the famous Audrey Hepburn? And how did that make you feel?

EMMA
I must have been five or so when I first realized that the face on popular women's handbags was that of my grandmother. Then there was the time when I recognized her photo in a frame on a friend's kitchen wall. The real answer is that I'm still not fully aware that Audrey Hepburn was my grandmother because the concept of her

and what she represents changes and morphs. I transform, and so does she, or the way I hold her within me. I'm always learning about what she really meant to people and the lasting impact she had—and still has—on their lives. These moments of realization help me form my own idea of who she was. I hope that I never fully "learn" who Audrey Hepburn is. It's a constant discovery.

INTERVIEWER
I know you were born after she passed, but have you a sense of who she was through her films and from talking to your father?

EMMA
I learned to celebrate my grandmother like the rest of her admirers who loved her movies. I laughed when she laughed, I cried when she cried, I rejoiced with her, and my heart broke a little bit every time hers did. *That* is how she first found her way into my heart; that is the magic of cinema. But as I grow as a woman, and the more people I meet around the world who love her, the more personal and intimate this concept of Audrey becomes for me.

INTERVIEWER
And what did you make of her then?

EMMA
That she was an incredible role model and continues to be. That's simply who

she was. Each and every one of us must
learn, in her honor, to be ourselves.

INTERVIEWER
And what about her style? Is it
something you try to emulate?

EMMA
Up to a point, of course, because her style is
timeless. I have in my repertoire a number of
items that she iconized—the black turtleneck,
the penny loafer (often with a white sock, in
my case), and a simple pashmina in the evening.
The ultimate lesson here is that certain items
never go out of fashion. Simplicity is key.

INTERVIEWER
Do you have anything of hers that feels really
special and celebrates who she was as a person?

EMMA
Yes, I have her coffee-stained white linen teddy
bear that's always waiting for me on my childhood
bed when I return to my father's home. On my
seventeenth birthday he also gave me a gold chain
with seventeen gold hearts that belonged to her.
I also have a patent leather handbag with her
initials monogrammed on the clasp, and some of
her sweaters. Ironically, my favorite of these
shrank to an unwearable size in the wash. At the
risk of sounding careless, I have a theory that
the things I have lost or can no longer wear

are somehow lessons from the afterlife sent by my unmaterialistic grandmother as a reminder that objects are not what is precious in life.

INTERVIEWER
And which is your favorite photo of her, one of the most photographed women of her century?

EMMA
The one she chose herself when asked the same question by a magazine. She was in Ethiopia carrying a child on her back and refused to have the photo retouched.

INTERVIEWER
How does that make you feel about her?

EMMA
I love her reaction because it seamlessly illustrates how truthful she was about her appearance, how *real* she was. When I look at that photo, I feel a love and an affinity with her. She looks so *human*. We need this so desperately today—to see a woman aging gracefully.

INTERVIEWER
Can you sum up what makes her so special, so unique?

EMMA
She lived by a few key principles, and she practiced them every day of her life. She always

put kindness first. Guests who stayed with her told me that every single morning she woke them with freshly cut flowers from her garden. People tell me she had the ability to make you feel like the most special person in the room. She singled people out and saw their beauty, what they have to offer to the world. She loved.

INTERVIEWER

Yes, I think you're right. Audrey really was one of a kind, wasn't she?

EMMA

(smiling)

My father and I would say that there's been no one like her before or since. One of my favorite things he says about her, and something we must take a moment to appreciate, is how truly remarkable this is: "No one ever had a single bad thing to say about Audrey Hepburn." Maybe Billy Wilder summed it up best when he said, "God kissed her on the cheek and there she was."

JUST AS MY MOTHER SAID soon after my birth that she hoped I would play my "own small part in making the world a better place," so I wished the same for my children, and those wishes have already come true.

My daughter, Emma, who was born in La Paisible less than a year after Mum died, has especially always known on a deep, visceral level that her purpose in life is to do whatever she can to help improve the lives of others. As she says, she has some large penny loafers to fill.

Like my mother and the generation before her, as a family we've worked closely with charities and nonprofit organizations in service to others, and after she died, Rob, Luca, and I set up a fund to help malnourished and orphaned children around the world. In her memory I also became an advocate for people with rare diseases under the banner of the European Organization for Rare Diseases (EURORDIS).

My mother was a dreamer, and she refused to give up on her hopes or her dreams, starting with the hope that her father would come back one day. She continued to dream throughout the war, praying for the killing and the hunger to end. She carried that dream forward into middle age with her fervent hope for world peace and the firm belief that every child would one day matter.

It was her deepest desire that we continue to keep the flickering flame of those dreams alive and not give up until we have each played our own small part in making the world a better place. One of her favorite things to say to those asking about her humanitarian work was, "Parents are not enough, teachers are not enough, doctors are not enough, friends are not enough, but all of us together have a chance."

A part of me is glad she is no longer alive to see more wars ravaging ever more communities and ethnic cleansing going unchecked along with human trafficking, famine, poverty, and sexual and physical abuse. Man's inhumanity to man sometimes seems to have no limit, and the results are always devastating, but in the spirit of the phenomenon that was and still is Audrey Hepburn, we must continue to do what we can to redress the balance and fight for humanity, justice, and compassion.

Everyone who knew her promises me she was a true, living manifestation of her principles of integrity, decency, and empathy. "Be kind" was the essence of her message. "Think of others before yourself." If you do one thing in her memory, do that, and her legacy will live on.

If there were an Oscar for the way a person conducts themselves in life, then my mother would have won it every single year. Fittingly, she kind of did at the end of her life. After being awarded the Screen

Actors Guild Life Achievement Award not long before she died, which she asked the actress Julia Roberts to accept for her, she was awarded the Jean Hersholt Humanitarian Award, gifted by the Academy of Motion Picture Arts and Sciences, which I accepted from Gregory Peck on her behalf only a few weeks after her death.

"If ever someone lived up to the ideals of this award with dedication and conviction, it was Audrey Hepburn," Greg said, his eyes glistening. Embracing me onstage, he stepped aside as I told the tearful audience, "On her behalf, I dedicate this to the children of the world."

I knew that, somewhere, the woman I carry forever in my heart was listening.

Read at My Mother's Funeral

Sam Levenson

For attractive lips, speak words of kindness.
For lovely eyes, seek out the good in people.
For a slim figure, share your food with the hungry.
For beautiful hair, let a child run its fingers
  through it once a day.
For poise, walk with the knowledge that you never
  walk alone.
People, even more than things, have to be restored,
  renewed, revived, reclaimed, and redeemed…
  never throw out anyone.
Remember, if you ever need a helping hand, you
  will find one at the end of each of your arms.
As you grow older, you will discover that you have
  two hands: one for helping yourself, and the
  other for helping others.

ACKNOWLEDGMENTS

My mother was interviewed so often that many of the things she said have been repeated over and over, by others and by herself, as—after a while—she tended to stick to a kind of script, even with her own family.

We are indebted to all those journalists, authors, interviewers, and radio and television stations that have chronicled so many of her words and placed them in the public domain. There are far too many sources to cite individually, and we have employed the rule of "fair use" wherever possible. If we have failed in places, then please forgive us in the spirit of Audrey Hepburn, from whom these quotes originated.

Several people were able to help with our research, and we acknowledge and thank them for their assistance and time. These include Christa Roth, Ian McLeod, Gary Stahl, Helena Coan, Janis Blackschleger, Peter Charlesworth, Hoang Chiem Bang, and my daughter Emma Ferrer.

Anyone who would like to read about my mother's life in more detail will discover that there are books about almost every aspect of her life. Many are listed in the bibliography below. Here are a few that Wendy and I would recommend:

- *Audrey Hepburn: A Biography* by Warren G. Harris, Simon & Schuster, 1994

ACKNOWLEDGMENTS

- *Audrey Hepburn* by Barry Paris, Putnam, 1996
- *Dutch Girl: Audrey Hepburn and World War II* by Robert Matzen, GoodKnight Books, 2020

The End

P.S. And I still do... sometimes... just before falling asleep... smile in the dark.

◆

BIBLIOGRAPHY

Books
Audrey Hepburn: An Elegant Spirit by Sean Hepburn Ferrer
Audrey at Home: Memories of My Mother's Kitchen by Luca Dotti
Audrey Hepburn: A Biography by Warren G. Harris
Audrey Hepburn by Barry Paris
Dutch Girl: Audrey Hepburn and World War II by Robert Matzen
Enchantment: The Life of Audrey Hepburn by Donald Spoto
Audrey Style by Pamela Clarke Keogh
Warrior: Audrey Hepburn by Robert Matzen
Nobody's Perfect: Billy Wilder; A Personal Biography by Charlotte Chandler
Hubert de Givenchy by Jean-Noël Liaut
Fred Zinnemann: An Autobiography; A Life in the Movies by Fred Zinnemann
Gregory Peck by Michael Munn
William Wyler: The Authorized Biography by Axel Madsen
Blake Edwards: Interviews edited by Gabriella Oldham
George Cukor, Master of Elegance: Hollywood's Legendary Director and His Stars by Emanuel Levy
James Stewart: A Biography by Donald Dewey
Colette by Joanna Richardson

BIBLIOGRAPHY

Yesterday, Today, Tomorrow: My Life by Sophia Loren
Timeless Audrey by Sean Hepburn Ferrer and Emma Ferrer (unpublished)
A Single Seed by Phoebe Fraser
Arnhem: Ten Days in the Cauldron by Iain Ballantyne
Roman Holiday: The Secret Life of Hollywood in Rome by Caroline Young

Interviews

- Sean Hepburn Ferrer
- Emma Ferrer
- Christa Roth
- Ian McLeod
- Gary Stahl
- Peter Charlesworth
- Hoang Chiem Bang

Letters, Photographs, and Film Clips
from Sean Hepburn Ferrer's files

ABOUT THE AUTHORS

SEAN HEPBURN FERRER was born in Bürgenstock, Lucerne, Switzerland, on July 17, 1960, to Audrey Hepburn and Mel Ferrer. He lived in Switzerland, Marbella, Madrid, London, Paris, Los Angeles, and Rome until he started school in 1965. His parents divorced in the late sixties, and in 1970 he moved to Rome to live with his mother and her second husband, where he attended the French Lycée Chateaubriand. In the mid-1970s he attended a Swiss boarding school, where he completed a French baccalaureate.

For forty-seven years, Sean has worked in every aspect of the entertainment industry: from film and television development, production, and marketing to the management of legacy-related intellectual properties and their related commercial applications. To protect and foster his mother's name, in 1993 he founded the Audrey Hepburn Estate, which monitors intellectual property rights as well as a series of nonprofits dedicated to continuing her humanitarian legacy as a UNICEF ambassador. In 2013 he was appointed honorary chair of the Audrey Hepburn Society at the US Fund for UNICEF (raising US$250 million). He was also the ambassador for EURORDIS, the European Organization for Rare Diseases (2013 to 2017).

Originally educated in French, English has been his professional language for the past five decades. He is also fluent in Italian and

ABOUT THE AUTHORS

Spanish and speaks basic Portuguese. Sean lives in Madrid, Spain, and Florence, Italy, with his wife Karin. Their five respective children are all adults.

WENDY HOLDEN was a respected journalist and war correspondent for the London *Daily Telegraph*, covering news stories around the world. A fellow of the Royal Historical Society, she is the author of more than forty nonfiction books featuring inspirational men and women, many of them set in WWII. Her bestselling titles include *The Teacher of Auschwitz*, based on the true story of a young, gay German prisoner who risked his life for children in Auschwitz. She also wrote *Born Survivors*, about three young mothers who hid their pregnancies from the Nazis, and *One Hundred Miracles*—the memoir of musician Zuzana Ruzickova, who survived three concentration camps.

Tomorrow to Be Brave is the memoir of the only woman in the French Foreign Legion. *Behind Enemy Lines* tells the story of a French Jewish spy, and *A Woman of Firsts* is the memoir of the "Muslim Mother Teresa." She also wrote the ghosted memoirs of Goldie Hawn, Barbara Sinatra, Patricia Gucci, and the No. 1 bestselling memoir of Cher.

A public speaker and teacher of creative writing, her first novel, *The Sense of Paper*, was published by Random House, New York. Her second, *The Cruelty of Beauty*, is to be made into a European film. She is currently working on a screenplay and another WWII book. She lives in Suffolk, England, with her husband and dogs, and is a passionate swimmer and gardener.

www.wendyholden.com